Sport Ethics

Applications for Fair Play

Jake Laurie

Second Edition

Sport Ethics
Applications for Fair Play

Angela Lumpkin, Ph.D., M.B.A.
Dean, College of Education
State University of West Georgia, Carrollton, Georgia

Sharon Kay Stoll, Ph.D.
Director, Center for ETHICS*
University of Idaho, Moscow, Idaho

Jennifer M. Beller, Ph.D.
Assistant Professor, Teacher Education
University of Idaho, Moscow, Idaho

With the Endorsement of the
National Association for Sport and Physical Education

Boston   Burr Ridge, IL   Dubuque, IA   Madison, WI   New York   San Francisco   St. Louis
Bangkok   Bogotá   Caracas   Lisbon   London   Madrid
Mexico City   Milan   New Delhi   Seoul   Singapore   Sydney   Taipei   Toronto

WCB/McGraw-Hill

A Division of The **McGraw·Hill** *Companies*

SPORT ETHICS: APPLICATIONS FOR FAIR PLAY, SECOND EDITION

This book is printed on acid-free paper.

2 3 4 5 6 7 8 9 0 DOC/DOC 9 3 2 1 0 9

ISBN 0-07-092117-2

Vice president and editorial director: *Kevin T. Kane*
Publisher: *Edward E. Bartell*
Executive editor: *Vicki Malinee*
Editorial coordinator: *Tricia R. Musel*
Senior marketing manager: *Pamela S. Cooper*
Project manager: *Mary E. Powers*
Senior production supervisor: *Mary E. Haas*
Coordinator of freelance design: *Michelle D. Whitaker*
Compositor: *Carlisle Communications, Ltd.*
Typeface: *10/12 Galliard*
Printer: *R. R. Donnelly & Sons Company/Crawfordsville, IN*

Freelance cover designer: *Kristyn A. Kalnes*
Cover image: © *Jim Cummins/FPG International*

Library of Congress Cataloging-in-Publication Data

Lumpkin, Angela.
    Sport ethics : applications for fair play / Angela Lumpkin, Sharon
Stoll, Jennifer Beller. —2nd ed.
        p.   cm.
    Includes bibliographical references and index.
    ISBN 0-07-092117-2
    1. Sports—Moral and ethical aspects—United States. I. Stoll,
Sharon Kay.   II. Beller, Jennifer Marie.   III. Title.
GV706.3.L85   1999
796'.01—dc21   98-38662
                                                              CIP

www.mhhe.com

Preface

The popularity of competitive sports continues to increase. Other than the media exposés associated with multi-million dollar salaries for free agents, no subject related to sport seems to command the interest of the media, sport managers, coaches, athletes, and fans more than the erosion of ethical values. Almost daily, another point-shaving incident, bench-clearing brawl, positive result on a drug test, or athlete failing to maintain academic eligibility brings disgrace or embarrassment to a sport organization.

Some individuals argue that sport ethics has become an oxymoron because of the violations undermining fair play. There are people involved in sport who have lost or have never developed the ability to reason morally within a sporting context. Since fair play necessitates that all competitors have the same chance for success, moral knowing, moral valuing, and moral acting are viewed as essential. Too often, though, the quest for winning and gaining awards overshadows individuals' beliefs in sportsmanship and playing within the spirit of the rules.

This text addresses many issues confronting the essence, and possibly even the survival, of competitive sport. We advocate moral reasoning in sport as essential to the attainment of values in sport, such as character development, teamwork, cooperation, and self-discipline. Within these pages, the reader will find philosophic theory that has proven effective in the moral development of athletes. Students preparing for sport management careers will find this book valuable in their exploration of how to preserve ethical values in sport.

Most people want sport cleansed from corruption and abuse so it will be characterized by fair play and beneficence. The issue remains how to eradicate the problems while preserving what is good in sport. The application of moral reasoning to sport can lead the way.

SPECIAL CONTENT FEATURES

Among the unique features of *Sport Ethics: Applications for Fair Play 2/e,* students will find an easy-to-read text, filled with a balanced mixture of theory and application and thought-provoking questions. Through real-life dilemmas that regularly challenge athletes, coaches, and sport managers, students are challenged to examine how they would respond to moral issues in sport.

Theoretical Basis for Moral Reasoning in Sport

Chapters 1, 2, and 3 provide the foundation for a philosophic understanding of moral reasoning. Moral character, comprised of moral knowing, moral valuing, and moral acting, requires impartiality, consistency, and reflective judgment. A reasoned moral inquiry based on these three tenets uses individuals' values (both moral and nonmoral) to determine each person's universalizable principles. A consistent value system based on justice, honesty, responsibility, and beneficence leads to a moral standard that will withstand scrutiny.

Thematic Description of the Major Challenges to Morality in Sport

Differing from existing books on sport ethics, this text describes the leading areas threatening the development and application of moral values in sport. Chapters 4 through 11 focus on thematic areas of sport in which individuals are challenged to use moral reasoning to decide how they will respond to ethical dilemmas. The chapters provide historical and sociological perspectives on issues facing all levels of sport. Chapter 4 examines the increasing amount of intimidation and gamesmanship and how these impact sportsmanship, while Chapter 5 describes the pervasiveness of violence in sport. In Chapter 6 students look at how sport drop-out and burn-out may adversely affect athletes. Chapter 7 presents eligibility issues that challenge moral values. Chapter 8 raises questions about legitimate and unethical uses of drugs and about drug testing. Chapter 9 looks at how commercialized sport has led to an emphasis on the nonmoral value of winning and at all the benefits associated with being "number 1." Chapters 10 and 11 discuss the ethical issues associated with racial and gender equity in sport respectively. Chapter 12 summarizes the importance of applying moral reasoning to sport.

The information in this text leads students to engage in critical and reflective thinking about what values they believe should characterize competitive sports. Students are asked to determine whether the moral values of justice, honesty, responsibility, and beneficence should guide the development and continuation of sports in this country.

Theory Boxes

To provide readers with a more in-depth understanding of moral principles and philosophic theory, Chapters 1 through 11 include numerous theory boxes. These boxes elaborate on terminology, concepts, definitions, and philosophy. By separating this information in boxes, the flow and continuity of the text are preserved. These boxes include knowledge vital to a comprehensive understanding of morality in sport.

Issues and Dilemmas

Students and teachers will value the opportunity to apply moral principles by resolving the *Issues and Dilemmas* in each chapter. Chapters 1 through 3 follow an open-ended discussion format.

The *Issues and Dilemmas* in Chapters 4 through 11 are written in case study format with real-life situations that challenge each student to begin a reasoned inquiry. Follow-up questions conclude each situation so that students can demonstrate their value systems and universalizable principles.

The moral reasoning process requires impartiality, consistency, and reflective judgment in answering each question. The *Issues and Dilemmas* will facilitate an in-depth personal analysis as well as lively student interactions. This feature makes the text come alive with timely applications.

ORGANIZATION

Sport Ethics: Applications for Fair Play 2/e begins with Chapters 1 through 3, providing the foundation for the rest of the book's information. Chapters 4 through 11 can be sequenced as the instructor prefers since they present a variety of issues in competitive sport.

The Epilogue, Chapter 12, summarizes and links the major content areas presented in the text and emphasizes moral principles and values as they relate to the thematic chapters. Here students are urged to apply to sport their developing moral reasoning abilities.

PEDAGOGICAL FEATURES

Several pedagogical aids will assist students in benefiting from *Sport Ethics: Applications for Fair Play 2/e.*

Chapter Opening Issues

Each chapter begins with a series of questions that introduce the content to follow. The questions are phrased to alert students to significant information, as well as to get readers to start a reasoned moral inquiry.

Chapter Summaries

The key content areas in each chapter are reemphasized in the summary. By reading the summaries that highlight the main points and reinforce salient concepts, students can solidify their knowledge base and the application of morality in sport.

References

Chapters draw upon the latest and the best documentation for this text. Each source quoted or referred to in the text is cited in full in the reference list.

Additional Readings

Selected readings are provided in each chapter because added resources will guide students in learning more about the topics discussed.

Internet Resources

This edition provides addresses to a variety of resources on the Internet, resources that lead student searches for more information on moral reasoning and ethics in sport.

Glossary

A comprehensive glossary at the back of the text reinforces for students the understanding of new terms.

ACKNOWLEDGMENTS

We would like to express our gratitude to all those involved in the preparation and development of *Sport Ethics: Applications for Fair Play* 2/e. We particularly appreciate the insights provided by the reviewers' helpful comments. These aided greatly the development of this edition.

Jan Rintala, Ph.D.
Northern Illinois University

J. William Douglas, Ph.D.
West Virginia University

C. Newton Wilkes, Ed.D.
Northwestern State University

Carol Alberts, Ed.D.
Hofstra University

As indicated on the cover, the National Association of Sport and Physical Education (NASPE) endorses this text. We appreciate NASPE's dedication to the field.

Lastly, we wish to express our appreciation to the McGraw-Hill professionals with whom we worked on this second edition. An especial "thank you" is extended to our families for their unending support and love.

Angela Lumpkin
Sharon Kay Stoll
Jennifer M. Beller

Contents in Brief

Contents

Moral Reasoning in Sport

◆ What is moral reasoning?

◆ What does morality have to do with sport?

◆ What do you think constitutes a moral issue in sport?

◆ How did you come to this view?

◆ How do people arrive at their moral opinions?

◆ What do you think are two moral issues in sport today?

A PLAN FOR FAIR PLAY

During a volleyball game, Player A hits the ball over the net. The ball grazes off Player B's fingers and lands out of bounds. The referee does not see Player B touch the ball. Should Player B tell the referee that she touched the ball? What do you think? Which of the following do you agree with?

1. "Why should I tell the ref? It's her job to catch it."
2. "Why should I help the other team? Gaining the advantage is the name of the game."
3. "Of course, I'll tell the referee. Isn't the purpose of the game to find out who is the best player, not who has the best eyesight?"

In this scenario, what is the reasonable and right thing to do for fair play?

Thinking about what is the right thing to do and why it is right is called *moral reasoning*. This is the systematic process of evaluating personal values and developing a consistent and impartial set of moral principles to live by, which is not an easy task.

Thinking is not an automatic process; rather, it requires self-discipline, time, knowledge of personal beliefs, and a systematic approach. Thinking about difficult issues and placing yourself in cognitive dissonance is also necessary to increase your moral development (Stoll and Beller, In press; Kohlberg, 1981). (See Box 1-1).

Unfortunately, most competitive people are so involved in personal and professional activities, whether practicing a sport, preparing for a game, studying for classes, visiting with friends, or just making it through the day, that thinking about fundamental moral issues seems unimportant (see Box 1-2).

1

THEORY BOX 1-1

THE STUDY OF MORAL DEVELOPMENT

The study of moral development is concerned with asking how and through what process human beings learn or develop morally and ethically. It is a difficult study; difficult because of the volume and complexity of the material to be studied and because there are opposing views regarding moral development.

The opposing views, or theories, are internalization and constructivist. Internalization models include the (1) psychoanalytic and (2) social learning theories.

Sigmund Freud (1933) in his psychoanalytic theory, which was the first major moral development research, hypothesized that the superego, id, and ego function together to govern aggressive and sexual instincts. He hypothesized that internalization of social norms occurs because of dynamic processes concerning the superego, id, and ego relative to feelings of guilt. Essentially, the superego (an internalization of societal norms and parental values) controls the id (the pleasure seeking/hedonistic instincts) and the ego (personal thoughts and decisions).

In comparison, the social learning theorists (the second internalization model) hold that morality is learned through socialization processes. Moral development is the process by which individuals adopt society's notion of acceptable values and behaviors (Bandura 1977; McGuire and Thomas 1975). Essentially, an individual who consistently internalizes norms is viewed as a greater moral person. Typically, social learning theorists apply the "bag of virtues"

approach (Kohlberg 1981). These theorists believe that individuals model their behaviors after others who personify the particular trait, value, or virtue desired. Moral education through this framework uses operant conditioning, reinforcement, and modeling (Bandura 1977; Aronfreed 1968).

Researchers in social learning theory posit that modeling and rewarding of behaviors in particular situations encourage generalization to all areas of life and theorize that throughout an individual's life the same underlying moral processes exist. While social learning theorists posit that moral behavior is the product of social environments, set standards, and the modeling of virtuous behaviors, constructivist theorists concern themselves with cognitive development relative to moral growth (Shields and Bredemeier 1995; Weiss and Bredemeier 1990; Kohlberg 1981). They believe that morality reflects the extent to which individuals use principles to guide moral action. Moral understandings are logically structured and developed through the stages of growth, with reasoning the foundation to moral functioning. Cognitive moral development is based on (1) what is considered right and fair, (2) what are the reasons for doing right, and (3) what are the underlying sociocultural perspectives (Reimer, Paolitto, and Hersh 1990).

Piaget (1932), the first to study moral development from a cognitive moral developmental approach, formulated a model and theory that emphasized cognitive development in children. Morality included the individual's respect for both rules and justice (a concern for reciprocity and equality among individuals). Piaget was concerned with the shift in morality from respect, constraint, and obedience to self-governance and control. He identified two broad moral development categories: (1) heteronomous stage morality of constraint/coercive rules and (2) autonomous stage morality of cooperation/rational rules (Piaget 1932).

Individuals in the heteronomous stage base their moral judgments on unilateral obedience to authority such as parents, adults, and established rules. Because rules are sacred and cannot be altered, individuals feel obligated to comply; right and wrong are usually viewed as black and white, with rightness and wrongness viewed in terms of consequences and punishments. The autonomous stage (morality of cooperation and reciprocity) is characterized by the individual's ability to develop a more subjective sense of autonomy and reciprocity. Right and wrong are situationally dictated, with rules subject to modification, relative to human needs or situational demands. Duty and obligations are relative to social experiences, peer expectations, and reversibility (the placing of oneself in another's position). This stage is typified by respect and cooperation with peers, rather than obedience to adult authority. Lawrence Kohlberg (1981) in his work at Yale and Harvard picked up Piaget's banner, expanded it, and spent more than thirty years attempting to make sense of how people learn and develop morality. Kohlberg expanded Piaget's stage theory by positing that moral development follows an invariant, culturally universal, six-stage sequence, organized into the following three levels:

Preconventional
Stage One—Punishment/obedience; avoid punishment

Stage Two—Follow rules for own interest, others do the same; to serve own needs

Conventional
Stage Three—Good Boy, Good Girl; reacts to expectations of parents, peers, other authorities

Stage Four—Social system and conscious maintenance; duty to social order, society

Postconventional (Principled)
Stage Five—Contract and individual rights

Stage Six—Universal ethical principles; based on consistent, universal ethical principles.

Kohlberg posited that higher stages require more complex reasoning and that through maturation and education, moral reasoning increases. As individuals interact with people and their environment and are challenged to cognitive dissonance (the questioning of one's values and beliefs), construction and transformation of personal moral understanding occurs. He also hypothesized that moral development could arrest at any stage especially during highly stressful conditions. Although many theoreticians have posited different variations of Piaget's and Kohlberg's models, most have the foundation that moral development is influenced by the following three major factors:

1. Moral education
2. Moral role models
3. Moral environment

By themselves, each is ineffective in developing moral growth, but together they influence and effect moral development.

The passionate controversy between the internalists and constructivists lies in the question of whether moral development can be empirically measured. Internalists believe that morality cannot be measured or *should not* be measured, and they argue that doing so is a dangerous practice because a test cannot be constructed to measure the slippery and complex moral issue in its developmental process. If this is true, they argue, then measuring cognitive knowledge of morality is impossible. They also typically argue against an empirical measure, in that we know moral value when we see it. Constructivists would argue that the concept of knowing moral value is not true and that a cognitive process (if it can be defined) can be measured, and if measured, can be taught through a cognitive process. (Stoll and Beller, in press).

It is ironic that both internalists and constructivists are concerned with the same end—better moral growth for all people in the sense of respect and concern for others.

THEORY BOX 1-2

RESEARCH SHOWS . . .

Researchers have found that athlete populations are significantly more affected than non-athletes in their reasoning process and thus appear to be less morally developed than their peer populations (Beller and Stoll 1992, 1995; Beller, Stoll, and Rudd 1997; Beller and others 1996; Hahm 1989; Bredemeier 1984; Bredemeier and Shields 1986; Krause and Priest 1993; Penny and Priest 1990; Stoll and Beller 1992, 1997, 1998; Stoll and others 1995. Stoll and Beller (1993, 1994a, 1994b, 1995) and Rudd, Stoll, and Beller (1997a) have posited that this is a result of an unconscious masking of the moral reasoning process. Because of the competitive process practiced in America, athletes learn "not to think" about the weighty issues of ethics. Instead, they blindly and passively follow the accepted behavioral norms. If everyone else practices behavior A and wins, we will practice behavior A. Beller and Stoll (1992, 1995) and Rudd, Stoll, and Beller (1997a) also posit that this masking can be raised through intense reasoning processes. In their studies they have found that athlete populations can meet or move beyond their peer groups in morally reasoning in a relatively short period of time such as eighteen weeks. (Beller 1990; Beller and Stoll 1992). In later work, with other competitive populations, Stoll and Beller, in various studies individually and collectively with other authors, have noted that this specific masking of behavior is also found in other competitive populations including business students (Reall, Bailey, and Stoll, in press), law students (Stoll and Beller 1993), and military personnel (Penny and Priest 1990; Krause and Priest 1993; United States Air Force Academy 1994).

THEORY BOX 1-3

MORAL UNDERSTANDING

Kohlberg (1981) and Rest (1986) state that moral understanding should directly affect moral motivation and behavior. Kohlberg, however, states that the strength of the relationship is only moderate. At this point, he and others state that too many other factors such as emotion, empathy, guilt, social background, experiences, and so on are involved for a high correlation. Lamb (1991) at Harvard University posited that children are born with empathy and that empathy can be summarily developed or stifled by the environment. This notion of biological traits for empathy places an even greater burden on the parent, teacher, and coach. Should we teach against empathy, if empathy is biologically a part of our very being?

TO KNOW, TO VALUE, TO ACT

As you will learn in this text, moral issues are very important because they affect what you do on and off the field of play. On the field, moral reasoning has a direct effect on the concept of fair play, which repre- sents the position that all players have the same chance for success. The quest in this text is to address certain moral issues in sport and offer some basic tools to help you think about what is right and why it is right. In the volleyball scenario (or all of life's moral questions), deciding the right thing to do depends on

1. what we *know* about the game, feelings of others, our values, beliefs, and expecta- tions of others;
2. how we *value* the win or advantage, the love of the game, ourselves, others, com- petition; and
3. what we actually decide and then how we *act* on that decision.

To Know

To know in the formal sense is called *moral knowing*. Moral knowing is the cognitive phase of learning about moral issues and how to resolve them (see Box 1-3). It is the ability to know that a moral dilemma exists, to know what you believe and value concerning the dilemma, to know how to look at the greater picture surrounding the dilemma, and finally, to know how to reason through the dilemma to find the right thing to do.

TO KNOW, TO VALUE, TO ACT

Lickona (1991) describes the components of good character in his seminal work, *Educating for Character.* Lickona believes that one must have the qualities of moral knowing, moral feeling, and moral action. Each of these components of character have subsets that must be fostered to develop good character. Under the subset of moral knowing, he lists moral awareness, knowing moral values, perspective taking, moral reasoning, decision making, and self-knowledge. Under moral feeling, he lists conscience, self-esteem, empathy, loving the good, self-control, and humility. Under moral action, competence, will, and habit are listed.

Each of the character domains are unequivocally linked. The domains do not function separately; each penetrates and influences in many ways. What we know and feel may affect our behavior and, reciprocally, how we behave may affect how we think and feel. Although we may know what is right and wrong, for many reasons and factors we choose to do wrong. Just knowing does not mean we empathize or have the self-control to follow with moral actions.

The concept of moral reasoning has been challenged by a new breed of moral educators known as the Virtuecrats. Led by Bennett (1993) in his work, *Book of Virtues,* the Virtuecrats argue that moral reasoning has really no place in the development of character. Rather, we learn the basis of good character through reading "good works" and following correct or acceptable behavior. Unfortunately, most ethicists, especially those in the Aristotelian fashion, would argue against such a perspective. Aristotle said that character is the composite of good moral qualities, whereby one shows firmness of belief, resolution, and practice about such moral values as honesty, justice, and respect. He also said that character is right conduct in relation to other persons and to self and that our humanness **resides in our ability and capacity to reason** and virtue results when we use our reasoning ability to control and moderate our self. Hence, reading about good virtue—even if the readings are the world's greatest masterpieces—is useless unless we have the capacity to reason and think through our actions.

To Value

Moral valuing is the basis of what we believe about ourselves, society, and others around us. Valuing asks such questions as: What is most important to me? Is the game the most important thing? Is the win or the advantage the most important thing? Is my gain more important than others? Is performance more important than results? Is there something more important than the win, and why?

Moral valuing takes into consideration your empathy, self-control, humility, and conscience as you direct actions toward others.

To Act

Moral action is your outward behavior that you manifest that is contingent on your values and cognitive processes. Moral action depends on your competency about moral issues and your own values. What exactly do you believe, and do you know it well enough to take action? Moral action also depends on your "will" to do what you believe. Do you have the courage and the will to accomplish what you believe? And finally, moral action depends on your daily habits. Is "doing the right thing" something that you value enough that it becomes a habit in your life?

TO KNOW, TO VALUE, TO ACT IN APPLICATION

The three phases, to know, to value, and to act, work in concert to help you make moral decisions. Much has been written about these different phases of moral development (see Box 1-4). In the volleyball scenario, examine what you value about playing a game.

To Value

Which of the following do you value the most?

1. The win, no matter how it happens
2. Gaining the advantage

3. Playing, winning, or losing is not important
4. Winning, but only within the letter of the rules
5. Winning, but within the spirit and letter of the rules

If you chose 1 or 2, you probably value the results of a performance more than the performance itself. If you chose 3 or 5, you probably value performance more than the results. If you chose 4, you may value winning but only if it follows the accepted social parameters of rules.

To Know

Why you value what you do is directly affected by how you have been educated and socialized about sporting events, though recent research now argues that we may be born with innate empathy. You might argue that you chose numbers 1, 2, and 4 because that is the reality of playing the game today. You know that this is the only successful way to play a game. Why do you know this? Is it because you experienced it, either through playing the game, through coaching techniques, or through what others have told you?

If you chose number 3 or 5, you know that performance, or how you play the game, is more important. You have come to this perspective because of what you have learned from your sport experiences. Interestingly, although the answers may be directly opposed to each other, you come to know them through the same process.

To Act

If you consider the volleyball scenario, you would probably act according to what you know and what you value. Your will and habit depend on your value structure and your knowledge of the subject, society, and your own perspective.

A PARTICULAR PERSPECTIVE

In deciding, resolving, and evaluating any issue (including our volleyball scenario), some form of reasoning is needed. The greater the ability to reason, the better able we are to address moral issues.

Moral reasoning is a problem-solving activity, a way of trying to find answers. It is no different than any other logical and systematic process except that it involves offering reasons for or against moral beliefs. Moral reasoning is a way to critique questions and answers. It is not limited to a defensive position of what we believe or know to be right, rather, our purpose in moral reasoning is to discover the truth. In moral reasoning, opposing positions are analyzed to decide whether we should agree or not.

Let's look at a specific scenario involving one of football's greatest innovative coaches, Paul Brown. Brown began his coaching career at Massillon High School in Massillon, Ohio. In 1928, his high school team was a little slow in the backfield. Brown analyzed the rules to find an advantage and found one. The rules made no mention of what a uniform could or should look like, except that there must be a number on the back. Coach Brown seized the opportunity. He took footballs and cut them into halves. He sewed one half on the front jersey of all the backfield players' uniforms. When the quarter-

BROWN'S ROUSE

The rouse that Brown played could be traced to Pop Warner. It seems that Warner used the same tactic earlier. The tactic were found to be unethical and rules were developed against such tactic. Apparently, the high school league that Brown was in had not heard of the *slippery rule*. (Jerry Gems, North Central College, Naperville, IL, October, 1997).

back passed off, everyone appeared to have a football (see Box 1-5).

1. What are the opposing positions in this scenario?
   a. It is acceptable because it is within the rules.
   b. It is acceptable but highly questionable.
   c. It is unacceptable even if it is within the rules.
   d. It is unacceptable because it is against the spirit of the rules.

   What is your position concerning Coach Brown's behavior? Ask four friends their positions. Do you all agree? Why or why not? You may find that you will not all agree on the moral action in this scenario. Some people will state emphatically that Brown was cheating. Others will say that he was not cheating but being very clever. Others will argue that it is perfectly acceptable to do what Coach Brown did and that rules need to be written to address the problem. Whatever position you take, you may find that not everyone accepts your arguments. Be advised that conflicting views are commonplace, and you and your friends may never resolve them. Other positions may be right and you may be wrong, or you may be right and they may be wrong. Because the purpose of moral reasoning is to seek moral truth to guide day-to-day conduct and to regulate social institutions, discussions about moral issues may result in arguments. Such arguing is not necessarily bad, as some people believe. Moral arguing may help you reach agreement through a sys-

tematic reasoning process. Arguing is bad if it is irrational or if the persons engaged in it are unreasonable. At the same time, such unreasonableness may be good if it is used to make progress in discovering moral truth. Arguing does not necessarily mean fighting or even heated disagreements. Rather, argumentation is attempting to demonstrate that some beliefs are true based on the truth of other beliefs.

Before continuing the moral reasoning process, you need to develop a particular philosophical perspective. This perspective is based on your ability to be as impartial, consistent, and reflective as possible.

REQUIREMENTS OF MORAL REASONING
Impartiality

Being impartial in determining any issue is always difficult and perhaps impossible. Humans tend to seek their own personal preference. Your value system is bombarded with intuition, emotion, and a myriad of values from science, logic, sense experience, and authoritarian perspectives.

What is difficult is quieting your own wants and *attempting* to develop an impartial reasoning system. To do so means to become concerned with other points of view. Since we all must live in the world with others, we must come to realize that our wants and desires must be tempered by how those wants and desires affect others. In developing a reasoned view, you must grow beyond, "What's in it for me?" Rather, your goal should be to consider your own values and the ramifications of each decision in relation to those who may be affected by your action.

Interestingly, if you are like most of us, you expect better behaviors from your friends. You may expect them to be altruistic even if you are egotistic. For example, most of us choose friends who demonstrate certain altruistic virtues (a particular moral excellence that promotes the general good or a special manifestation of specific moral values). That is, we choose friends for certain basic virtues, such as fairness, honesty, and truthfulness, and we

From a moral point of view, being fair or impartial is attempting to be free from bias, fraud, or injustice. Being fair and impartial is trying to be equitable and legitimate, or not taking advantage of others. Such qualities are essential in making decisions about moral issues. Without such qualities, all decisions become biased and centered on the good of one, or what is considered good for one. If you wish to be considered fair, or if you wish to hold traits esteemed by others, you work toward impartiality in your reasoning. Obviously, you will fail because of your own mortality . . . but the point is to at least try.

Place the concept of impartiality into the volleyball scenario. If you remove yourself from the scenario, does it make a difference in your answer? In other words, should all volleyball players call an infraction when one occurs? Or, should infractions be called only by the referee? This is difficult to answer because the norm today—and the rule—is to let the referee make all calls. However, you must be careful if the referee is the judge of all behavior. What if the referee does not see all the action? Does the game then become trying to outsmart the referee? Should our goal of playing the game rest solely on how good the referee's eyesight is? What exactly is the purpose of the game? How you answer these questions refers directly to what you think is the purpose of the game.

In the Brown scenario, can you apply the rule of impartiality? For example, should rules be seen only as obstacles that must be overcome? That is, are rules made only so that clever ways can be found to get around them? What exactly is the purpose of the game rules?

usually trust our friends and believe that they will not fail us. Would you choose friends who you know would lie to you, cheat you, or steal from you? Probably not! Of course, the same virtuous traits you find imperative in your friends are traits that you want others to think you demonstrate. Most of us want others to know us as being honest, truthful, responsible, and altruistic, and to think of us as being fair and concerned for others, even if we are not.

To be fair means developing an awareness of others' feelings and needs. Being fair also demands imagining and understanding others' interests and the effect of our actions on their lives (Frankena 1973). To be otherwise is to risk loss of friendship or companionship and loss of our own civility.

Consistency

To reason morally, you must also be logical and consistent. Being logical is the essence of moral reasoning, which involves an exact process. To be consistent when making moral decisions, past and present decisions must be taken into account. If you hold two positions that contradict each other, both cannot be truthful or acceptable. For example, suppose that you and Jill are about to play a game of squash. You decide to play by a certain set of rules, whereby you will each call your own errors. You expect each other to follow these rules. Before the game begins, you agree that the serving line is out. If you call a ball that hits the serving line out, then Jill has an obligation to do the same. Suppose, though, that in the heat of the game, you hit a line shot on the front boundary line. The score is 8-6, your favor; one more point and you win. You have worked hard in this game, and Jill ALWAYS beats you. Jill does not see the line shot. She asks you, "Was it out?" You saw it, and you KNOW that it was out.

1. What should you say?
2. What would you say?
3. What should you say to be consistent?

In a reasoned sense, Jill expects you to tell the truth, thus you should tell the truth: the ball was out . . . even though you may want to believe it was in.

In this scenario, you must overcome your own emotional wants and realize that if you hold a different set of standards for yourself than what you expect of others, then you are being inconsistent and untruthful to yourself and your opponent. If you truly give your word to follow the rules, then the rules stand for you as well as Jill. In the heat of a close game, if you do not call your serving errors, then you are blatantly lying. Thus you violate two psychological perspectives of moral reasoning, being impartial and being consistent. Apply this reasoning to the volleyball scenario and the story of Coach Brown.

Reflection

You must decide your moral and ethical dilemmas through reflective judgment based on clear moral and nonmoral values. Reflective thinking is exercising careful judgment in all moral issues, based on your moral and nonmoral values. Unfortunately, few of us exercise reflective thinking. Often, we take a stand on an issue because we are biased by our own cultural, sociological, or biological presuppositions.

For example, XZY University believes it has gender equity in its distribution of funds for men and women. There are an equal number of sport teams for men and women. There are an equal number of coaches. The men's teams are football, cross country, golf, tennis, track and field, and basketball. The women's teams are volleyball, golf, tennis, cross country, track and field, and basketball. The budget for the men's program, including football, is approximately three times larger than the women's. However, if figured without football, the budgets are approximately equal. Football as the number one revenue sport brings in about 60 percent of the working revenue. Without this revenue, there would be no programs for the nonrevenue sports. Therefore, XZY University states that equity exists as is.

1. Do you agree?
2. What are the issues in this case?

In traditional ethical inequity, the emphasis has always been on rationally determining moral issues, which in turn justifies your choices to behave in certain ways. Specifically, critical, reflective thinking is exercising careful judgment or observation about an issue. Critical means to be accurate, exact, and precise about an issue, to take into account all sides of an issue, and to determine its present and future implications. Use critical thinking to examine the different sides of the gender equity issue at XZY.

Case One: Equity exists.
Case Two: Equity does not exist.
Case Three: Equity does not exist, but inequity is acceptable.

Which of the three cases is true? All three cannot be true.

Rebuttal to Case One: Does equity exist? If equity is defined as equal access to all goods for all people, equity does not appear to exist. If football uses or has access to twice as much funding as the women's programs, equity cannot exist.

Rebuttal to Case Two: Equity does not exist. As with Case One, the statement must be true. Equity does not exist.

Rebuttal to Case Three: Inequity is acceptable in this case, since without football there would be no other programs. This scenario may be true, or it may be untrue. Put another way, this argument for inequity rests on justification of unequal distribution of goods to men because without men there would be no football and without football there would be no money. Therefore, because of football, men are special. This argument rests on the assumption that men are more of some quality than women more of what: brighter, industrious, special, talented, or productive? If you can access the quality that men are more of, then you have the reason why inequity is acceptable. A different supporting argument to Case Three might be: "But without football there would be no other programs." The reply might be: "Why have a program that by its very nature discriminates against others? Should we have programs that benefit only one class of people—men?"

For a thorough discussion of gender equity, check out the following Web sites:

◆ Christine Grant of the University of Iowa has a thorough Web site addressing the current research and arguments dealing with gender equity in collegiate sport: http://www.lib.uiowa.edu/proj/ge/
◆ The Women's Sport Foundation: http://www.lifetimetv.com/sports/index.html
◆ Another current site that will give much research data about this difficult topic is the work of R. Vivian Acosta and Linda Jean Carpenter: http://www.lib.uiowa.edu/proj/ge/Acosta/womensp.html

The counter to this statement is that without football, there are no funds and no programs. And, are we not advocating the demise of sport, period? This also may be true, or it may be untrue. Perhaps in the discussion of football "funding" the other programs, we must examine how the monies are distributed beyond the "basic needs" of any one given program. For example, the common practice of athletic departments sending their football teams to bowl games is to spend every dime earned, and more, on the trip. Most of the central administration, their families, their children (and, in some cases, the nannies for these children), and other significant individuals receive travel, hotel, and food as well as tickets to the game. In addition, each individual player, coach, and significant other receives warm-ups, gym bags, brief cases, and so forth—all emblazoned in team colors, logos, and bowl insignia.

It is not uncommon for an athletic department to spend the maximum payout, which can be anywhere from $300,000 to several million dollars for an overall four-hour event.

The discussion about equity, therefore, must account for all actions in relation to all individuals involved in the athletic program. Does equity exist in the distribution of excess funds throughout the program? Does the overall quality of the experience and program exist for all no matter the gender or sport?

It is certain that distribution of funds will change what sport is today. The change may be good or it may be bad; in any case, change will occur. What we do know is that if equity is to occur either belt tightening will happen or administrators will become creative in how to address the problem. Presently, many institutions have found solutions to their gen-

THEORY BOX 1-6

ETHICS, MORAL—THE TERMS

Etymologically, the word *ethics* is derived from the Greek, *ethiké*, meaning science of morals or character. Typically, the formal study of ethics is concerned with the principles of human duty, or the study of all moral and mental qualities that distinguish an individual or a race relative to other individuals or races. Ethics is an analytical, scientific study of the theoretical bases of moral action. The study of ethics is often categorized according to professions, such as the ethics of law, business ethics, the ethics of medicine, sport ethics, the ethics of teaching, the ethics of coaching, and so forth. Ethics may also be called meta-ethics, analytical ethics, or critical ethics.

In contrast, the word *moral,* from the Latin *mos,* refers to an individual's actual custom or manners. In a technical sense, moral pertains to an individual's *actions* as being right or wrong, virtuous or vicious, or good or bad in relation to the actions, intentions, or character of responsible people carrying out the deed. For example, let's return to the squash game. We are in the midst of an intense rivalry. You think I have gotten completely out-of-hand. I begin to shove and push. I also have an unnerving habit of

hitting the ball directly at myself when you are behind me. This strategy forces you to somehow reach around me, which results in some physical contact. The physical contact gets increasingly worse, and I push you three more times. You finally have had enough, and the next time I push you out of the way for a shot, you "waylay me with a haymaker." Your reaction may seem justified considering the circumstances; however, such retributive actions are suspect. The history of societies tells us that violence begetting violence is a poor solution to a moral dilemma. I might say correctly that "although you are a good person, you acted wrongly—perhaps with good motives and intentions—when you struck me. The consequences were bad even though I provoked you. Surely, there is a better way to solve this problem." Note that in the case of moral action, there is a subtle but important difference between right and wrong and good and bad. "Right and wrong" apply to an individual or agent's acts, whereas "good" and "bad" refer to (1) the person who is the agent of a particular act, (2) the effects of the agent's acts, (3) the agent's motives from which the act was done, and (4) the agent's intention.

---

der equity dilemmas through creative fund raising. The state of Florida legislated a head tax on every game, professional and amateur, played. The tax is directly funneled to girls' and women's sports. It appears their gender equity problems have been reduced. The University of Michigan, as well as many other large Division I schools, has found that great amounts of funds are raised through merchandising the university's logo. For years, collegiate institutions did not or were not able to control the unsanctioned use of their logos. Within just a few years, through controlled licensing of its logo and products, the University of Michigan's budget was almost doubled. Today their budget is in excess of $400 million dollars.

Such scrutiny about any difficult issue may or may not bring about new enlightenment. As you can see, we may all agree about the issues after critical reflection, or we may disagree. It is possible that several different theories may survive the reflective

process. You have no guarantee that your means to finding the truth through moral reasoning will support only one view. Even if you do find different views, you will have begun to understand how to defend your moral positions and you may learn about yourself and your beliefs.

DEFINING ETHICS, MORALITY, "GOOD AND BAD" TERMINOLOGY

Before considering further issues, morality and ethics should be defined. (The words *good, bad, right,* and *wrong* are commonly used in the study of ethics; such usage does not necessarily connote moralizing.) *Ethics* and *morals* are usually interchangeable, but technically they connote two very different perspectives (see Box 1-6).

Moral specifically refers to your motives, intentions, and actions in dealing with others, while *ethics* is the study of morality. Therefore we say that

THEORY BOX 1-7

NONMORAL VALUES

Frankena (1973) has placed nonmoral values into six different categories:

A. *Utility values:* Things are valued as good because of their usefulness for some purpose, that is, a racquet is good because it allows you to play your squash game.

B. *Extrinsic values:* Things are valued as good because they are a means to what is good. You may rate extrinsic values highly because of the benefits they bring you. Winning, an extrinsic value, is most important. Being successful is imperative to the good life. By winning, you have access to a variety of goods, success, esteem, fame, and so forth.

C. *Inherent values:* Things are valued as good because the experience of contemplating them is good or rewarding in itself. Thinking about a winning shot or the beauty of an athletic movement may be inherently good.

D. *Intrinsic values:* Things are good in themselves or good because of their own intrinsic properties. Being courageous, dedicated, and self-sacrificing are examples of intrinsic values. They are good because of their own properties.

E. *Contributory values:* Things are valued as good because they contribute to the intrinsically good life or are parts of it. Money is contributory; it contributes to a good life.

F. *Final values:* This includes all things or the combination of things that are good on the whole.

Nonmoral things most often fall into several of the above categories. These things can be good in more than one sense, that is, both extrinsically and intrinsically.

---

this text studies the ethics of modern American sport and the morality or immorality of cheating, performance-enhancing drug use, and exploitation of athletes. Ethics studies the underlying issues, while morality is concerned with actions, motives, and intentions of the sport participants.

Moral and Nonmoral Value

The study of morality is much more than defining words, even though understanding terminology is essential. Morality deals with all human acts, intentions, and motives that affect or impinge on others. Relationships are the determinants of how you value morality. The issue of values therefore comes into play both in a moral and nonmoral sense (see Box 1-7). *Values* are defined as anything having relative worth. It is relative in the sense that what you think is valuable, someone else may think has no value. Some may value a new red sports car, while others may value a land-rover. In morality,

values are placed into two general categories: nonmoral and moral (see Box 1-8).

Examples of nonmoral values are money, fame, power, position, and winning. They are not moral in the sense that they are not people, intentions, motives, deeds, or traits of character that affect other persons. These values are usually extrinsically based on "things".

Winning, success, fame, and pleasure fall into several of these different categories. Nonmoral values and the good they bring determine how you make moral decisions. In America, capitalism rewards those who value material goods, success, and winning. Anyone who says winning is unimportant in American society is unrealistic and naive. The moral question, however, is: How important is winning? Is winning more important than how you treat others? If winning or other nonmoral values are "the bottom line," moral values may be seen as useless or silly. As a Division I athlete said, "Hey, it's nice to talk about morality, and I'm as moral as the next guy, but the only thing that matters is winning.

THEORY BOX 1-8

VALUE SOURCES

In his provocative book on how we develop our value system, Lewis (1990) states that values come from various sources. He places these value-development sources into six categories; you use a little of several to come to your value beliefs. These six categories are the following:

1. *Authority:* Values are placed into perspective by taking someone else's word, having faith in an external authority. Authority figures have a great deal of power in determining what you value and what you do not.
2. *Deductive Logic:* In this case, you subject your beliefs to various consistency tests that underlie deductive reasoning. You decide what you value by deciding whether the value functions with your value structures.
3. *Sense Experience:* You decide whether something is of value by placing that value into your internal testing scenarios. You gain direct knowledge through your own five senses.
4. *Emotion:* You determine whether something is right or wrong by your emotions, that is, feeling that something is right.
5. *Intuition:* You decide whether you believe something is good or bad by your own unconscious thinking, which is rational rather than emotional.
6. *Science:* Finally, a synthetic technique relies on sense experience, intuition, logic, and sense experience again.

Using several is not necessarily bad if you consider that Albert Einstein, Karl Barth, and Mahatma Gandhi were products of several different types of value systems. However, it could be very bad if you combine these value types irrationally and unsympathetically (to others). You should remember that your value systems are often highly biased and really very illogical. Fox and DeMarco (1990) have stated that by asking three questions, you may find answers to the nature of your own moral value biases.

1. How do you state your beliefs and what do these beliefs imply? (In other words, the very tone of your voice may actually moralize how you feel about an issue or another person. Do the beliefs have hidden meanings?)
2. How do you practice your beliefs? How do you praise and criticize others? (Are you faithful to your beliefs and do you have a hidden agenda about moralizing as you praise or criticize?)
3. What reasons do you use to defend your point or view or to criticize others? (Is the reasoning impartial, consistent, reflective, or highly biased?) The answers to these questions may show that inconsistency lies between your beliefs and your actions. As you try to become consistent, you will develop a more reasoned moral view.

I'll do whatever it takes to win, even if I have to knee him in the groin or kick him in the head." Or, "Nobody cares about number 2. Winning is all that matters" (Stoll and Beller, 1992).

Moral Values

Moral values are the relative worth that is placed on some virtuous behavior. Moral values are internal, subjective, and immeasurable in an objective sense. They are traits or dispositions that you esteem and portray. Moral values are usually esteemed

in America because human relationships would be difficult to maintain without moral values.

Let's use a racquetball game as an example. Before beginning the game, John tells you that he does not particularly like rules and that he intends to do whatever necessary to beat you. John really does not care if he hits you or follows the rules. After all, the real game is beating you. What would be your response? Would you play the game? Or, would you decide that John is the world's biggest jerk and tell him where to "put it"? Or, would you join in to beat him by whatever means possible?

The answers revolve around what we believe to be important in human affairs. Moral beliefs are elusive. They come to us through a labyrinth of experiences. Most of us have only vague ideas about what we believe, or we hide or constantly change our beliefs.

What is a moral issue?

A moral issue can arise from various concerns. An overly narrow view of morality tends to block moral reasoning and inquiry by excluding relevant and important human interests. To have a moral point of view is simply to be concerned about how other people are affected by the things that we do. We take others' interests into account. We are not only moral agents of moral actions, intentions, and motives; we are also moral subjects affected by what others do to us.

A classic moral issue is found in the opening volleyball scenario. What is the motive and intention of not telling the referee?

Motive:	To win the game through referee deception
Intention:	To gain an advantage by deceiving the referee

In the Coach Brown scenario, what is the motive and intention?

Motive:	To win the game at any cost
Intention:	To gain an advantage by deceiving the referee and opposing players

If you do not agree, what do you think the motive and intention are in both scenarios?

SUMMARY

The process of moral reasoning demands a specific perspective as well as knowledge of basic terminology. Moral character is made up of three different components: moral knowing, moral valuing, and moral acting. This chapter specifically addresses the need for impartiality, consistency, and reflective judgment. The terminology of ethics and morality is defined; the former as the study of the latter, which refers to the motives, intentions, and actions as they affect others. The differences between nonmoral and moral values are discussed. Your value system is probably part of at least six different forms. From the discussion, you can understand that there may be no right answers to moral dilemmas and that others may or may not agree with you. In the next chapters, the actual study of moral reasoning begins.

ISSUES AND DILEMMAS

1. Find the moral issue in each of the following scenarios, the moral and nonmoral values, or any inconsistency of action.

   a. Jim believes that using performance-enhancing drugs is no one's business but his own.

      Position 1: No person is an island . . . your actions do affect others. As a sentient being, you have effects on others and are loved by others. Any decision that adversely affects humanity is a moral concern to others.

      Position 2: Each person's destiny is his or her own. Because the action affects only Jim, it is not a moral question.

   b. Coach Smith motivates his players by saying that they have a moral responsibility to give 100 percent at all times.

      Position 1: Motivation to win a game is not a moral issue; rather, it is a nonmoral issue. Responsibility is not always a moral issue. For example, you have a responsibility to brush your teeth each day, but it is hardly a moral responsibility. Though it could be argued that teeth brushing is an example of what is necessary for good health. Again, because none of us are insular, we are all responsible for our own good health.

      Position 2: Responsibility is a moral issue because the players have implicitly given their word to do their best. They are obligated to morally do the best that they can at all times.

   c. Mary is opposed to drug testing, because she believes it is morally wrong and an invasion of her rights. When challenged that testing probably deters drug usage, she states that such is irrelevant because morality has to do only with how you control your own actions.

      Position 1: Mary is perfectly right. Testing does not make one moral, nor should testing be the means to legislate morality. Morality is not mandated by social decree or law. Morality has to do with what you value as a person.

      Position 2: Mary is wrong. Testing deters drug usage and, thus, sport authorities have a moral obligation to administer drug tests. Performance-enhancing drug use places the participant in grave jeopardy and destroys the sanctity of the sporting experience. Therefore, to remove or reduce drugs in sport, drug testing is morally mandated.

   d. Team A played its arch-rival, Team B, on B's court. Team B's
   fans yelled obscenities and developed obscene cheers. When
   asked her opinion after the game, Team A's coach replied, "Such
   behavior is not a question of morality. It is a question of who is
   the most prepared to handle the stress. It's all in the game."

   Position 1: Coach is wrong. Fan behavior is a moral question. Whenever people offend other people, it is a question
   of morality. To justify such behavior as a part of the game
   places sport in the position of amorality . . . anything goes.
   Position 2: It is the nature of the game to play through ad-
   versity. What the fans do has nothing to do with it. As long
   as the players are under control, who cares what the fans do.
   A good coach prepares players for fan behavior. That's what
   coaching is all about, being prepared.

2. Consider the following:

   a. What exactly is a moral issue?
   b. How do people arrive at their moral opinions?
   c. What do you think are two major moral issues in sport today?

REFERENCES

Aronfreed, J. 1968. *Conduct and conscience.* New York: Academic Press.

Bandura, Albert. 1977. *A social learning theory.* Englewood
Cliffs, New Jersey: Prentice Hall.

Beller, J.M. 1990. A moral reasoning intervention program for
Division I athletes. Ph.D. diss. University of Idaho.

Beller, J.M., and S.K. Stoll. 1990. Moral development of student
athletes: Can athletes learn not to cheat? Unpublished research. Center for ETHICS, University of Idaho.

———. 1992. A moral reasoning intervention program for Division I athletes. *Academic Athletic Journal.* (Spring): 43–57.

———. 1995. Moral development of high school athletes.
Journal of Pediatric Science 7(4) (November): 352–63.

Beller, J.M., S.K. Stoll, and Andrew Rudd. 1997. The "Great
Character experience": Assessing the effectiveness of a Great
Books approach to teaching moral character with competitive
populations. *Research Quarterly for Exercise and Sport* [Ab-
stract]. Supplement.

Beller, J.M., S.K. Stoll, Barbara Burwell, and Jack Cole. 1995
(September). The relationship of competition and a Christian
liberal arts education on moral reasoning of college student
athletes. ERIC Data Base, Resources in Education, Red #ED
382 620.

———. 1996. The relationship of competition and a Christian liberal arts education on moral reasoning of college student athletes. *Research on Christian Higher Education.*
3:99–114.

Bennett, William. 1993. *Book of Virtues.* New York: Simon and
Schuster.

Bredemeier, B.J. 1984. Sport, gender, and moral growth. In *Psychological Foundations of Sport,* edited by J.M. Silva and R.S.
Weinberg. Champaign, IL: Human Kinetics.

Bredemeier, B.J., and David Shields. 1986. Moral growth
among athletes and non-athletes: A comparative analysis.
Journal of Genetic Psychology 147: 7–18.

Fox R.M. and J.P. DeMarco. 1990. *Moral reasoning: A philosophical approach to applied ethics.* Forth Worth, TX: Holt,
Rinehart, and Winston, Inc.

Frankena, W.K. 1973. *Ethics.* 2d ed. Englewood Cliffs, NJ:
Prentice Hall.

Freud, Sigmund. 1932–33. *New introductory lectures on psycho-
analysis,* XXII. New York: Morton Publishing Co.

Hahm, C.H. 1989. Moral reasoning and development among
general students, physical education majors, and student athletes. Ph.D. diss., University of Idaho.

Kohlberg, Lawrence. 1981. *The philosophy of moral development:
Moral stages and the idea of justice.* New York: Harper and Row.

Krause, J.V., and Bob Priest. 1993. Sport values choices of
United States Academy cadets—A longitudinal study of the
class of 1993. Unpublished manuscript. Office of Institutional
Research, United States Military Academy.

Lamb, Sharon. 1991. First Moral Sense: Aspects of and Con-
tributors to a Beginning Morality in the Second Year of Life.
In *Handbook of moral behavior and development.* Volume 3,
edited by Wm. M. Kurtines and J.L. Cewirtz.

Lewis, H. 1990. *A question of values.* San Francisco, CA: Harper
and Row.

Lickona, T. 1991. *Educating for character.* New York: Bantam
Books.

McGuire, J. and M. Thomas. 1975. Effects of sex, competence, and competition on sharing behavior in children, *J Personal & Soc Psych* 32(3): 490–4.

Penny, W.J., and Bob Priest. 1990. Deontological sport values: Choices of United States Academy cadets and selected other college-aged populations. Unpublished manuscript. Office of Institutional Research, United States Military Academy.

Piaget, Jean. 1932. *The moral development of a child*. Glencoe: Free Press.

Reall, M., J. Bailey, and S. Stoll. n.d. Moral reasoning "on hold" during a competitive game. *Journal of Business Ethics*. In press.

Reimer, J., D.P. Paolitto, and R.H. Hersh. 1990. *Promoting moral growth: From Piaget to Kohlberg*. Prospect Heights, Il.: Waveland Press.

Rest, James. 1986. *Moral development: Advances in research and theory*. New York: Praeger.

Rudd, Andrew, S.K. Stoll, and J.M. Beller. 1997a. Expressed coaching behavior and its effect on athlete moral development. *Research Quarterly for Exercise & Sport* [Abstract]. Supplement.

———. 1997b. Moral calluses in sport. Paper presented at annual conference of the International Philosophic Society for the Study of Sport, Clarkston, Washington.

Shields, and Bredemeir, Sperber, M. 1990. *College Sports Inc.* New York: Henry Holt and Co.

Stoll, S.K., and J.M. Beller. 1992. Qualitative research of moral reasoning in sport populations. Unpublished research. Center for ETHICS, University of Idaho.

———. 1993. Effect of a longitudinal teaching methodology and classroom environment on both cognitive and behavioral moral development. *Research Quarterly for Exercise and Sport*. (Supplement), 64 (March): A-112.

———. 1994a. The effect of a longitudinal teaching methodology and teaching environment on both cognitive and behavioral moral development. Ref #ED 359180, Resources in Education ERIC Data Base.

———. 1994b. Methodology and its effect on cognitive moral reasoning. *Research Quarterly for Exercise and Sport*. (Supplement), 64 (March): A-97.

———. 1995 (September). The importance of teaching methodology in moral education of sport populations. ERIC Data Base, Resources in Education, Ref #ED 382 619.

Stoll, S.K., J.M. Beller, Michael Reall, and C.H. Hahm. n.d. The importance of teaching methodology in sport education. *Academic Athletic Journal*. Forthcoming.

Stoll, S., J.M. Beller, Barbara Burwell, and Jack Cole. 1995. Moral reasoning of Division I and Division III athletics: Is there a difference? Resources in Education, Ref #ED 382 681.

———. n.d. Comparison of moral development of Division III and Division I athletes. In press.

———. 1998. A comparison of moral reasoning scores of student athletes in Division I and Division III NCAA member collegiate institutions. *Research Quarterly for Exercise and Sport*. (Supplement), 66 (March): A-81.

United States Air Force Academy. 1994. Longitudinal study of United States Air Force cadets' moral reasoning. Colorado Springs, CO: United States Air Force Academy (Office of Research and Development).

Weiss, M.R., and B.J. Bredemeier. 1990. Moral development in sport. In *Exercise and sport science reviews*. Vol. 18, edited by K.B. Pandolf and J. Holloszy. Baltimore: Williams and Wilkens.

ADDITIONAL READINGS

Ashmore, R.B. 1987. *Building a moral system*. Englewood Cliffs, NJ: Prentice Hall.

Evans, J.E.D., ed. 1987. *Moral philosophy and contemporary problems*. New York: Cambridge University Press.

Fischer, J.M., ed. 1987. *Moral responsibility*, Ithaca, NY: Cornell University Press.

Hospers, J. 1953. *An introduction to philosophical analysis*. Englewood Cliffs, NJ: Prentice Hall.

Kohlberg, Lawrence. 1980. *The meaning and measurement of moral development*.

Marx, Karl, and Fredric Engels. 1955. *On religion*, Moscow: Moscow Foreign Language Publishing House.

Rawls, J. 1971. *A theory of justice*, Cambridge, MA: Harvard University Press.

Woodhouse, M.B. 1980. *A preface to philosophy*, Belmont, Calif: Wadsworth Publishing.

CHAPTER 2

A Reasoning Strategy
for Fair Play Behavior

- ◆ What are moral values?
- ◆ How do moral values relate to principles?
- ◆ Why are principles written in the negative?
- ◆ Why and how do you stack principles?
- ◆ How do you develop rules from principles?

AN APPLICATION OF MORAL VALUES AND PRINCIPLES

You are the new assistant athletic director for Small Town University, known for its competitive athletic teams. You are told and you feel that there is a true *esprit de corps* about the athletic programs: One for all and all for one. Everyone seems directed toward and believes in the values of the athletic program. At this school, cheerleaders and the pep band are a large part of the aura of game nights. At your first home women's basketball game, you are seated next to the athletic director and the president of Small Town. Fan support is tremendous, and the crowd is loud and boisterous. When the opposing team is introduced, the home cheerleaders hold signs that say, "You Stink!" "Who Cares?" "Where Did You Learn To PLAY?" "Go Home." The crowd and fans love it.

You watch the athletic director and president—no response. The game begins, and both teams seem to be well matched with good coaching and control on the floor. At the first time out, the pep band moves to the floor and does a quick maneuver that places the brass instruments facing directly into the visiting team's huddle. It is doubtful that the coach can hear or yell over the noise.

You sneak a peek at the athletic director and president—no response, again. During the visiting team's free throws, a group of students, apparently organized and lead by a band member, uses large black dots on white cardboard that they move back and forth and up and down to cause vision problems for the opposing team. No response still from the athletic director or president. The game concludes. The home team wins by two points. After the game, you mention to the athletic director that you thought the band and cheerleaders were out-of-hand. The athletic

director somewhat agrees but states that it is unreasonable to expect anything different in this day and age. The media publicizes that the professionals and larger universities are all doing the same thing. How can anyone expect the fans at Small Town to be any different? You respond that you think it was in very poor taste from everyone involved, and shouldn't Small Town want a better image? The athletic director agrees but states it is unreasonable to intercede during a good game, and besides the whole purpose of home court is *ADVANTAGE.*

What is the reasonable action in this scenario of home court advantage? To do nothing and to accept the present case as *quid pro quo?* Or should athletic administrators intercede to prevent such behavior? To answer such questions, you need a valid and consistent reasoning process to examine both sides of the issue. The reasoning process used must be subject to the same rules and general principles that apply to all reasoning. Good reasoning should guide your day-to-day sport conduct and help regulate sport teams, clubs, and organizations. Good self-reflective reasoning takes into consideration your own motives, intentions, and actions as they affect others. The reasoning strategy you are seeking is important, as important as any other human endeavor.

As discussed in Chapter 1, this reasoning process called *moral reasoning* is a form of argumentation. Simply, in moral reasoning, you attempt to find the truth about what you believe. As you remember, moral reasoning is the systematic process of evaluating personal values and developing a consistent and impartial set of moral principles to live by daily. You have already learned that what you believe usually comes to you via some abstract system through various sources. These beliefs act as guideposts for how you make moral decisions. In the athletic scenario, what you believe about the purpose of a game and the purpose of that game as viewed by spectators will serve as guideposts in deciding what action to take. Some questions you need to address should focus on what you believe is the purpose and role of the game, the players, and the spectators.

1. What do you believe is the purpose of playing a basketball game?
2. What do you believe is the role the visiting team should play?
3. What do you believe is the role the fans and spectators should play?

The answers to these three questions are yours alone. No one else can tell you what you believe. However, self-serving beliefs or unexamined personal beliefs will probably fail as a means to solve weighty issues facing the new assistant athletic director.

MORAL VALUES

Because beliefs are abstract, your goal is to place the abstract into something concrete. In moral reasoning, this "something somewhat concrete" is known as *moral values.* You seek to discover what you value, think, feel, deduct, and intuit through what you believe. What is the purpose of the game?

Belief 1:	To score points and win
Belief 2:	To score points and win, but only by working cooperatively with your opponent
Belief 3:	To play and have a good time; points and winning are not important

Let's examine each of the three beliefs. If the purpose of the game is only to score points and win (Belief 1), you may not value how the game is played or under what conditions. In other words, the game is valued only for its results.

If the purpose of the game is to score points and win, but only under the conditions of working and cooperating with your opponent (Belief 2), you may value how the game is played and under what conditions more than you value the final result. The game is valued not only for its results but for the performance that occurs.

If the purpose of the game is play and fun (Belief 3), you value the experience rather than results. Performance may or may not be important. What matters is the quality of the experience.

In the three cases, something different is valued in the game. The valuing in these cases is based on essentially nonmoral values, winning versus performance versus experience. However, you must realize that your nonmoral values will directly affect how you morally value other people. That is, if winning and scoring points are what you value most, you may easily justify cheating or other questionable moral behavior. In contrast, if experience or performance is more important, you will be less likely to commit questionable acts. That is, if at Small Town University, the only important thing is winning, then the cheerleaders', band's, and fans' behaviors are acceptable. Any behavior becomes acceptable because the purpose of the game is to win at all costs.

However, if performance or experience is more important, the cheerleaders, band, and fans would be ancillary and unimportant for the good of the game. There would be no need for their behaviors because the purpose of the game is performance or experience (see Box 2-1 and Fig. 2-1).

PRINCIPLES

In a moral reasoning process, values are usually written in a special way called *principles* (see Box 2-2). Principles are universal guides that tell which kinds of actions, intentions, and motives are prohibited, obligatory, or permitted in human interactions. Principles are "universal rules of conduct" that identify and define what is valued (see Box 2-3). By placing your values into a universal form, universality, you will have a usable measuring stick to examine tough issues. In the assistant athletic director quandry, is there a universal way applied to sport to examine the fans', band's, and cheerleaders' behaviors and then to develop a general

THEORY BOX 2-1

THE PERCEPTION OF SPORT

The motive, intention, and action of the experience are very different considering the perceived reality of action today and the proposed ideal of what sport should be. In Figure 2-1, notice the differences in motive, intention, and action. In the perceived reality, any action is acceptable to gain the final goal—the win. In the perceived ideal, motives, intentions, and actions are governed by what the goal should be—excellence.

THEORY BOX 2-2

FIRST RULES

Principles are general written statements, or *First Rules*. These rules are first because all other rules of action stem from them. Specifically, principles justify other rules and there are no other rules more important. Principles are First or ultimate Rules which cannot be reduced further. For example, the Golden Rule (Do unto others as you would have them do unto you), which most of us have learned, is an ultimate, universalizable rule, or a First Rule. Because of its universal nature, you can derive other rules from it, and, if all goes well, you can apply the First Rule in all situations.

statement about it, based on what you believe and value? (See Figure 2-2.) Look at the scenario again and see if you can make some general operational comments that can be developed into First Rules (see Box 2-4).

1. If you are results oriented, you might say, "Any behavior is acceptable as long as I win."
2. Or, you might place the comment into the ethic of "Win At All Costs."

In contrast, if you are performance or experience oriented, you might say,

3. Winning is acceptable, but only if you follow the rules.

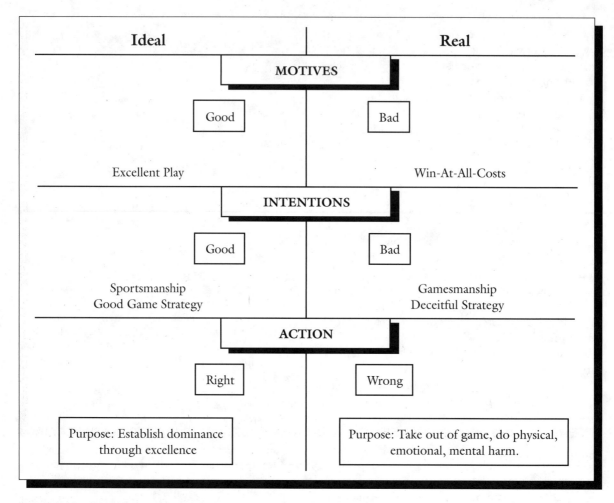

FIGURE 2-1 The Perception of Sport.

THEORY BOX 2-3

KANTIAN ETHICS

We will use the Kantian term, *universality*, meaning applied to all persons the same. Kant stressed two widely accepted principles of morality: (1) that moral judgments must be founded on universal rules, which are applicable to all persons in the same way and (2) that persons must always be treated with respect. His concept of universality requires you to test moral rules by seeing if you can apply them universally in the same way to all persons. His "categorical imperative" stated that duties are prescriptive and independent of consequences. Kantian ethics are widely held today as a standard of reasonableness and rationality.

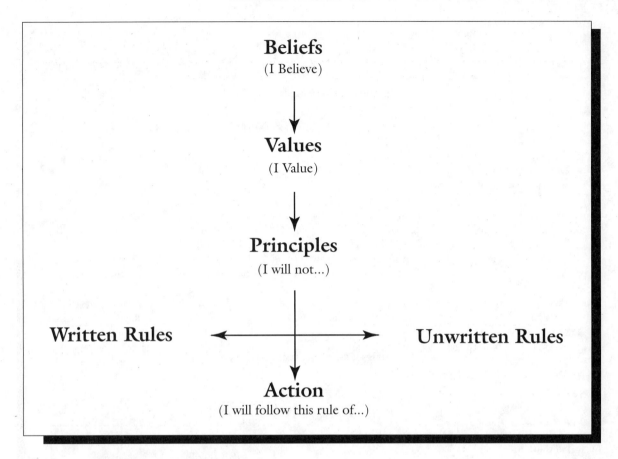

FIGURE 2-2 Paradigm: From Beliefs to Action.

4. Or, winning or losing is always a possibility, while following both the spirit and the letter of the rules.
5. Winning or losing is unimportant; playing well is the key.

EXAMINING VALUES AND DEVELOPING PRINCIPLES

You now need to examine your comments about your values and see if you can develop them into First Rules (see Fig. 2-2). Is it possible to reduce these comments about sport into some form that you could use for all of life's moral decision making? Remembering the concern for universality, assume that it is possible to develop a set of First Principles that you can readily use. Also assume that you can limit these First Rules

to a workable number, like three or four. Assuming that it is possible, how would you go about it?

SELECTING FOUR MORAL VALUES

Moral values are numerous and varied, including honesty, honor, truth, respect, sincerity, integrity, justice, duty, cooperation, and so on. How can you select or choose just one or two or three? This is not an easy task, but certain historical guides can help. For example, if you examine certain general, historical, and cultural parameters that can be found in the Bible, the Pali Canon, the Q'uran (Koran), and most societal ethics, you might find some explicit, simple, common, and shared values. That is, in all of the above cases, four moral values surface: justice, honesty, responsibility, and beneficence. These

THE NUMBER OF FIRST PRINCIPLES

How many or how few moral values and principles are there? Moral values are varied as we have discussed. Your task is to limit your values so that you can develop a workable set of principles. Too many universalizable values and principles may conflict with each other; however, only one moral value like love and its accompanying principle of "love your fellow human" may be too general, too abstract, or too vague to be useful in making moral determinations. Therefore, more than one is preferable, but more than five is probably ineffective. Writers on the subject of universalizable principles agree somewhat on the content. Most favor principles based on justice, freedom, and beneficence or nonmaleficence. For example, Frankena (1973) reduces the universalizable principles to (1) distributive justice and (2) beneficence. Fox and DeMarco (1990) state that the universalizable principles are (1) Do No Harm, (2) Do Not Be Unfair, and (3) Do Not Violate Another's Freedom. Lickona (1991) calls for only two universal principles of (1) respect for others and (2) responsibility.

Fox and DeMarco (1990) state two general conditions for establishing moral principles, conditions that you can apply to both examining your values and developing principles.

1. Principles must be explicit and simple (no abstraction, just basic concrete statements). In developing principles, simplicity is imperative because difficult moral questions must be easy to understand. Complicated principles affect your efficiency in deliberation and judgment of moral issues; too complicated a principle and you may never resolve the problem.
2. Principles must also be shared, common, and universalizable. (That is, the principles you choose are actually cited by people in many different societies and cultures in various ways.) Common principles are shared by the world's major religions, cultural laws, and knowledge of basic human nature. Because of the universal nature of the principle in relation to other people, the wider the acceptance, the stronger the ability to settle disputes. Realize, however, that universal agreement about a principle is not the complete test. History has shown that some cultures have accepted deviate behavior as the norm. For example, the people of Germany seemed to accept Hitler's genocide of the Jews, which would imply that genocide of Jews was acceptable. Principles must pass various tests of reasonableness and rationality.

The reasonable and rational tests center on: Are your thoughts coherent? Do your thoughts support your convictions? Are you willing to test your reasons by taking others into account? Are you willing to place your principles against the test of impartiality, consistency, and reflection? Can you submit your principles to the scrutiny of others?

ETHICAL THEORY

Ethical theory is broad and complicated. Theories range from social contract perspective, to self-actualization theory, to classical teleologic utilitarian, to deontic non-consequential, to hedonism. Our purpose here is not to study the history of ethical theory but rather to say that most of these theories are concerned with moral values. For overall histories of ethics, see the reading list at the end of this chapter or check the Internet references listed here:
A directory of sources on ethical theory:

http://truth.wofford.edu/~kaycd/theories.htm
A slide show about deontological theory:
http://www.kwu.edu/religion/REPH325/week04/slide1.htm
Sample information about consequential ethics:
http://voled.doded.mil/dantes/exams/dsst/sf474.htm
A contemporary list of utilitarian writers and philosophers:
http://www.acusd.edu/ethics/utilitarianism.html

shared values have a universal appeal because they are imperative to human relationships, without which morality can and does not exist (see Box 2-5).

Justice: Moral Value One

The first moral value is justice. Four general types of justice exist: (1) distributive, (2) procedural, (3) retributive, and (4) compensatory. Distributive justice involves the perceived fairness and distributions of benefits and burdens relative to outcomes. Procedural justice involves the perceived fairness of the policies, procedures, and agreements used to determine outcomes. Retributive justice involves the perceived fairness of punishment of a lawbreaker or evildoer. Compensatory justice involves the perceived fairness of making good on a harm or unfairness that a person or persons may have suffered in the past.

Each of these types of justice is inherent in moral reasoning and decision making in sport. For example, organized sport organizations have rule books stating what are considered acceptable and unacceptable actions on the field of play (procedural). If these guidelines or rules are violated, sanctions are imposed, such as penalty and foul shots, banishments from play, and so on (retributive). In the most general sense, teams have rules that players must follow in order to participate (procedural) and sanctions if those rules are not followed (retributive).

Distributive justice can also be seen in the passing and implementation of Title IX legislation. The compensatory justice factor is awarding monetary relief or some form of goods for past misconduct. That is, distributive and compensatory justice must be considered in issues of equity, as discussed in Chapters 10 and 11. Equity refers to gender and racial opportunity, plus opportunity for persons with disabilities (see Box 2-6).

We believe justice is also inclusive of what is known as distributive justice, or the equity of treating others, especially competitors, fairly. Theoretically, distributive justice is based on integrity for doing the just and equitable right. Equitable does not necessarily mean being treated equally or the same in this case. Suppose that you and Joe are both swimmers and swim for health reasons. Joe is an able-bodied swimmer; you, however, are a paraplegic. If you and

THEORY BOX 2-6

OUR CULTURE IN AMERICA

Culture in America is based on the concept of equal intrinsic dignity and value of the individual. That is why the federal and state governments subsidize the poor and handicapped for various social needs from food and lodging to social services.

Joe are treated the same, there would be no special accommodations for you. You would have to access the facility the same as Joe—no wheel chair ramps and no hydraulic devices to lower you into the pool. In this case, it is not fair for you and Joe to be treated the same. "Justice asks us to do something about cases of special need . . . because only with such attention can people have something comparable to an equal chance of enjoying the good life" (Frankena 1973, 50). This does not mean that justice demands that all lives must be equally good in a nonmoral sense, that is, distribution of money, wealth, goods, winning, and success. Rather, it means that justice asks that we treat others equally in the sense that they have the proportionally same contribution to the goodness of their lives, in a moral sense. It does not mean that once a certain minimum has been achieved by all, you must distribute all your goods to help others meet the same competitive standard that you have achieved. To do so would be unproductive and possibly fanatical.

Honesty: Moral Value Two

Honesty is the condition or capacity of being truthful or trustworthy in dealing with others, including competitors. Honesty is dealing fairly and uprightly in speech and action. The moral value of honesty is based on the premise that the actor or agent will not lie, cheat, or steal. (*Moral actor* or *moral agent* is common terminology referring to the person who is acting, based on motives and intentions.) For example, honesty refers to the honest person as one who, after accepting the rules and laws as a necessity to playing the game, follows them. If you decide the rules are ineffective, then you must make a decision. You have three choices: (1) accept

MORAL REASONING OF ATHLETES

In studies using the Hahm-Beller Values Choice Inventory (© 1989) at the University of Idaho (Hahm, Beller, and Stoll 1989; Beller 1990; Beller, Stoll, and Hahm 1992; Beller and Stoll 1992), and at the United States Military Academy at West Point (Penny and Priest 1990; Krause and Priest 1993; Beller and Stoll 1995), honesty was found to be the lowest value relative to other moral values of responsibility and justice. However, this is not to say that athletes or non-athletes score high on such inventories. The Hahm-Beller has been criticized as being reductionary—meaning that the authors have arbitrarily selected three first principles to act as guidelines for ethical conduct. However, even with ten years of criticism, the Hahm-Beller has stood the test of time with over 35,000 inventories charted (Beller, Stoll, Burwell and Cole 1995; Beller, Stoll, and Hahm 1992; Beller, Stoll, and Rudd 1997; Krause and Priest 1993; Penny and Priest 1990).

the supposed flawed rule and play the game, (2) accept the rule as is, but try to change the rules, or (3) refuse to play. Situations 1 and 3 are self-explanatory, but changing the rules may mean open protest and maybe even a rebellion against how the rules were developed. During this rebellion, you have two options, refuse to play by the rules (and accept the fact that the player may not play), or accept the rules as they are until new rules are developed. The conditions stated are such that an honest player is obligated to live within the three situations stated, because an honest player would not covertly violate the rules or cheat. Honesty is a difficult value to follow, especially for athletes (see Box 2-7).

Responsibility: Moral Value Three

Responsibility is accounting for your actions. Frankena (1973) discusses the three different ways we use the word *responsible*.

1. Jane is responsible, which says something about Jane's character,

2. Jane was responsible, meaning that Jane is and was responsible for some past action, and

3. Jane is responsible for Y (some action), meaning that Jane is responsible for some future action.

Situation one concerns moral value. Situation two may directly refer to some nonmoral action such as getting the equipment, or situation two may refer to moral action such as blatantly injuring an opponent. Situation three has the same possibilities as situation two, meaning it could refer to either nonmoral or moral values. In sport today, the word for responsibility is *accountability*, meaning both the nonmoral and moral values of situations one, two, and three. Athletes take pride in their accountability to the team, the coach, and the game. Responsibility is probably the most dominant moral value in an athlete's sporting life.

Beneficence: Moral Value Four

Beneficence is the condition of (a) not doing harm, (b) preventing harm, (c) removing harm, and (d) doing good. Considering the perspective of competition in this country, we have taken a moral leap by including this value. In the international sense, beneficence might be called "Fair Play," the act of giving to another above and beyond the call of game play, or the act of common civility. For example, in the 1952 Olympic Games, the Italian bobsledder, Carlo Monti, was winning the event, with one team to follow. When he heard that the last team had a broken brake, Monti immediately returned to the start and gave the opposing team his brake. The opposing team won, using Monti's brake. The international "Fair Play" award was given to Monti for his devotion to the concept of fair play (see Box 2-8).

The following scenario provides an opportunity for showing beneficence to opponents. Assume that you and Josie are playing squash in the national squash tournament semifinals. You have played Josie on several different occasions, and you know each other moderately well. You use the same kind of squash racquets, with the same handgrips. You have identical backup racquets. On the way to the court this morning (a thirty-minute drive), the van driver informs Josie that she cannot carry her rac-

THEORY BOX 2-8

A COMMENT ABOUT ATHLETES

In our work with college-age athletes, we have found that they seem to have no conception of the word *beneficence*—defined as (a) doing no harm, (b) preventing harm, (c) removing harm, and (d) doing good. They cannot accept this moral value in sport participation.

Many athletes would agree that conditions (a) and (b) are acceptable, (c) is marginally acceptable, and (d) perhaps never acceptable. Athletes are not necessarily unkind, rather it has to do with their concept of reality and competition (Beller and Stoll 1993). One could argue that this notion of beneficence really relates to the old notion of sportsmanship. For more on this topic see:

An article by Ken Fidlin—*Toronto Sun*
http://www.canoe.ca/BalCle/oct3_fidlin.html
Article about sportsmanship:
http://www.chronicle.duke.edu/chronicle/97/03/31/s04LackOf.html

THEORY BOX 2-9

WHAT DO ATHLETES SAY?

Many athletes would not give Josie the backup racquet; they rationalize that such is a "break of the game" and no one is responsible to do good, only to do no harm or non-maleficence. Therefore, they are not obligated to loan Josie the backup racquet. We disagree for various philosophical reasons, both from an idealistic perspective, or what is known as a Kantian perspective or a consequential perspective. (Consequential ethics, an ethical theory, holds that the rightness or wrongness of acts is based on the nonmoral consequences that the act brings.)

1. An Idealist or Kantian would say that the moral principle is to be kind, no matter the consequences. That is, the amount of money, the opponent's obnoxious personality, or other factors are irrelevant. The moral principle, beneficence, is held at all times for all people.
2. A consequentialist might say that the loss of the backup racquet was due to no irresponsibility of the moral agent, that is, the player.
   a. To not play the match would deny the reason for being there, which is competing with the best in the tournament.
   b. A forfeit win, in this scenario, is tainted. Is the win a win or a manipulation of rules outside the game itself?

quet bag on board. Josie personally places her racquet bag in the rear of the van. When she arrives at the court, Josie discovers that the van driver removed her racquet bag to repack equipment and inadvertently forgot her bag. She asks the driver to return to retrieve her racquet bag. In tournament play, a fifteen-minute forfeit time is allowed before disqualification. The round trip for the van to the hotel is about sixty minutes. Josie proceeds to the court; by tournament rules, no racquet means a forfeit. If Josie forfeits, you advance to the national championship. Josie checks around and finds you are the only person at the tournament with a backup racquet the same as hers. She explains the circumstances about her racquet and asks to use your backup racquet (see Box 2-9).

1. Would you give Josie your backup racquet?
2. Would any of the following affect your answer?
   a. You don't especially like Josie.
   b. The winner is guaranteed $1,000, and a forfeit is as good as a win.

c. What if the prize is $5,000?
d. The two other players in the semifinals bracket are not of the quality of you or Josie. It is likely that whoever wins this match will win the championship and the $10,000 top prize.

Allowing Josie to use your backup racquet also may address other moral values, but essentially this is an issue of beneficence, item (d) doing good (see Box 2-10). The first three conditions, (a) not doing harm, (b) preventing harm, and (c) removing harm, may have already been met; there is no intention

THEORY BOX 2-10

RESPONSIBILITY AND JUSTICE

In this case, to loan the backup racquet is an issue of both justice and responsibility.

Responsibility states that you are accountable not only for your action but your actions in relation to competition and the game itself. You have a responsibility to play to your best ability and to seek your highest competitive level. For competition to occur at the highest possible level, the backup racquet must be shared. The concept of distributive justice is not necessarily giving the racquet but believing in the concept of equal distribution of competition. If you want to have the best competition, you would want Josie to have an equal opportunity to compete. You would do everything in your power to see that Josie, your opponent, can play in the competition. Therefore, you would offer your racquet (probably before Josie even asked).

THEORY BOX 2-11

NONMALEFICENCE

For our work with athlete populations, we begin our study of treating others kindly with the concept of "doing no harm." "Doing no harm" is the moral value of nonmaleficence. Athletes on the whole seem to agree that intentionally harming an opposing player is totally unacceptable. Once they agree that this is true, we can begin examining beneficence. However, some athletes, especially those in contact and revenue-producing sports, never accept this concept (Beller 1990; Beller, Stoll, and Hahm 1992; Beller and Stoll 1992; Beller and Stoll 1993; Beller, Stoll, and Rudd 1997; Beller and others 1995; Beller and Stoll 1995). For more information on this topic see, the University of Idaho's Center for Ethics homepage and click on the HBVCI icon. http://www.ets.uidaho.edu/center_for_ethics/

here to harm the opponent. No rule requires you to give Josie your backup; however, the final element of beneficence asks you to do good, which in this case may be both moral and nonmoral—moral good in the sense of treating Josie kindly and nonmoral good in the sense of intrinsic, inherent things. Can you think of any others?

Because doing good plays an important role in sport, it has application in this text on sport ethics. Beneficence passes moral criteria: it is common to the world's religions and cultures and, from a reasoned and rational sense, is paramount to relationships with others (see Box 2-11).

FROM VALUES TO PRINCIPLES
Negative Versus Positive Principles

We have stated that we believe there are four universal values: justice, honesty, responsibility, and beneficence. We have tried to apply these values to sport. Now we must develop a set of universal principles by which to lead our sporting lives (see Box 2-12).

A *principle* is technically a statement, written in the negative, of our values and beliefs. It is a statement from which all rules are developed. For example, "I will not lie." Apply the concept of writing in the negative to the four moral values we selected.

Justice: Principle One—Do Not Be Unfair

We mean fair in the sense of simply treating all people by the same set of standards and by employing distributive justice, procedural justice, compensatory justice, and retributive justice. This principle simply stands as a measure of fairness. This principle or First Rule should be applied to everyone it touches. Such a perspective opens a wide array of questions when dealing with equity questions, rule interpretations, and so on.

Honesty: Principle Two—Do Not Lie, Cheat, or Steal

The moral value of honesty is framed within three possible negative precepts of lying, cheating, and stealing. Lying is verbal dishonesty. Cheating is be-

THEORY BOX 2-12

WRITING PRINCIPLES

Fox and DeMarco (1990) argue that principles should be written in the negative rather than the positive. Negative principles seem to cover all situations and cases and apply to everybody all the time. The negative seems to be more concrete; we seem to understand the negative more easily. Rules over time have been written from the negative, for example, the Ten Commandments or the National Collegiate Athletic Association's (NCAA) Manual. Positive principles seem to be more abstract. For example, "do not cheat" carries the implication that you should never cheat, under any circumstances; whereas to "play honestly" may not be possible, when out of ignorance you may not be playing honestly. That is, you may be violating a rule because it may be obscure or you do not know the rule exists. Cheating means that you consciously know and covertly act to violate rules; "don't cheat" means that you know the rules and choose to follow them. Negative principles are powerful in that more people can accept them because evils are being avoided. Our negative principles are being stated from a positive value system based on justice, honesty, responsibility, and beneficence.

ing dishonest in action after giving your word, implicitly or explicitly, to follow some specific rules. Stealing is taking something that belongs to someone else.

Responsibility: Principle Three—Do Not Be Irresponsible

This principle means that you knowingly take your actions into consideration and do what you say you are going to do. You do what you promise to do, and you accept praise or blame for what you have done. You act in such a fashion that others can depend on you to complete what you begin.

Beneficence: Principle Four—Do Not Be Uncivil

We have written this principle to take into consideration the four tenants of beneficence: (a) doing no harm, (b) removing harm, (c) preventing harm, and (d) doing good. We are using this principle as the concept of being civil to others and showing common decency. The concept is that you treat others with a certain sense of decency in which you do no harm, you remove harm, you prevent harm, and you attempt to do good.

APPLYING THE PRINCIPLES

In our athletic director scenario, which of the aforementioned principles apply? At least the following three apply: justice, responsibility, and beneficence.

a. Justice in the sense of treating others fairly.
b. Responsibility in the sense of acting responsibly in a game situation.

c. Beneficence in the sense of being civil to others, including opposing team members.

To apply the principles, you need to ask yourself some particular questions.

1. Is justice being served in the athletic director scenario? Does good competition have a chance to survive or exist when the external conditions are such that equal play cannot occur? If the coach cannot coach, is fair or equal play occurring?
2. Is responsible action occurring in this situation? Are the people involved being responsible for their actions? Should the band and cheerleaders be held to a higher degree of responsibility because of their representative positions for the school? Should the athletic director and president be responsible for holding them to a higher standard? Are the fans being responsible for their actions? Should they be responsible?
3. Is civility occurring around the court? Should opposing teams be treated with common decency? Would you want to be treated civilly in the same situation? Why should the standard be different at a basketball game? Can you universalize your answers?

"STACKING" THE PRINCIPLES AND FINDING EXCEPTIONS

If you have more than one principle, you may find that your principles may at times conflict. For example, which is more important—not telling a lie or being responsible? In the four principles that we have written, list which is the most important, the second most, the third, and the fourth. Now, use an example in which two of your principles will conflict, such as "Do Not Be Dishonest" and "Do Not Be Unkind." Decide how you will resolve the problem.

Mary is your good friend. You are both competitive dance skaters. Mary is always highly sensitive about her personal attire; in fact, Mary is sensitive about any negative comments directed toward her. You realize this and understand that though Mary may be too sensitive, she is worth the effort to be a friend. Mary buys a new competitive dance costume that is very expensive. She wears the outfit for a special dress rehearsal in which you and she are preparing to compete, though in different levels. She thinks the costume is gorgeous. When Mary sees you, she tells you about her expensive outfit and how beautiful she thinks it is. In your heart of hearts, you think her choice is just about the ugliest thing you have ever seen. You think it is the wrong style, the wrong color, the wrong length, and the wrong everything for Mary. Mary asks you what you think of the outfit. Considering the four principles, Mary is asking you to make a moral decision concerning at least two of them, "Do Not Be Dishonest" and "Do Not Be Unkind." What would you do?

1. Would you tell Mary the truth and bear the consequences of her response? Or,
2. Would you tell a little white lie, and tell Mary the outfit is okay? (Would it make any difference if you two were competing in the same event?) If you chose number one, perhaps you believe that the principle of "Do Not Be Dishonest" is more important than "Do Not Be Unkind." In this perspective, you believe that honesty is the most important value. You decide that truth is more important than Mary's feelings.

If you chose number two, then you may think that being kind is more important than being honest. You took into consideration Mary's sensitivity and think that honesty really is not that important. What is the more right action, not being unkind or telling the truth? At this point in our discussion, perhaps neither is. In stacking principles, though, you are forced to decide which is more important.

Or perhaps you believe that the issue is a matter of taste, which is a nonmoral issue. Therefore, you chose number two because in the sense of social tact it is permissible to tell a little white lie (see Beller and Stoll 1996).

The purpose of moral reasoning is to use a rational, impartial, reasoned system to find solutions to moral questions. When you decide your stacking order, you are bound or obligated to follow this order. Does this mean at all times? Yes, it does—*unless you can find specific exceptions.*

Suppose in this case you argue that "telling the truth" is really hurting Mary. Should you be so bound to a principle that the principle becomes more important than the person? Perhaps, but principles without context many times cause wrong actions and inconsistencies. In stacking your principles, you need to ask yourself if this moral question is an exception to your principles. If "Do Not Be Dishonest" is your most important principle, does it remain so at all times or does this become an exception? Is telling a friend what you see as the truth about a skating outfit an exception to your principle? Reason and rationality tell you that to all principles and ordering of principles there must be exceptions. However, what merits an exception?

3. Suppose that in the skating scenario, you chose an alternative approach. Is there a way to address both honesty and beneficence?

If you can find a way to place the two values on an equal plane, this may be an acceptable alternative and the best solution. You are able to take into consideration both principles and may even argue that the principle "Do Not Be Irresponsible" forces you to tell Mary the truth as kindly as possible. (This approach may not work either; Mary may be so sensitive that whatever you do will hurt Mary.) If you chose this position, you may have decided that the two principles, "Do Not Lie" and "Do Not Be Unkind," are at the same level of importance and have no difference in your hierarchical order.

When you order your First Principles, you decide which is the most and which is the least important. When conflict arises, ordering or stacking principles will give direction to which principle is more important. You must also take into consideration, when ordering your principles, if an exception exists. This ordering, though, must remain the same and consistent through all situations. If not, your ability to reason critically and find alternative solutions (the very nature of moral reasoning) becomes greatly diminished and mired in confusion.

FROM PRINCIPLES TO RULES

Your First Principles act as basic guides in developing day-to-day rules, which are subordinate to First Rules. The word *rules* in this case can be explicit (like actual written game rules) or implicit unwritten rules (like personal moral guides on being a friend, parent, or spouse). You expect your friends to be trustworthy, loyal, and honest. You expect your spouse to be loyal, responsible, and monogamous. Examples of other day-to-day written and perhaps unwritten rules, sometimes called *ethics,* include professional ethics, business ethics, and medical ethics. Sport also has day-to-day written rules such as game rules and unwritten rules like sportsmanship. When people talk of morality in sport, they often call it *sportsmanship* (see Box 2-13).

Other specific rules, written and unwritten, that could derive from our principles include the following:

Value: Justice
Principle: Do Not Be Unfair

  1. Rule: Do Not Violate Game Rules
  2. Rule: Do Not Use Performance-Enhancing Drugs

Value: Honesty
Principle: Do Not Lie, Cheat, or Steal

  1. Rule: Do Not Cheat While Playing a Game
  2. Rule: Do Not Lie to Opponents or to Officials

Value: Responsibility
Principle: Do Not Be Irresponsible

  1. Rule: Do Not Play an Injured Athlete
  2. Rule: Do Not Be Athletically Disqualified by Being Academically Deficient

Value: Beneficence
Principle: Do Not Be Unkind

  1. Rule: Do Not Intentionally Harm Another Player
  2. Rule: Do Not Let Others Harm Opposing Players

THEORY BOX 2-13

WHAT IS SPORTSMANSHIP?

Forgive us for using the word *sportsmanship*. Many individuals are offended by the use of this word and instead prefer *sportspersonship*. We checked with the majority of ruling organizations in this country and over 4000 sites on the Internet and they are still using the word *sportsmanship*. Therefore, since the majority still uses it, we will use the term here.

Few people can identify exactly what moral values, principles, or rules sportsmanship is supposed to portray. Historically, sportsmanship derives from the English heritage and is an unwritten moral rule based on the virtues of fairness and honesty. It used to be considered requisite to playing a game. Interestingly the groups' values may not be consistent within the group and each person within the group may have a different understanding of what that word means.

The word *sportsmanship* is also a misunderstood word. Sportsmanship is written into the playing rules today under the rubric of unsportsmanlike conduct. The word itself is probably a dying entity. Some—for example, Canadians—prefer the term, "Fair Play." The Canadian government has developed the Fair Play Commission to educate and address issues of sportsmanship, or as they describe it, "fair play within sport." See these two sources:

http://tiger.net-master.net/~sports/sportsma.htm

Illinois High School Athletics Association http://www.ihsa.org/feature/sawa/

SUMMARY

Thus far, you have discovered that reasoning strategies are very important to solve moral issues in sport. Before you continue, review the precepts of moral reasoning. Critical inquiry is based on rationally determining moral issues. A critical, reasoned inquiry demands accurate, exact, and precise thinking. A reasoned inquiry also takes into account all sides of an issue in its past, present, and future sense. To reason then, demands that you follow the

ISSUES AND DILEMMAS

Which of the following rules or comments can be matched with one of your *First Rules*?

1. Coach says you have a curfew of 9:00.
2. The time limit for the balance beam routine is 90 seconds.
3. Women in sport have a right to equality.
4. The rule book says, "Only two dribbles."
5. Can you list four more?

three tenets of moral reasoning, that is, to be impartial, consistent, and reflective.

In developing your reasoned inquiry, your personal philosophies also come into play. What you believe and who you are colors how you act. That is, your values, both moral and nonmoral, are the deciding factors in your moral inquiry. Values determine your principles and your obligations. If you can reason through your values and determine a consistent value system, you will be on your way to a moral standard that can withstand internal and external scrutiny.

Once you have discovered your values, you then pen your universal principles. These First Rules guide you in developing your personal and professional rules.

REFERENCES

Beller, J.M. 1990. A moral reasoning intervention program for Division I athletes: Can athletes learn not to cheat? Ph.D. diss., University of Idaho.

Beller, J.M., and S.K. Stoll. 1990. Moral development of student athletes: Can athletes learn not to cheat? Unpublished research. Center for ETHICS, University of Idaho.

———. 1992. A moral reasoning intervention program for Division I athletes. *Academic Athletic Journal* (spring): 43–57.

———. 1993. Sportsmanship: An antiquated concept? JOP-ERD (August): 74–79.

———. 1994. Moral reasoning of high school athletes and general students: An empirical study versus personal testimony. Manuscript submitted for review.

———. 1995. Moral development of high school athletes. *Journal of Pediatric Science,* 7(4), (November): 352–63.

———. 1996. Honesty and the "Little White Lie". *Strategies* 9(7) (May): 23–25.

Beller, J.M., S.K. Stoll, and C.H. Hahm. 1992. Moral reasoning and moral development in sport review and HBVCI manual. Center for ETHICS, University of Idaho.

———. 1993. The Hahm-Beller Values Choice Inventory in the sport milieu: A new sport moral reasoning inventory. Manuscript submitted for publication.

Beller, J.M., S.K. Stoll, Barbara Burwell, and Jack Cole. 1995 (September). The relationship of competition and a Christian liberal arts education on moral reasoning of college student athletes. ERIC Data Base, Resources in Education, *Red* #ED 382 620.

———. 1996. The relationship of competition and a Christian liberal arts education on moral reasoning of college student athletes. *Research on Christian Higher Education* 3: 99–114.

Beller, J.M., S.K. Stoll, and A. Rudd. 1997. The "Great Character experience": Assessing the effectiveness of a Great Books approach to teaching moral character with competitive populations. *Research Quarterly for Exercise and Sport* [Abstract] Supplement.

Fox, R.M., and J.P. DeMarco. 1990. *Moral reasoning: A philosophical approach to applied ethics.* Fort Worth, TX: Holt, Rinehart and Winston, Inc.

Frankena, W.K. 1973. *Ethics.* 2d ed. Englewood Cliffs, NJ: Prentice Hall.

Hahm, C.H., J.M. Beller, and S.K. Stoll. 1989. The Hahm-Beller Values Choice Inventory in the sport milieu. (available from Center for ETHICS, Room 109 Memorial Gym, University of Idaho, Moscow, ID 83843).

Krause, Jerry V., and Bob Priest. 1993. Sport values choices of United States Academy cadets—A longitudinal study of the class of 1993. Unpublished manuscript. Office of Institutional research, United States Military Academy.

Lickona, T. 1991. *Educating for character.* New York: Bantam Books.

Penny, W.J., and R.F. Priest. 1990. Deontological sport values: Choices of USMA cadets and selected other college-aged populations. USMA Publication.

ADDITIONAL READINGS

Ashmore, R.B. 1987. *Building a moral system*. Englewood Cliffs, NJ: Prentice Hall.

Beck, R.N., and J.B. Orr. 1970. *Ethical choice*. New York: The Free Press.

Carrett, E.F. 1984. *The theory of morals*. London: Macmillan Publishing Co.

Dubin, C.L. 1990. *Commission of inquiry into the use of drugs and banned practices intended to increase athletic performance*. Ottawa: Canadian Government Publishing Centre.

Hahm, C.H. Moral reasoning and moral development among general students, physical education majors, and student-athletes, Ph.D. diss., University of Idaho.

Johnson, O.A. 1969. *Rightness and goodness: A study in contemporary ethical theory*. Hague: Martinus Nijhoff.

Penny, William J., and Bob Priest. 1990. Deontological sport values choices of United States Academy cadets and selected other college-aged populations. Unpublished manuscript. Office of Institutional Research, United States Military Academy.

Rawls, J. 1971. *A theory of justice*. Cambridge: Harvard University Press.

Ross, W.D. 1930. *The right and the good*. Oxford: Clarendon Press.

Rudd, Andrew, S.K. Stoll, and J.M. Beller. 1997a. Expressed coaching behavior and its effect on athlete moral development. *Research Quarterly for Exercise & Sport* [Abstract], Supplement.

———. 1997b. Moral calluses in sport. Paper presented at the annual convention of the International Philosophic Society for the Study of Sport, Clarkston, Washington.

Smart, J.D. 1961. *An outline of a system of ethics*. Melbourne:

Stoll, S.K. 1993. *Who says this is cheating?* Dubuque, IA: Kendall/Hunt.

Stoll, S.K., and J.M. Beller. 1992. Qualitative research of moral reasoning in sport populations. Unpublished research. Center for ETHICS, University of Idaho.

Stoll, S.K., J.M. Beller, M. Reall, and C.H. Hahm. n.d. The importance of teaching methodology in sport education. *Academic Athletic Journal*. Forthcoming.

———. 1993. Effect of a longitudinal teaching methodology and classroom environment on both cognitive and behavioral moral development. *Research Quarterly for Exercise and Sport* (Supplement) 64 (March): A–112.

———. 1994. The effect of a longitudinal teaching methodology and teaching environment on both cognitive and behavioral moral development. ERIC Data Base, Resources in Education, Ref #ED 359 180.

———. 1994. Methodology and its effect on cognitive moral reasoning. *Research Quarterly for Exercise and Sport* (Supplement). 64. (March): A–97.

———. 1995. The importance of teaching methodology in moral education of sport populations. ERIC Data Base, Resources in Education, Ref #ED 382 619.

———. n.d. Do we teach character in sport? In *Sociology of Sport*, edited by J. Gerdy. In press.

———. Unpublished data. Center for ETHICS, University of Idaho.

Stoll, S.K., J.M. Beller, Barbara Burwell, and Jack Cole. 1995. Moral reasoning of Division I and Division III athletics: Is there a difference? Resources in Education, Ref #ED 382 681.

———. n.d. Comparison of moral development of Division III and Division I athletes. In review.

Stoll, S.K., J.M. Beller, J. Cole, and B. Burwell. 1995. A comparison of moral reasoning scores of student athletes in Division I and Division III NCAA member collegiate institutions. *Research Quarterly for Exercise and Sport* (Supplement) 66 (March): A–81.

CHAPTER 3

A Consistent Game Plan

- ◆ What are the steps to analyzing and criticizing moral principles and rules?
- ◆ How do you apply moral principles to a moral issue?
- ◆ What are the major fallacies to reasoning?

A STRATEGY TO ANALYZE MORAL REASONING

It is never easy to make good decisions, and it is definitely not easy to systematically think through a moral problem, taking into consideration your own values and beliefs while weighing them against what others value and believe. In Chapters 1 and 2, you found that sometimes principles and rules may clash. What do you do when this happens? How can you go about finding a consistent systematic reasoning process when things just do not seem to fit?

Assume that you are a girls' basketball coach in an inner city high school. Through your hard work, and that of the team, you have realized your dream of competing in the city championship. Your team is centered around Jody, an imposing six-foot, two-inch; 24 points-a-game player. Before joining the team, Jody was a discipline problem in school but now she appears to have found a new goal in life; she wants to become what she perceives you to

be—a sincere, honest, hard-working, caring teacher and coach.

The day of the big game, Mr. Wright, the newly appointed athletic director, informs you that Mr. Dud, the former athletic director (who dropped dead of a heart attack last week), did not keep accurate eligibility records for the girls' teams, and according to the rules, Jody is too old to play in the big game. In fact, Jody was too old to play the entire season. He also mentions that Jody probably does not know she is and was ineligible.

Jody has little else going for her except athletics. Her two brothers are in jail for drugs and violence, the father is missing, and the mother is questionable as a role model. Mr. Wright says he will understand if you decide to break the rule; Jody is worth more than a rule. However, he also states that breaking the rule and getting caught will probably place you in great jeopardy for future employment as a coach. Considering the state of affairs, Wright cannot make a decision but states that he will remain silent for the good of the school and will support whatever you decide.

You have always obeyed the rules and you set that example for your players. Now you must decide between obeying the rule or permitting Jody to play in what might be, for you and the team, the biggest game ever.

Should you play Jody? Why? You face a tough decision. Wright, who should have acted, refused, placing the burden on you. You are in a position where you must now act and make a choice. Making a choice is a voluntary behavior, and voluntary behavior denotes a moral dilemma.

Within this voluntary behavior, three factors define this case as a moral choice: (a) alternatives, (b) choice, and (c) acting. Your alternatives are: you can play the game as is, play the game without Jody, or not play the game. (Most rules state that playing an ineligible player forfeits all former games, causing the team to be out of contention for the championship game.)

You apparently have a specific moral value system in that you are known to be competent, honest, and caring, which we could translate to values of responsibility (competency), honesty (truthfulness), and beneficence (loving kindness). If the value system is developed, then you probably have a set of principles such as "Do Not Be Irresponsible," "Do Not Be Dishonest," and "Do Not Be Unkind." In this case, and before any final judgments are made, you must debate (with yourself), your own principles relative to the worth of the game. Should you follow the rules? Or are you justified in violating the rules? Should you follow your principles, considering all the mitigating consequences—Jody's self-worth (and perhaps her future), team pride, school prestige, and the former athletic director's ineptness? If you have developed your principles, you must weigh your moral obligation concerning what ought to be done.

What are your obligations in this scenario?

In this case, your obligation (see Box 3-1) may hinge on (a) obligation to yourself, (b) obligation to Jody, (c) obligation to society and the moral order, and (d) obligation to your own principles (not necessarily in that order).

In studying such issues, you may argue that the consequences of your actions or the nonmoral good that would come from playing Jody is better

than strictly following a set of austere guides like First Principles. If Jody is played, nonmoral extrinsic good could be revenue for the school; an intrinsic value could be playing a championship game; a contributory value for other team members could be their hard work all season (see Box 3-2).

Can you think of any others?

In this scenario, you as the coach are asked to make a decision between the worth of the individual and the rule. How do you decide?

1. Do you follow the rule because you are bound to follow rules?
2. Do you follow the rule because you are afraid you might get caught if you don't?
3. Do you violate the rule because you believe Jody is more important than the rule?
4. Do you violate the rule and justify that by saying Jody is more important than the rule, when in reality you need Jody to win?

In this case and all cases of conflicting values, there are certain steps that you may follow to help yourself systematically think through a moral problem.

1. Step One: Are Any Moral Principles Violated?

You chose four moral principles as the basis of your most fundamental obligations to others in sport. When you agree to compete, you agree to apply these moral principles at all times. If you

CONSEQUENTIAL AND NONCONSEQUENTIAL ETHICAL THEORY

Even though numerous varieties exist, ethical normative theory generally falls into two main classes, consequential (teleological or utilitarian) and nonconsequential (deontological, deontic, Kantian) ethics. Utilitarian, teleological, and consequential ethics are not exactly the same. Although the three viewpoints begin with concern for the greatest amount of good, the teleologian is concerned primarily with moral intention and the consequential with the ultimate action for the amount of good. For a good examination of these theories, see Frankena 1973 and Fox and DeMarco 1990, or check out these Internet sites:

A directory of sources on ethical theory:
http://truth.wofford.edu/~kaycd/theories.htm
http://voled.doded.mil/dantes/exams/dsst/sf474.htm

An ethics update on ethical theory and applied ethics:
http://ethics.acusd.edu

In the case of Jody, the basketball player, if you decided that you can justify a decision to play the game because of all the mitigating consequences, you are practicing a form of consequential ethics. That is, any act can be right or obligatory if it produces a greater balance of good than do any other possible alternatives. Consequential ethics are often referred to as relative in that the consequences of each situation decide the ethical position. Some philosophers state that such an ethical position does not violate ethical rules because good requires that each of us adhere strictly to the duty of doing the greatest amount of good.

Consequential theory states that the basic or ultimate criterion or standard of what is morally right, wrong, or obligatory is the nonmoral value that is brought into being. Frankena (1973) explained,

> . . . the final appeal, directly or indirectly, must be to the comparative amount of good produced, or rather to the comparative balance of good over evil produced. Thus, an act is right if, and only if, it or the rule under which it falls produces, will probably produce, or is intended to produce at least as great a balance of good over evil as any available alternative; an act is wrong if and only if it does not do so.

The consequential could argue that the good that would result from playing the game might be greater than the evil of violating the rule. What argument can you give for playing Jody? Give four conditions of nonmoral good that could arise from deciding to play Jody. We offer the following:

1. You and Jody had no intention of violating any rules. You have worked hard all year; shouldn't Jody be given the opportunity to finish the year?
2. The rest of the team knew nothing of these conditions, and they deserve the chance to play the game.
3. If Jody is told that she is ineligible, wouldn't that cause irreparable harm?
4. Consider also all the revenue and public good that is brought to the school because of playing in a championship game.
5. Consider the good that will come to you and vicariously to all the future players you will work with when you are promoted after the win.

On the other hand, if you decide that the team should not play the game and should reveal the truth concerning Jody's eligibility, then you may be practicing what is known as nonconsequential ethics. Nonconsequential, or deontic (deontological), ethics holds that there is an inherent rightness apart from all consequences. In other words, there are acts that are obligatory regardless of the human condition or misfortune, or as the old adage states, "Let justice prevail though the heavens may fall." It may be thought that such a position is cruel and heartless to the human condition; however, deontic principle states that certain ethical laws must never be violated, for example, do not lie, do not kill, and do not cheat.

Deontic theory, therefore, holds that rightness is a fundamental, irreducible ethical concept. Deontics believe that holding to principles is a duty. For example, it is your duty to keep your promises, not because doing so will produce the best possible consequences, but simply because you have made the promise. Promise keeping is right because it is promise keeping. Ross (1930) called this kind of example a "*prima facie* duty."

"*Prima facie* duty" or "conditional duty" is a brief way of referring to the characteristic (quite distinct

Continued.

CONSEQUENTIAL AND NONCONSEQUENTIAL ETHICAL THEORY—cont'd

from that of being a duty proper) an act has (for example, the keeping of a promise) of being an act which would be a duty proper if it were not at the same time of another kind which is morally significant.

Deontic theory such as Ross' *prima facie* duty has an inherent rightness of all actions that you ought to follow, rather than considering the consequences. In the Jody case, the deontic would say that all consequences mean nothing; you have only one course of action. You must publicly declare Jody ineligible. All games must be forfeited.

From our discussion, it would appear that you as coach could ethically make either a deontic or consequential choice and justify it. However, this is not the case. It must be remembered that our ethical questions require consistency, impartiality, and reflection. Remember also that you profess the values known as (1) obeying laws and rules, (2) professional

honesty, and (3) professional competency. It would appear that you have a certain set of professional rules based on First Principles. We are not sure exactly what these First Principles are, but it could be argued that they may include (1) Do Not Be Dishonest, (2) Do Not Be Irresponsible, and (3) Do Not Be Unkind. If this is true and if you consequentially justify your decision to play the game with Jody, you abrogate your own moral position and are not being consistent with your own beliefs and practices. If you act in conflict (which is your prerogative) with your values, you deny the essence of what you believe. Such behavior would portray you as being confused and inconsistent with your values. Because of your own past behaviors and purported ethical beliefs, if you truly value honesty above any nonmoral value, you have no recourse but to act non-consequentially.

---

violate any of your principles, then you must decide whether this action is an exception to the rule or whether your action is morally unacceptable. How do you know when a principle is violated? The answer lies in knowing what you believe, what you value, and what principles you have developed. If you do not know, you will have continual problems with making moral decisions. Your purpose in developing these principles is to influence a sport society that is just, honest, responsible, and civil. In the scenario, what do you believe about the worth of the rules in setting criteria for sport events?

    a. Should rules be followed at all times?

    b. Are there times when rules should not be followed?

    c. Are any moral principles being violated?

2. Step Two: Are Any Moral Rules Violated? Numerous moral day-to-day rules follow directly from each principle. These rules govern all behavior in sport settings. These role-specific rules should guide you as you participate; if they do not, you need to address why they are exceptions.

3. Step Three: Is This Case An Exception? Rules may have exceptions, but the exceptions must be justified. The burden of proof of whether this is an exception means that you must show that there is a good, overriding reason for allowing this exception. For example, you may have an exception if a moral rule is in conflict with a moral principle. Examine a situation involving the moral principle, Do Not Be Unfair. An athlete has asthma and requires a specific drug to compete at the minimum level. The drug, however, is on the "banned drug" list of the governing body. The "banned drug" is a rule—Do Not Use This Drug, but the asthmatic athlete cannot compete in a distributive justice sense. This case is an exception. Therefore, if you have many of these exceptions, you may need to change the rule to, "Do not use this drug, unless authorized by a physician for medical conditions to meet minimal performance levels."

4. Step Four: Are The Rules Justified? Sometimes rules are immoral, such as a rule that arbitrarily harms or is unjust. When you apply rules, you must ask whether the rule is a good rule. If the rule violates one of your moral principles, you may

truthfully say that it is morally wrong, even though there appears to be a good reason for the rule. For example, in 1991 the NCAA Rule Book stated,

16.10.2.7—An institution or its staff member may not provide transportation (e.g., a ride home with a coach) to an enrolled student-athlete even if the student-athlete reimburses the institution or its staff members for the appropriate amount of the gas expense.

The purpose of this rule was that a coach or any athletic personnel could not give an athlete a free or reimbursed ride. Its original intent and motive was good—to make sure that student athletes do not receive special favors. However, its resultant effect could bring about bad actions. Suppose that coach A is driving through a rain storm and sees athlete B walking without benefit of umbrella or raincoat. If coach A gives athlete B a ride, she is violating a rule. The NCAA had good reason for the rule, in that the governing organization was trying to keep a rein on unfair inducements or free gifts and benefits. However, the rule in this case was violating two moral principles, "Do Not Be Irresponsible" (letting a human being walk in a rain storm without benefit of protection, when we have protection to offer) and "Do Not Be Unkind" (offering someone a kind service). The rule in this case violated two basic moral principles. The rule appeared to be in error in its application to this situation, although maybe not under other circumstances.

5. Step Five: How Can The Rules Be Changed?

If the day-to-day rules are your personal rules, you can readily make a change. However, if the changes affect a large social group, such as those made by sport governing bodies, a change may require political action, a demonstration, or a legislative move. If you cannot morally function within the rules and change cannot be effected, you may even be morally justified in breaking or violating the rule as long as it is done consistently, within the parameters of our moral principles.

If you choose to play Jody, you might use the following reasoning process.

1. Does your choice violate any of your moral principles? Yes, it does. It violates the principle of justice (playing by the rules, procedural justice) and the principle of honesty (you implicitly gave your word to follow the rules of the sport organization). Because your choice does violate at least two principles.

2. Is this case an exception? Yes, you say. The exception becomes "Do not be unjust except in cases where being unjust does a greater good." Or, "Do not be dishonest except in cases where being dishonest is a greater good. . . ."

3. Does the burden of proof state that it is an exception? Can you use this exception in all cases? At this point, you may become hard pressed to meet the burden of proof. For the burden of proof asks if you can generalize this exception to all cases. Would you want others to follow the same line of reasoning? Would you want other coaches to apply this same exception? What might

occur if you do have such an exception to the rules? "Do not be unjust except in cases where being unjust does a greater good." Our problem now becomes defining the greater good and controlling the interpretation of the "greater good."

4. Should the rules be changed?

If the exception is strong enough, the rules should be changed. Should the rules now state, "All players must be of a certain age by a certain date. However, if some players don't know how old they are, the rule is flexible." Or, "All players must be of a certain age by a certain date, except in cases where age cannot be determined." Or, "All coaches must follow the rules of the organizations, except in those cases in which rules are unknowingly violated." As you can see, such exceptions become difficult to formulate. Can you write your exception so that it can bear the burden of being universalized to the greater society?

OBSTACLES AND FALLACIES IN REASONING

Now that you have an idea of how you can systematically think through a moral problem, what problems will you face in placing your system into action? Because of the very nature of moral reasoning, you will be faced with many personal and social challenges to carry out your game plan of moral reasoning.

Your first challenge is to muster the courage to stand for what you value in the face of doubt, ridicule, and misgiving by those around you. Many people will not believe that moral values, principles, and rules have any merit. They will set forth various arguments about why moral reasoning is useless, manipulative, and silly. Following are a few of the basic obstacles (a reasoning obstacle is a limited thinking perspective that obscures an enlightened point of view) and fallacies that you will encounter that will work against your moral valuing and moral reasoning.

Skepticism

Some people will show extreme skepticism that any reasoning about moral issues can exist. Skeptics purport that it is not possible to reason about moral judgments. They believe that any determination of morality is simply an expression of feelings or emotion. For example, these skeptics might say, "That act is good only because it is nothing more than a matter of taste such as 'I like that,' 'Well, that's the way I feel about it and that's all there is to it,' 'You are entitled to your feelings and I to mine,' or 'Well, there really isn't a right answer, is there?' "

If you examine these statements, you will notice that the skeptics use words such as "simply," "merely," or "nothing more." The study of ethics is complicated, difficult, and hardly, if ever, "nothing but this" or "nothing but that." Morality does involve feelings and emotions, but moral reasoning is more than feelings. Even if moral reasoning were only feelings and emotion, you could still reason about emotions and desires and about how you should or should not morally act. You could still make moral judgments, according to moral rules, principles, and values, on these feelings and emotions. You must keep your mind open to the possibility of solving problems by rational means and improve your reasoning, rather than assume you are defeated before you start.

Cultural and Relative Ethics

Relative Ethics (see Box 3-3) is a second challenge to your reasoning. All of us have heard others say, "It is all right with me, as long as it does not bother me," "Who am I to judge?" "Everyone has the right to their own beliefs," or "They have a different standard, one I have no right to infringe upon." These statements underlie an ethical dilemma that most of us will face—that moral judgments are judgments with no objective solution and as such are relative. They change by degree as to different times and places. The relativist will use various arguments to show that no standard exists, and any exceptions to a standard prove that it does not exist.

Dogmatism

Dogmatists have all the answers. Because they feel strongly about an issue, they confuse subjective certainty with objective certainty. Obviously, you need strong convictions, but dogmatics refuse the

CULTURAL RELATIVISM

A cousin to relative ethics is cultural relativism. Cultural relativism states that different religious, ethnic, or socioeconomic groups are contradicted by moral judgments in another cultural tradition. Cultural relativism states that moral judgments are relative to the culture, religion, socioeconomic circumstances, or background of the agent. This argument, as well as relative ethics, is typically used to excuse immoral behaviors of many disadvantaged athletes. [The Ben Johnson debacle is a prime example. Johnson was an international track and field sprinter from Canada who tested positive for steroids in the 1988 Seoul Olympic Games. The Commission of Inquiry that investigated the incident noted that Johnson's poverty may have been a deciding factor in taking the drug (Dubin 1990).]

The argument states that because disadvantaged athletes are raised in deprived socioeconomic backgrounds and environments of constant crime, they cannot develop the abilities to be moral. They are morally deprived through no fault of their own, and they are in essence coerced to act immorally by societal standards. They are not responsible for their immoral actions. The true villain in this case is society. Therefore, what right has society to judge, condemn, or inquire into their moral or immoral actions?

Though we agree that judgment and condemnation is not our goal and society may be part of the problem, we disagree that we should abnegate moral reasoning on the grounds of relativism. We believe the relativist's position is logically flawed.

The cultural relativist argument can be simplified into the following threefold premise:

1. Athletes from different cultural, religious, and socioeconomic backgrounds have different and conflicting moral beliefs.
2. Because different groups have different beliefs and there probably is no one way to act morally, each group is responsible only for its own morality within that group.
3. Therefore, you have no moral right to criticize their moral positions or place your morally reasoned standards on them.

The above argument, however, is flawed if you consider the criteria for moral reasoning. Reflect on this case. Is premise (1) true and consistent in all cases and at all times? No, premise (1) is not true.

Not all athletes from different backgrounds have conflicting standards to the norm. Many athletes from deprived backgrounds have flourished and are considered moral ideals. (A *moral ideal* is someone who serves as a moral model. His or her actions are just, honest, and responsible. Historical moral ideals were Jesus Christ, Mohandas K. Gandhi, and Socrates. It may be difficult to find an athletic moral ideal, but it is possible. (For example, think of Bob Richards, Olympic pole vault gold medal winner, or Eric Liddel who refused to run the heats of the 100 meters at the 1924 Paris Olympics due to their being held on a Sunday. Liddell went on to win the gold medal in the 400 meter race and set a world record. He truly had an uncompromising spirit.)
See Internet site for Bob Richards.
http://www.usatf.org/athletes/hof/richards.shtml
A short caption on Eric Liddel
http://www.britannia.com/history/prime/prime45.html

Some of the athletes who exercise immoral behaviors according to the societal norm do not hold to premise (1). They have moral principles that agree with societal norms such as caring for their children. It is true that in *some cases* and at *some times* socioeconomically deprived athletes may have conflicting moral actions. Because the above logical statements are true, premise (1) cannot be true.

Premises (2) and (3) are also flawed because they do not logically follow from premise (1). Even if there were no universally accepted ethical values and even if every judgment were unique to every culture, this does not prove that moral reasoning cannot solve moral problems. Just because different socioeconomic groups or persons disagree, it does not follow that no correct answers exist to moral problems. You could just as well argue that because Adolph Hitler in his slaughter of 6 million Jews, and the recent Chinese government in their execution of the pro-democracy students believed their positions were for the moral good of the people, that only their moral answer to quell different races or different opinions is the right answer. The mere suggestion that a moral disagreement exists does not prove or suggest that there is no correct

Continued.

CULTURAL RELATIVISM—cont'd

moral answer. Neither does it suggest that different fundamental moral principles apply to different groups. Also, the mere fact of ethical disagreement between cultures, religions, or socioeconomic classes should not deter moral reasoning. Only by your attempting to reason critically through moral problems can moral views be tested. To assume that people agree that no right answers exist is a blind prejudice that cannot withstand reasoned criticism.

For Internet discussion and a pro-cultural relativism position see:

http://www.worldculture.com/relative.htm
http://www.faklen.dk/en/the_torch/cultrel.shtml

possibility of error or acknowledgment that they may be wrong. "Reasoning is unnecessary because the answer is known; I know and I do not care what anyone says." The dogmatic has a closed mind and refuses to acknowledge any alternative.

One of the aims in moral reasoning is to help straighten out dogmatic thinking. If not, you can oppose yourself in your own thinking, denying responsibility for your own opinions and acts and making it virtually impossible to communicate with others in a rational or coherent way.

False Obstruction of Theory and Practice

Also, some people believe that ethical theory is after all only a theory and not factual, realistic, or practical. You will hear, "The real world is not like that." You, however, must not reject theories simply because they are theories. You should reject theories only if evidence shows they are inadequate. A theory is not inadequate just because it is a theory. All civilized human activity involves theorizing in the sense of generalizing or hypothesizing, and nearly all theories are practical to the extent that they have at least potential applications.

Other Obstacles: Fallacies in Reasoning

As a moral reasoner, you must realize that if you do not follow a standard, logical pattern you may be duped into using fallacious reasoning. If you are very observant, you will notice that most people use psychological, rather than philosophical, reasoning. Specifically, the way that they use the argument is the strength of the argument. They are highly convincing not because of what they say but how they say it. Such reasoning appeals to things people want to believe or to prejudices they hold.

The Fallacy of Authority

Coach Jones, the commissioner, the official, or God has greater plausibility in that it was said by someone in authority. The fallacy of authority is claiming that something is true simply because someone in authority says it is, rather than because it is supported by evidence.

Ad Hominem Arguments

"You cannot believe a word he said, because he is a jerk." In this fallacy, an opinion or belief is wrong solely because the person saying so is known to be bad or disreputable. Name calling is difficult to refute and is the most subversive and cowardly method to win an argument. The method is quite effective because it is so vicious. People often try to defeat their opponents by making fun of them. Name calling also is used in other ways, "Do not believe the coaches' argument that they need more money; they are biased." "Look who is talking" is another variation, suggesting that one flawed person cannot evaluate another.

Misplaced and Improperly Placed Authority

For some reason, you tend to trust experts or people who have professional degrees or important positions. You listen when they have something to say about anything, even when the supposed expert has little experience on that subject. This flawed reasoning is employed by marketers using professional athletes to endorse and advertise products hoping people will buy the products because of the athletes' endorsements.

The Appeal to Force

Might makes right. This position supposes that the opinion of the bigger, stronger, greater number is the correct opinion and probably should determine the morally correct position. This position is often thought to be the most realistic conception of ethics because its standard is not some lofty ideal but the real way the world works. Large numbers of people may be very wrong about a moral issue; for

example, Nazi Germany succeeded for almost ten years because of its political and military power.

The Appeal to Pity and Ridicule

The appeal-to-pity threat is typified in, "Woe is me. Please help me. I am always wrong. Why are you picking on me? You do not like me. Nobody likes me."

Begging the Question

This threat is known as a circular argument. Often thought to mean the argument is illogical, rather it means that the argument is based on incorrect information or the same information again and again. The individual tries to win the argument simply by repeating, insisting, or shouting the same information over and over.

Equivocation

This threat is using words incorrectly or choosing words with the wrong meanings. It also represents arguments in which the words change meanings within the argument. The threat of equivocation is one reason why it is important that we understand ethical terminology.

Psychological Obstacles

The use of psychological obstacles is simply poor reasoning. For various reasons, individuals never learn how to think. They express themselves in slogans or cliches and mimic what Karl Marx called "herd behaviors."

In the cases of Jody, Coach Brown, the volleyball scenarios, and all the other issues discussed thus far, did you fall prey to any of the fallacies and obstacles to moral reasoning? Most of us do. The task is to try to overcome this problem.

A Final Comment on Courage

Even if your moral reasoning does not yield correct answers, the process of moral reasoning may free you from your own prejudices, lead you to discard beliefs based on false premises, and help you better understand the views of others. If nothing else occurs other than being able to distinguish that moral actions are reasonable or unreasonable, then you have grown in your moral abilities.

Finally, once you have developed the ability to reason morally, you will then need the spirit and the courage to speak out for what you have reasoned is the right thing to do. Taking a stand for the moral right will not be easy. In fact, you may find that, to use the words of Robert Frost, it is "the road less traveled." Courage, however, to reason morally and to stand for what is right is the only solution to address "the new morality." A serious examination of morality requires both courage and humility—courage because you may find that others oppose you in your beliefs, and humility because you may need to recognize your own mistakes and limits.

SUMMARY

Before we examine numerous ethical issues in sport, let us review the precepts of moral reasoning. Critical inquiry is based on rationally determining moral issues. A critical, reasoned inquiry demands accurate, exact, and precise thinking. A reasoned inquiry also takes into account all sides of an issue in its past, present, and future sense. To reason, then, demands that you follow the three tenets of moral reasoning, that is, to be impartial, to be consistent, and to be reflective.

In developing your reasoned inquiry, your personal philosophies also come into play. What you believe, and who you are colors how you act. That is, your values, both moral and nonmoral, are the deciding factors in your moral inquiry. Values, therefore, determine your principles and your obligations. If you can reason through your values and determine a consistent value system, you will be on your way to a moral standard that can withstand internal and external scrutiny.

Once you have discovered your values, you then pen your universal principles. These First Rules stand for you in developing your personal and professional rules or guides. You have five steps to follow in using these First Rules and you have numerous obstacles and threats to overcome. Use these tools to examine critical issues in sport today.

ISSUES AND DILEMMAS

In the following five questions, what threats or fallacies can you find?

1. Look who is calling me a cheater. You are the biggest cheater on this team.
2. Hey, don't pay attention to Smith. He is one of those born-again Christian athletes!
3. The commissioner of major league baseball should do away with designated hitters. That's not the way the game was intended to be played.
4. Research shows that football athletes do poorly in college; it is obvious that they are not too bright.
5. You never have liked me, have you? Admit it, that is why you disagree with me.

In the following, discuss the issue from two different positions.

6. Athletics at the NCAA Division I level is big business. It brings in millions of dollars in gate receipts and contributions from fans. Even though the NCAA rules state that athletes are limited to twenty hours of practice per week, student athletes in revenue sports typically spend forty to sixty hours per week preparing for competition. It is time that you recognize that the student athlete is a myth and free yourself from your own hypocrisy. Pay the athletes and establish semi-pro leagues.

   Position a: This question has to do with the purpose of playing games. Exactly why do we have collegiate athletics? If you can answer this question, then you can write reasons for keeping the sport.

   Position b: The purpose of athletics is to bring money, fame, and publicity to the university. The athletes know their place in this purpose. The athletes get their pay through the grants-in-aid that they are given. That is all that they need and deserve.

The following questions deal with the four principles. Which of the scenarios are prohibited by which principle? More than one principle may prohibit an action.

7. Coach Smith wants his high school basketball players to win college scholarships. He does have a respectable placement record. He believes it is acceptable to overstate the facts about his players, especially concerning their character.

8. Coach Carlton refuses to allow any athlete to object to any of his coaching policies. He believes objections or criticisms are a sign of disrespect.

9. Mr. Black, the school athletic administrator, states that more money is allotted to the boys' program because more people come to the boys' games. If they earn more, they should get more. It is simply capitalism at work.

10. Bill uses anabolic steroids. He justifies the use by saying that if he wants to compete, he is forced to use them because competitors do.

REFERENCES

Dubin, C.L. 1990. Commission of inquiry into the use of drugs and banned practices intended to increase athletic performance. Ottawa: Canadian Government Publishing Centre.

Fox, R.M., and J.P. DeMarco. 1990. *Moral reasoning: A philosophical approach to applied ethics*. Fort Worth, TX: Holt, Rinehart and Winston, Inc.

Frankena, W.K. 1973. *Ethics*. 2d ed. Englewood Cliffs, NJ: Prentice Hall.

NCAA Manual. 1991. Overland Park, KS: National Collegiate Athletic Association.

Ross, W.D. 1930. *The right and the good*. Oxford: Clarendon Press.

ADDITIONAL READINGS

Ashmore, R.B. 1987. *Building a moral system*. Englewood Cliffs, NJ: Prentice Hall.

Beck, R.N., and J.B. Orr. 1970. *Ethical choice*. New York: The Free Press.

Beller, J.M., and S.K. Stoll. 1994. Moral reasoning on high school athletes and general students: An empirical study vs personal testimony. Manuscript submitted for review.

Carrett, E.F. 1948. *The theory of morals*. London: Macmillan Publishing Co.

Hahm, C.H., J.M. Beller, and S.K. Stoll. 1989. The Hahm-Beller Values Choice Inventory in the sport milieu. (available from ETHICS, Room 109 Memorial Gym, University of Idaho, Moscow, ID 83843).

Johnson, O.A. 1969. *Rightness and goodness: A study in contemporary ethical theory*. Hague: Martinus Nijhoff.

Lickona, T. 1991. *Educating for character*. New York: Bantam Books.

Penny, W.J., and R.F. Priest. 1990. Deontological sport values: Choices of U.S.M.A. cadets and selected other college-aged populations, West Point, NY: USMA Publication.

Rawls, J. 1971. *A theory of justice*. Cambridge: Harvard University Press.

Smart, J.D. 1991. *An outline of a system of ethics*. Melbourne: Melbourne Press.

Stoll, S.K. 1993. *Who says this is cheating?* Dubuque, IA: Kendall/Hunt.

4

Intimidation, Competition, and Sportsmanship

◆ What is intimidation?

◆ What is the role of intimidation?

◆ Should we want to take out the other player?

◆ Can we be intimidating without trying to be?

◆ What does it mean to play a good game?

At a recent meeting on sportsmanship, a professional football player was discussing what it meant to be a good sport. He argued that good sportsmanship is linked to how a player treats the opponent before the game, during the timeouts in the game, and after the game. Good sports shake the opponent's hand before and after the game. Good sports help the opposing player up after a good hit; good sports follow the rules; good sports win humbly and lose with little, if any, negative trash talking to the opponent; good sports value the game and what it means to play fair. In contrast to his fair play rhetoric, this specific professional player is portrayed by the media as an "in your face" opponent. When asked what is the place of intimidation in competition his response was, "Hey, I'm a good sport between plays and when the game is over. But the bottom line of my job is to physically, mentally, and spiritually take the opponent out of the game." So then, who would he play? His re-

sponse, "The second player and then do the same thing to him." When asked: "If this is the case, why not go into the opponent's locker room before the game and just shoot the opponent? Then, you could play number two, or, on second thought, shoot him too. Maybe shoot them all and then you would win for sure." His response, "I would if it were legal, but it's not. The point is that we want to take the other guy out so that we can win. Football is about life and death, as long as everything is done within the rules."

INTIMIDATION AND ITS ROLE IN COMPETITION
Defining Intimidation

Should intimidation be used as a tool to win sporting events? Should one physically, mentally, and emotionally want to take the opponent out of the game? Should one want to play the second best individual, or perhaps the third best?

Intimidation is the act of causing someone to be fearful, withdrawn, or coerced. Intimidation is a polar activity in that it can occur under two cases: purposeful or non-purposeful intimidation.

Coaching Intimidation: Purposeful

Intentionally intimidating another, either by our actions or words, is a conscious decision. While it has been argued that such behavior is questionable as a moral action, the issue will be addressed more in-depth later.

Intimidation has long been used as a means to control the behavior of others. Coaches often use intimidating practices to motivate athletes to behave in certain ways—to be more aggressive, to do better in classroom performances, or to attend to and meet the responsibilities of being an athlete. The moral agent—in this case, the coach—believes that intimidation will motivate the athlete to act in a certain fashion, through fear of what may occur. Typical methods of intimidation can range from mild tactics like glaring at the athlete or raising the pitch and tone of the voice, to stronger physical and emotional tactics, such as cursing, throwing objects, kicking, berating, grabbing the jersey or face mask, pushing the athlete, or spitting in the opponent's face. In the psychology literature, these forms of motivation are typically called *negative feedback* (Dieffenbach 1998). The constant negative verbal and physical assaults are typically used to "motivate" an athlete to perform to his or her best. Oftentimes, however, these forms of negative feedback set a motivational climate that is outcome/ego oriented. The focus is on the individual in relation to the goal, the win. The focus is not on performance/task/mastery. On the other hand, positive motivation (*positive feedback*) tends to set a climate focused toward the performance/task/mastery environment. Thus, according to researchers, performance is best improved if the motivational climate is set using positive feedback.

The authors once asked a highly intimidating coach why he used such strong negative feedback practices to motivate, considering that most of the psychological research today supports the notion of positive motivational techniques (those that uplift the athlete) rather than negative motivation (those that tear away at the athlete's psyche) (Stoll and Beller 1992). It has long been documented that though both techniques work, positive motivational techniques, in the long run, are better for the athlete, better for the coach, better for the sport, and even better for the fans. The coach responded that although the research might be true, negative motivation gets the job done more quickly and with little investment of his time. We noted that in a baseball game during the seventh inning stretch, he swore twenty-seven times. What exactly does profanity accomplish? Wouldn't the athletes become immune after about the tenth time? His response, "A coach doesn't have the time or energy to be worried about who needs what form of motivation—positive or negative. Cursing and screaming get the job done quickly so I can spend my time concentrating on strategy." He also noted that his method has been highly successful and is based on the military model. History and tradition were in his favor. He had won numerous local, regional, and even national titles, and several of his athletes have been drafted into the professional leagues. Little doubt exists that his technique works; the question is whether positive motivational techniques may be as good, if not more productive, in motivating the athlete (see Box 4-1).

If intimidation is intentionally practiced, then the action becomes a moral issue. As noted in the first three chapters, if the moral agent has motive and intention to violate another, the agent's action becomes a moral issue. At this point we need to take intimidation and the practice of negative intimidation a step further.

Coaching Intimidation: Non-Purposeful

Intimidation can occur with no purposeful motive, intention, or action of the moral agent. That is, the demeanor and professional position of many individuals, without any overt decision to be intimidating, may cause others to be intimidated. Because of college professors' professional demeanor, professional position, or even professional dress,

college students often find their professors intimidating. Employees may be intimidated by their supervisors not because of any direct action, but because of the employees' perception of what the supervisors might or might not do. Children may be intimidated by adults, not because of anything the adults do, but because of the adults' size, the depth and strength of their voices, or the manner in which they walk or wear their clothes. Athletes may often be intimidated by a coach because of reputation. The reputation may be the success ratio of wins to losses, or the coach's professional experience, or just being awed and intimidated by the coach's position.

Perception is the key to the problem. The moral agent is perceived as an intimidating individual and thus the moral receiver behaves in a certain way, fears the agent, and may avoid contact with the agent at all costs. If the moral agent has no intention or motivation to intimidate, the resultant perception of the receiver is not the fault of the agent. Though some could argue, IF the moral agents know that their position, dress, carriage, voice, size, or position intimidates others, then they should seek out different practices. That is, if children are overtly intimidated by the size of the agent, the agent could speak gently to the child, kneel down to speak with the child, or be less brusque in physical actions. However, many times the moral agent has no notion that others are intimidated by them. As such, the moral agent is not responsible for the ensuring intimidation. But remember that each of us perceives our world and the motives and intentions of others differently (Kretchmar 1994). What one of us may perceive of as intimidating in an individual, another

THEORY BOX 4-1

VIOLENCE, INTIMIDATION, AND GAMESMANSHIP

Violence means physical force exerted for the purpose of injuring another. Many professional sport administrators have expressed concerns about heightened violence among players, fans in the stands, and city celebrations after the winning of championships. For example, the stabbing of Monica Seles by a crazed fan during a 1993 tennis tournament in Germany illustrates how violence continues to encroach into sport. More prevalent problems, though, may be the dramatic increases in intimidation and gamesmanship displayed by athletes seeking to gain advantages. *Intimidation* is an act intended to frighten or inhibit others or render them too timid to do certain behaviors. *Gamesmanship* refers to pushing the rules to the limit without getting caught, using whatever dubious methods possible to achieve the desired end.

may not. Because perception is an individual view of the world and our perception of another's motives and intentions is unknown, perception cannot be the basis for deciding moral issues.

Intimidation From The Player's Point of View

Intimidation is also one of the bag of tricks that athletes use to gain an advantage over an opponent. An athlete will argue that if the opponent is intimidated, the feeling of intimidation will psychologically take the opponent out of the game. If the opponent is cowed, then the athlete or moral agent will have an opportunity to gain the edge and win the game. Intimidation for the player is a double-edged sword as well; it can again be purposeful or non-purposeful. (see Box 4-2).

Intimidation By The Athlete: Purposeful

Purposeful intimidation by the athlete is the direct motivation, intention, and action to somehow take the opposing player out of the game.

THEORY BOX 4-2

YOU BE THE JUDGE: IS THIS CONDUCT ETHICAL?

1. A lineman or a defensive back is beaten by the opposing lineman or wide receiver, resulting in a big play for the offense. On a subsequent play, the lineman or defensive back takes out his opponent with a vicious blindside hit to the knees meant to cause injury, even though neither player is involved with action near the ball. Is this hit ethical? If not, how should this intimidation be punished? How should the lineman or defensive back be educated? What changes are needed to reduce the potential for injury?

2. In his first at-bat after his grand-slam home run, Mike is prepared for the expected brushback pitch. He is not ready for the inside fastball aimed straight at his head. He attempts to bail out of the batter's box but is hit on the arm. He jumps up and charges the mound, bat in hand, as both benches clear. The ensuing brawl results in the ejection of several players from the game. Why is the brushback pitch seemingly accepted in baseball? Is your justification based on relativism? Why? Does a ball thrown at a batter's head justify his charging the mound? Why are teammates expected to join in the fray? How can these behaviors be changed for the better?

3. The shoving match underneath the basket has escalated without any fouls being called. Finally, Jack has had enough. The next time Pat pushes him to clear the lane, Jack grabs him and refuses to give ground. Pat retaliates by hitting Jack. Before the referees can break the scuffle up, punches from several players have landed. Who is violating sportsmanship rules in this situation? Is the absence of a whistle calling a foul on Jack, Pat, or are both tantamount to condoning their intimidation of each other? Does the failure to penalize minor shoving under the basket ever result in violent assaults? If you were the coach, how would you attempt to change these behav-

iors, especially if players from opposing teams play this way?

4. Tony is the best player on his ice hockey team, and without him the team does not have a chance to advance in the playoffs. Ray has been given the job of taking Tony out, legally or illegally; that is his role on the team. He must get Tony out of the game by means of penalty or injury. Ray uses his stick to break the arm of an unsuspecting Tony immediately after Tony scores. Ray gets a two-game suspension; Ray's team eliminates Tony because he cannot play with a broken arm. Why have (some) sports moved to the point where opponents are enemies and objects of the other players' physical and psychological abuse? Is the only objective winning, regardless of the method used?

5. The rivalry between East High School and West High School has escalated each year. Three years ago, a few of the West players started a fight late in the game because they felt East players were trying to embarrass them by running up the score. The next year, some of the East and West students in the stands started taunting and cursing each other. Last year had been the worst; the two sides brawled on the field after West pulled out an upset on the final play of the game. As the two undefeated teams prepared to play on Friday, school administrators urged fans and athletes to act responsibly, while arranging for more police officers. Volatile emotions erupted on an official's questionable call in the second period. The fighting on and off the field resulted in cancellation of the game. Is a fight among players in a football game ever justifiable? Do coaches ever use fights among opponents, teammates, and fans as motivational tools? What other strategies do coaches employ to motivate their players? Can the concept of fair play be used to positively motivate athletes? (See Box 4-3).

THEORY BOX 4-3

SITUATIONAL ETHICS APPLIED TO SPORT

The term *situational ethics* suggests that every ethical or moral decision is made on the spot, with no consistency between acts. People justify their behaviors by stating that nonmoral values, such as money, outweigh moral values. Is any action justifiable because money is riding on the outcome? When played for fun, sport can help teach moral values. But when a sport championship hangs in the balance, is it acceptable to bend the rules? Do individuals' values change because the nonmoral values of fame and fortune increase in importance?

Are moral values for sale? If so, at what price? Non-big-time college and high school sport appears fraught with unethical practices, although little or no money rests on the outcome of contests. Could it be that the imbalanced price of moral values is the inordinate value placed on winning?

In earlier chapters, principles were established on values, rules were developed, and any mitigating circumstances whereby a rule might be violated were taken into consideration. If money and winning cause a change in values, where is the burden of proof about the issues? It is doubtful that anyone would want to reverse or universalize a value that changes when more money is riding on it. Still, in the situations described in Box 4-2, many would endorse the athletes' actions if they were professionals but might not condone them in youth leagues or school programs. Does the skill level or amateur or professional status discount sport rules? Should adherence to ethical principles of conduct apply regardless of the competitive level?

Usually the purposeful activity revolves around psychological tricks such as preening or strutting before, during, or after the game. For example, a gymnast might practice psychological intimidation by purposefully and repeatedly throwing her hardest trick so that the competition will worry about their ability to meet the challenge. Or, a basketball player during warm-ups might make numerous difficult shots and strut his or her stuff, so that opponents will notice and have concern about the game.

Generally, intentional psychological intimidation occurs through trash talking. Though outlawed by most amateur sport ruling bodies, trash talking is as common as putting on a game uniform. Trash talking is the verbal act of berating the opponent. The athlete will chide the opponent on his/her lack of skill, physical size, competitive demeanor, or any other attribute that might be in question, "Is that all you got? My Momma plays better than you!" The Hollywood movie, "White Men Can't Jump" not only has a trash talking title, but is replete with every creative notion of how one can trash other players. Trash talking exists in youth sports, school sports, collegiate sports, and professional leagues. Women practice it, children practice it, and the fans practice it. The question becomes—if it is common practice, why not let it exist? And, if it is so commonly practiced, is it really a moral issue?

Harrison[1] has argued that trash talking grew from the jive of the intercity playground. Some trace its origin to an inner city game called "Playing the Dozens," "Basing," or "Jonesing," whereby the goal is to use words and trash talking to put someone else's momma down—often termed their "T Jones." As a cultural practice, trash talking moved from the playground to the court and the playing field. Its purpose may be intimidation but Harrison argued that the trash talking is not about doing any type of physical or emotional damage. Rather, the athlete may use trash talking as a way of bringing the game up to a higher level. Athletes will argue that trash talking makes them more psyched to play the game, and if they are denied the use of trash talking, they will lose a motivational edge. Trash talking, in this sense, may actually be a way of celebrating the very act of competition. Harrison argued that trash talking has been outlawed because of its African American roots and that the outlawing is really a form of racism—denying the worth of a cultural practice. Harrison also noted that trash talking today is definitely not limited in practice to African American players. He told us that Larry Bird, while he played the game of basketball, was supposedly the icon of trash talking.

Eassom noted that name calling is only what we make of it. He stated that just because a "crazy old man" down the road says nasty things to us, it does not mean that we have to listen, and there's nothing personal meant by it anyway. Just like ignoring the crazy old man, the athlete learns how to "not listen," to tune out the trash talking that occurs with sport.

In contrast to Harrison's and Eassom's points of view, Dixon argued that trash talking with all the notion of cultural practice is still words, and "words hurt." He asked, "Have we learned nothing about hurtful words from the history of racism and sexism? Have we not learned that it is hurtful to call women and different ethnic groups names? Have

we not learned that words are hurtful? And, have we not as a culture learned that such words can be legally interpreted as sexual and racial harassment? Is it necessary to say hurtful words to play the game and to play it well? Is sport supposed to be about psychological games of hurtful words?"

Rudd argued that trash talking was a moral issue because when trash talking is practiced ". . . individuals . . . show disrespect toward others for their own personal gain." (Rudd 1996, 18). Hence, if the action of trash talking occurs and is purposeful, a moral dilemma occurs. The athlete has a choice, whether to trash talk or not, and if the athlete chooses to trash talk, disrespect does occur.

Physical Intimidation: Purposeful

If an athlete goes onto the court or field and intentionally acts to "take out" the opponent through a physical act, physical intimidation occurs. The direct purpose of physical intimidation may not be long lasting injury but just enough to make the opponent think twice before acting, to ring his bell hard enough and long enough that fear exists. This issue of physical intimidation becomes cloudy when the practice of sport is about physical aggression, as in ice hockey, lacrosse, football, and today, basketball. The athlete uses the body against an opponent's body to gain the prize. The football player blocks and tackles; ice hockey, lacrosse, and basketball players all "check"—keeping a player from making progress. Players involved in physical contact sports argue that the physical contact and the aggression of the game are what the game is about: "There's nothing better in sport, especially football, than the sound of two bodies hitting as hard as they can." "Lacrosse is about violence." "Wimps don't play ice hockey."

All of these comments may be true, and we do concede that physical aggression and physical contact are part and parcel of contact sports (see Physical Intimidation: Non-Purposeful). However, if the athlete as the moral agent intentionally tries to "take out the opponent," a moral issue is raised. Marten, a former football player, wrestler, and coach said, "If any player goes out intentionally to take out another player, he is a coward. If you aren't

---

[1] The comments made by the following sport sociologists and philosophers were made at the 1996 annual meeting of the International Philosophic Society for the Study of Sport (held in Clarkston, Washington). Andrew Rudd gave a paper, "Moral Callousness As Evidenced by Trash Talking," which precipitated the discussion of the topic.

willing to put your best against his best, and you have to revert to violence to win, you are a coward. Such is the coward's methods."[2]

Hard words . . . "a coward." Marten's point may seem too strong; however, what he says is food for thought. If the intention is to take out the player, who does one play? The second string person, the trainer? Or, is the playing not the point? Therefore, the only purpose at this point would be to increase the chances of a win. If playing games in sport is about using one's mental finesse and physical skills, it is illogical, to want to decrease the opportunity to use one's best skills to play the game.

Giamatti, former commissioner of baseball and president of Yale University, wrote a book on baseball, *Take Time for Paradise* (1989). In that text and other works, he has noted that the beauty of competition lodges in one's purpose and intention. He wrote:

> *To toughen the body and temper the soul . . .*
> *To emphasize integrity and develop courage . . .*
> *To be obedient to the letter and spirit of the rules . . .*
> *. . . so winning is sweeter still.*

If the intention and motivation is to psychologically and physically take the opponent out of the game, a moral issue arises—because the athlete is neither being just nor responsible in the action toward the opponent. It does not matter what is accepted practice.

Non-Purposeful Psychological and Physiological Intimidation

As in the case of unintentional intimidation the coach, the same case can and does occur for the athlete. Athletes by their very nature—but without intending to—can intimidate their opponents; that is,

their size, their demeanor, and their physical skills may cause the opponent to be intimidated. However, this case is not a moral issue because the athlete is not going about his or her activity with any purposeful negative motive or intention toward the opponent. It is true that the resultant action of a sport practice may intimidate, but in this sense the athlete is not responsible—as it is a matter of perception. Remember, in this case, the moral agent is not responsible for how an athlete interprets the final action. The world would be better if good motives and good intentions were interpreted as right action, but in sports many times they are not.

For example, before a high school gymnastics meet started, the gymnasts from opposing teams warmed up by going through their routines. I watched a particularly talented gymnast from the opposing team. After the young girl dismounted from her beam routine, I told her she had a great routine and wished her team luck. The gymnast never responded to me but did say to her coach, "What did she mean by that?" Her coach turned toward me and said in disgust, "Ignore them; they're just trying to psyche you out." I had no intention of psyching out the young gymnast I enjoyed the routine, and truly wished her luck. An athlete, who watched and participated in the drama, had a different perception of the unfolding events. She thought the opposing coach was being rude and obnoxious and said loudly, "Coach, why don't you punch out her lights!" As pedagogists would say, this was a teachable moment, as the situation was discussed; good motives and good intentions are still good no matter how the other individual interprets the final action. Interestingly, the opposing gymnast must have been psyched out, because she was a good practice performer but a poor meet performer. She fell numerous times which she had not done in practice, and her performance doomed her team's chances of success as measured by winning—they lost that day. Perhaps the coach's negative perspective had an influence or perhaps good motives and good intentions had an effect. Perhaps the athlete and her coach had some other psychological performance problem. One coach and her athlete learned a great deal that day about non-purposeful intimidation. They had

---

[2] Dr. Marten and two of the authors were having a discussion one day about the purpose of competition. We were developing our paradigm on the ideal and the real sports contest. As we were discussing the nature of the intentional physical act to take out the other player, Dr. Marten noted that the old-time athletes would consider this nothing more than the act of a coward. His comments are here captured as he made them.

no control over the interpretation of an innocent, supporting remark. In future meets, when she finished her tenure as a high school coach, she was careful not to make any comments to this team or other opponents. She buckled under and played the game with no positive comments, no supporting remarks, and no appreciation for another's skill. Sport took a real hit that day. The coach, her athletes, and opponents were all the worse for it.

Physical Intimidation: Non-Purposeful

Injury and physical harm may occur to an opponent with no intention on the part of the offending athlete; in this case, the same sort of thinking applies that occurs with non-purposeful intimidation. Injuries do occur. Physical contact does happen. Accidents do occur. However, if the motive and intention is not about causing injury, then the resultant action is not a moral question. Athletes take the risk, the chance, that injury may occur. Playing sport is risky behavior. Sport is not for the faint of heart. The players go out and give it their best shot. They give their all. It is not about half-hearted activity. If one is blocking in football, one does it with every fiber of his being. If one is blocking a shot in basketball, one does it with the whole self. When activity is physical and opponents are physical, the chance of injury always exists. The injury becomes questionable as a moral issue only if the motive and intention of the athlete is to physically harm. Basketball players intentionally use their bodies, arms, and legs to "clear the boards." Football players intentionally use all of their strength, mass, and accumulating force to "hit" as hard as they can. Hockey players "check" with determination and gusto. However, it is a different concept entirely if the athlete does all of the above with "malice afore thought" as the lawyers call it. One can go out to give the hardest hit ever without intentionally thinking about "hurting the guy." Even though the activity might appear brutish, the resultant action may be innocent of intentional moral harm.

Of course, one could always argue that any activity that celebrates aggression is morally questionable. However, such an argument, if supported, would necessitate the end to numerous activities in which physical aggression is necessary to play the game. Perhaps it is so . . . that all activities that abound with physical aggression should be banned.

EXTERNAL FORMS OF INTIMIDATION

While intimidation occurs between players, coaches, and referees, a major piece to the puzzle involves external intimidation. In this sense, we mean influences that affect the game, influences which are external to game play itself. Under this category fall the influences and actions of fans, parents, coaches, administrators, media and others not directly involved in the game play itself. Many believe since they have bought a ticket, they not only have the right but the obligation to their team to influence the game through all sorts of intimidating practices. Mild forms of purposeful intimidation involve such practices as: (1) the distribution of various objects to fans so they can wave them behind the basketball goal in an attempt to throw off the shooter's focus and (2) musical bands standing behind opposing players' benches during time outs and playing loudly. Individuals practicing these actions argue that it is the coach's responsibility to teach his or her players to ignore such actions and that, after all, the opposing team fans have the same opportunity to intimidate. In other words, "All is fair in love, war, and sport."

While many sport enthusiasts argue that these forms of intimidation are just a natural part of the game, as well as "being a true fan," purposeful intimidation has taken on new detrimental practice lows. For example, in a recent basketball game that one of the authors attended, the student section chanted disparaging remarks targeted at the opposing team. The chant became so loud that the Public Radio station broadcasting the game had to turn down the volume—as they could not broadcast the statements and language on a "family" radio station. The following morning, the local newspaper also carried a column abhorring the student section's actions, claiming the students were worse than the coach in verbal abuse. When administrators, who were in attendance and heard the chants were queried, their response was that "They don't mean it; it's not meant personal; they are just supporting their team." Interestingly though, the tactic appeared to work. This player was held to 18 less points than his season average and his team lost a close game.

External intimidation though is not limited to game time. For example, a high school coach decided that for his team to gain an edge over the cross-town rival team in the district championship game, he needed to intimidate the team. He called a local florist, hired a hearse and driver, and had delivered to each opposing player and coach a wilted, dead rose and a card that said "Wishing you the worst in Saturday's game."

The question then becomes, "What is the purpose of competition?" If the answer is "to win at all costs," then external intimidation is acceptable. However, if the purpose of the competition is about placing an athlete's skills against another athlete's skills, then external intimidation is unacceptable. No self-respecting athlete should want an unfair win. Almost all good athletes are purists—they want fan support, they enjoy spectators, but there is a limit to how far the spectators should be a PART of the game.

SUMMARY

It appears that the goal today in sport is to take out opponents physically, mentally, and emotionally, to play number two, and thus increase the chances of a win. It also appears that fans and sport enthusiasts, in their attempt to cheer a team, are misguided in their intentions and actions. While their intentions may be to support their team, the actions (how they carry out their intentions) actually involve an attack on others, which reduces the overall quality of competition. It seems that Giamatti's concept that we need our opponents to play their very best—challenging us to be our very best, thus improving the overall quality of the competitive experience—is lost on players, fans, coaches, and sport enthusiasts today.

What then is the purpose of competition, and what is the role of intimidation in that purpose? The answer lies in the competitor's point of view and his or her value of the game and the competition. Robert Simon (1985) has said that competition should be a "quest for excellence." We agree. Do you?

ISSUES AND DILEMMAS

1. Two rival basketball teams in a conference played a basketball game on team A's court. During the game, team B's star player was consistently heckled whenever she missed a basket, pass, or rebound. In the return game on team B's home court, the home crowd took revenge by heckling team A's players. Such action is fair and acceptable because both crowds have equal opportunity to heckle.

2. Ice hockey is often a violent game. Players get hurt by hitting hard and smashing opponents into the boards. Players A and B are opponents playing in a championship game. While trying to control the puck, player A smashes player B into the boards. Even though the puck is on the opposite side of the arena, player B, a few minutes later, retaliates by smashing player A into the boards. Because "hitting hard" and "smashing players into the boards" are an inherent part of the game, player B's action was acceptable.

3. Yolanda is the best player on XYZ's team. She is a consistently high scorer and when she's on, XYZ wins. Lately, she's been on a lot and XYZ is in the championship game with ABC. ABC is a better team statistically but they are worried about Yolanda. A week before the big championship game, Yolanda's grandmother dies. Yolanda decides to play in the big game, "because MaeMa would have wanted me too." Because of Yolanda's notoriety the whole state knows about "MaeMa." During the championship game, Yolanda performs at the highest quality. ABC decides to revert to serious trash talking. Two players assigned themselves "trash duty." Typical derogatory comments are: "Hey Yo . . . miss MaeMa?" "Yo, drive this way and you'll get to meet MaeMa again." The tactics work and Yolanda is thrown off her game and ABC wins. Is this behavior acceptable or unacceptable? Give reasons why.

4. During a hotly contested women's basketball game, the fans sit directly behind the visiting team. A contest begins to see who can harangue the coach and players more. As the harangue contest between both fan clubs goes to a higher level, the coach and players are not able to communicate during time-outs. The players and coach have to move to the middle of the floor for time-outs. Finally the coach protests to the home team athletic facility manager. His response, "That's the breaks." Every facility has home team advantage. The visiting team does win the contest. Acceptable or unacceptable and why?

5. A field hockey player is permitted to hit the ball hard, providing the ball is not hit purposely at an opponent. Delphine on team A (intently concentrating on the net) hits the ball toward the goal,

but unintentionally hits Maria on team B. Maria complains that Delphine purposely hit the ball into her; however, the foul is not called. Down the field, Maria gains possession of the ball, retaliates, and hits Delphine with the ball. Maria's action was deemed acceptable.

REFERENCES

Dieffenbach, K. 1998. Letter to author, 23 February.

Giamatti, A. B. 1989. *Take time for paradise: Americans and their games*. New York: Summit Books.

Kretchmar, R. Scott. 1994. *Practical philosophy of sport*. Champaign, IL: Human Kinetics.

Mihalich, J. C. 1982. *Sports and athletics: Philosophy in action*. Totowa, NJ: Rowman and Littlefield Publishers, Inc.

Rudd, Andrew. 1996. Moral callousness as evidence by trash talking tee shirts. Master's thesis, University of Idaho.

Simon, R. 1985. *Sports and social values*. Englewood Cliffs, NJ: Prentice Hall.

Stoll, S. K., and J. M. Beller. 1992. Unpublished raw data.

Rules and Violence in Sport

- ◆ Were sport rules ever established specifically to attempt to prevent violent behavior and questionable conduct?
- ◆ What is violence?
- ◆ Does violence include only physical acts, or does it involve psychological ploys, too?
- ◆ Why does violence in sport exist, and why is it condoned?
- ◆ What are constitutive rules?
- ◆ How did the establishment of sport rules affect the amount and extent of violence in sport?
- ◆ How has the emphasis on winning influenced violence in sport?
- ◆ What are six categorical imperatives that could present violent behaviors in sport?
- ◆ What are several controls that could curtail or prevent violence in sport?

People recognize that bench-clearing brawls in baseball and fisticuffs in basketball occur outside the rules, although seldom do they classify such behaviors as violence. Fans acknowledge that vicious hits after whistles have sounded in football and hockey sticks used as weapons to cause injuries to knees and heads are malicious, but these occurrences are accepted in these sports. Many state that physical harm, and even injury, is just a normal part of the game (see Box 5–1).

Some people condone and praise behaviors that are psychologically and ethically abusive. Justified on the basis of gaining an advantage, players, fans, and coaches take violence to new heights (or depths).

It has been suggested that violence is so pervasive in sport that some athletes are indifferent when an opponent is injured. In fact, often the intent is to "take out" or debilitate an opponent as a desirable part of trying to win. Another issue related to violence concerns violence to self, as many athletes play with injuries that may permanently debilitate themselves, practice unsafe weight-cutting methods, or subject themselves to harmful drugs.

This chapter starts with an examination of why constitutive, proscriptive, and sportsmanship rules were developed. Categorical imperatives, or moral principles that underlie these sport rules, are suggested as ways to control violence in sport. After

MORAL CALLOUSNESS

Kretchmar (1995) discusses to some extent the effect of moral callousness. Kretchmar argues that human beings develop something called moral callouses around our hearts just like we do on our hands. As callouses become so hardened on our hands that we are prevented from feeling what we touch, so moral callouses around our hearts keep us from feeling ethical right and wrong. To remove the callousness, we must critically examine who we are, what we believe, and how that affects our perspective of the game. Kretchmar says that callouses come with symptoms such as: "everyone else is doing it", if no harm is done or no rule is caught broken, it's okay; problems distinguishing what is a rule and what is not; as well as difficulty in understanding the difference between sound strategy and moral trickery.

discussion of how violence affects sports, controls and moral education are recommended.

TYPES AND PURPOSES OF RULES

The absence of standardized rules in sport frees participants to play without constraints, to agree to a few control measures before the game begins, or to devise rules during the competition as the need arises. Although this may seem appropriate for children's games or impromptu contests, organized sport (especially when fans are present or records are maintained) needs rules. Three types of rules—constitutive, proscriptive, and sportsmanship—exist in sport.

Constitutive Rules

Rules that guide play within a specific game are *constitutive rules*. Such regulations developed gradually out of the need to equalize competition, and they govern such areas as length of the game, number of players, eligibility of the participants, and the need to be able to compare team and individual ac-

complishments. Besides stipulating game-specific skills, strategies, and techniques that make football different from basketball and both dissimilar to baseball, constitutive rules specify to all players what actions are permissible during games.

Constitutive rules also place boundaries on players' actions. These rules constrain behaviors to those deemed appropriate to the sport and the specific action taking place. For example, the rules of basketball restrict the amount of permissible contact. Unacceptable touching, hitting, and holding beyond that point are punished with a foul, or for more severe violations, with disqualification. Baseball and softball rules specify when and how one may slide into an opposing player defending a base. In these and other incidents, when players disregard the rules out of ignorance or blatant antipathy to gain advantages, violence occurs, often in retaliation for perceived intent to harm or to gain an unfair edge.

Constitutive rules give structure to sport, helping make the contest fair for all. They standardize the playing environment so that each athlete has an equal opportunity to excel. These rules regulate such factors as the age, weight, skill level, and maturational status of youth in certain leagues. They stipulate the ages, genders, residences, and academic performances required of school-aged athletes. Colleges are constrained by rules governing academic progress, eligibility, recruiting practices, financial aid, and time involvement. Thus constitutive rules are legislated by sport governing organizations.

Proscriptive Rules

Proscriptive rules expressly forbid specific actions, such as spearing in football and undercutting in basketball, often because of the associated high risk of injury. In some sports, scoring and winning may be predicated on the utilization of one's body and equipment as weapons against opponents, resulting in pain, serious injury, and even death.

Thus, proscriptive rules were established to prohibit players from intentionally trying to harm opponents; for example, rules were legislated after previous incidences of athletes' behaviors were judged as violent.

Many proscriptive rules were enacted in response to stick-wielding hockey players, pitchers throwing at batters' heads, linemen using chop blocks, and bench-clearing brawls. Some proscriptive sport rules exist to prevent interference from governmental authorities. Increasingly, sport leagues and governing organizations have imposed rules on their participants to control physically violent actions during competitions—to keep these situations out of the courts. That is, injuries inflicted on opposing players in hockey, basketball, baseball, football, soccer, and other sports are punishable by severe fines or suspensions. Had these actions occurred outside of sport, they would be punishable by imprisonment or large fines. Violent behaviors are not restricted to the professional leagues, either; youth, school, and college athletes imitate their heroes' and heroines' actions.

Sportsmanship Rules

Another type of rule, *sportsmanship rules,* refers to the inherent quality in playing a game in which one is honor bound to follow the spirit and letter of the rules. Many of these rules preclude behaviors that place winning above everything else, including opponents' welfare and competition between equitable opponents. Sportsmanship rules are designed to prevent ethically questionable and sometimes violent conduct.

ETHICAL CONDUCT OR NOT

Some violence in sport occurs because athletes choose to violate the rules. They participate in and condone ethically questionable conduct to gain an advantage. When an athlete does something that may not violate the letter of the rules but certainly is marginally within the spirit of the rules, the opposing player affected may retaliate violently, either through physical attacks or psychological intimidation.

Often, people defend violent and ethically questionable conduct on the premise that "everyone else does it." Is violence in sport deviant behavior? Many people seem ignorant of the purpose of sport when they say that behaviors they condone and ap-

plaud are not violent but, rather, are used to gain an advantage through craftiness or clever coaching or playing. The rationalization becomes, "Because everyone else is doing it, I must do it, too, or get beaten." Should the fact that everyone commits rule-violating actions make these actions fair, honest, or responsible? Others say that their actions do not directly violate rules. Even if this is the case, does such action infringe on the spirit of the rules? For example, volleyball players often tell officials that they did not touch balls that go out-of-bounds, even when they did. Should honesty have a place in sport?

Sometimes these actions lead to violence when athletes feel that their opponents' behaviors toward them are unfair. Relativism abounds in sport, often with regard to violence. Should the fact that seemingly one's opponent is in violation of the rules or seeks to intimidate give them license to do likewise? Many athletes state that they choose to initiate rule-violating behavior, hoping that they will not be penalized and that their opponents will retaliate and be punished.

Is Winning the Only Thing?

The degree of emphasis on winning directly influences the extent of physical and psychological violence in sport. That is, as winning increases in importance because of financial payouts, status, and symbolic rewards, many players will use any means at their disposal, even violence, to attain victory. This phenomenon can easily be seen in an assessment of violent actions at various levels of play. If violence occurs in youth leagues, is it usually associated with adults who have overemphasized winning? A too-common scenario finds parents and coaches maneuvering and pressuring young athletes, as if they were pawns on a chessboard, to achieve adult ego satisfaction and status. Violence in school sport has escalated because of overzealous fans, too much pressure to win, and the desire to capture media attention.

The absence of praise frequently parallels the presence of pressures to win. Not only do some adults model and bespeak the importance placed on winning, they also consider everyone else losers or

THEORY BOX 5–2

MORAL REASONING IN SPORT

Moral reasoning research on this subject is rather clear. It does not matter whether the athlete is a Division I athlete or Division III athlete. It does not matter if the athlete is a high school student or an Olympic athlete. It does not matter if the athlete is male or female, black or white, red or yellow. All competitive athletes are negatively affected in their ability to reason about ethical questions in sport. The way we practice competition in America today directly affects the sport competitor. Money does not seem to be the culprit. Rather, the need to win—for whatever price—appears to adversely affect the moral development of the competitor (Beller and Stoll 1995).

gain unfair advantages, and intentional injury of highly skilled opponents are examples of violent behaviors driven by the belief that only winning counts. At the pinnacle of sport, many professionals claim that they are expected to demonstrate violent behaviors and paid to win, not to care about their opponents or worry about the consequences of their actions. If they refuse to join in bench-clearing brawls on behalf of teammates or fail to punish, maybe illegally, opponents who sack their quarterback, they may find themselves not playing or cut from the team. The norms of sport, especially when exacerbated by expectations of aggression, seemingly demand increased physical abuse at each higher level of sport.

Some opponents see their opponents as objects rather than people. By objectifying opponents, athletes feel no remorse in injuring them intentionally. Either take out the opposing player with hard hits an athletic is taught, or be perceived as weak. The ethos of winning demands unquestioned loyalty to the team's goal of success by whatever means necessary.

One unconscionable example of objectifying opponents occurred just before the 1994 U.S. Figure Skating Championships when friends of Tonya Harding intentionally injured Nancy Kerri-

second best. In the winning-is-the-only-thing world, athletes seldom receive rewards, applause, or positive reinforcement for effort and improvement. Should adults condition young athletes to rant and rave when they lose by castigating them for not working hard enough or caring enough?

Since intercollegiate sport in most of the large universities has become business and entertainment, physical and psychological violence have increased (see Box 5–2). Taunting of opponents leading to fisticuffs, circumvention of the rules to gan. The elimination of skater Kerrigan from the national championships opened the door for Harding to win the title and qualify for the Olympic Games. The resultant media blitz surrounding the evolving saga included reports of FBI interrogations that implicated Harding as a conspirator, a threatened $25 million lawsuit by Harding against the U.S. Olympic Committee if she was denied the right to skate in the Olympics, shared practice time on the ice with Kerrigan in Lillehammer, Norway, and Kerrigan's silver-medal performance surpassing Harding's eighth place finish. In the quest for a national championship, an opportunity to skate for Olympic gold, and the millions of dollars awaiting the next champion on ice, did an athlete, Harding, choose to eliminate her closest competitor?

A disregard for the rules (constitutive, proscriptive, and sportsmanship) often leads to an objectification of the opponent as an enemy—someone to be overcome physically, mentally, and emotionally. Usually, athletes reveal that they do not wish to inflict career-ending injuries, just injuries that will prevent opponents from competing against them. This permits playing against less-skilled players and enhances the possibility of winning. Protective gear worn by football and ice hockey players may facilitate seeing opponents as objects because so little of the actual person is seen. Yet other athletes view their opponents, and even their teammates, as objects, too. For example, one college volleyball player stated that she would kick a teammate in the head for telling an official that she had touched a ball before it went out of bounds.

There is a clear connection between the emphasis on winning and a belief in the legitimacy of more aggressive and less sportsmanlike behaviors. Has winning gained predominance because winners receive the trophies, media attention, and popular status, and may continue to advance to higher levels of sport? Since these rewards are valued, and in order to keep them coming, athletes learn to do almost anything, including violence. Thus, sport perpetuates physical and psychological violence by condoning and rewarding it, especially when it is associated with winning. It seems noteworthy, however, that violence is acclaimed within the culture of sport and increases when it is effective.

Violence in sport evolved progressively as winning grew in importance. It was practically nonexistent when sport was played informally without rules. As constitutive rules were established to govern competitions, other regulations (proscriptive rules) were enacted to curb actions that could harm opponents or disrupt equitable play. Within structured sport, some players displayed ethically questionable conduct. Sportsmanship rules legislated against this, yet some actions within the letter but outside the spirit of the rules continued. Increases in violence in sport paralleled the emphasis placed on winning and its associated rewards.

CATEGORICAL IMPERATIVES

The pervasiveness of violence in sport provides a backdrop for establishing categorical imperatives. Needed are moral principles to serve as the basis on which one can judge whether any violent act is appropriate in sport. A *categorical imperative* is a universally accepted maxim that holds regardless of the situation because it is based on undeniable moral principles. The following represents a nonexclusive list of these categorical imperatives that, if adhered to, could eliminate violence in sport.

1. True sportspersons play to the best of their abilities within the letter and spirit of the rules (principles of justice, responsibility, and honesty).
2. Seeking to win is acceptable only if the letter and spirit of the rules are followed (principles of justice and responsibility).
3. An opponent is not the enemy but a worthy athlete deserving to be treated exactly as everyone would wish to be treated (principle of responsibility).
4. Retribution is never acceptable regardless of the unfairness or violence of the initial action (principle of beneficence).
5. Games are not played to intimidate; the ideal purpose is a mutual quest for excellence through challenge (principles of justice and beneficence).
6. Sportsmanship requires modesty and humility in victory, praise for winners, and self-respect in defeat (principle of responsibility).

HOW VIOLENCE AFFECTS SPORT
Why Violence Exists

Many psychological and sociological theories have been postulated about why violence occurs in sport. One suggests that sport both played and watched serves as a catharsis (that is, people relieve pent-up emotions and violent tendencies through enthusiastic cheering for well-executed plays on the field or court). Another proposes that athletes gravitate to sport because they have aggressive tendencies and need socially acceptable outlets for their release. A third theory suggests that sport nurtures violence through its structure and discipline. That is, only those who can submit themselves to an environment that stresses conformity, yet rewards individualistic, hard-hitting, violent behavior, can survive and advance in some sport settings. Last, the social learning theory speculates that violence occurs because it is modeled; that is, people mimic the successful or rewarded behaviors they observe on television or in the stands.

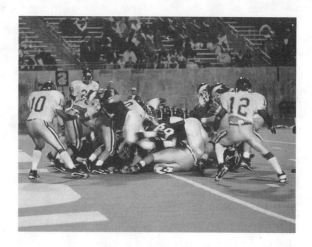

Additionally, societal values have changed markedly. The discipline problems of high school students in the 1940s, such as gum chewing in class and running in the halls, pale in comparison with today's concerns about drugs, guns in schools, teenage pregnancy, and AIDS. In sport, obscene language and gestures, verbal and physical intimidation, vicious hits intended to injure, psychological ploys, strategic advantage, fights and brawls, and gamesmanship are commonplace, although most are of relatively recent vintage. Many coaches and athletes covet the rights and privileges of sport involvement and occasionally stardom but refuse to accept the associated responsibilities of adhering to the categorical imperatives previously discussed.

Violence occurs in sport because the rules or the rule enforcers permit it and because players fail to hold themselves accountable to the spirit of the rules. Athletes at all levels quickly learn what they can and cannot do relative to every action. When a football player is not penalized for holding, he will repeat this action.

Legislating rules to curb and even eliminate violence from sport appears easy, yet many rules elude effective enforcement. Do sportsmanship rules exist because people violate others' rights? Do sport rules increase in number because people ingeniously find ways around existing rules? Some coaches and athletes seem to believe only in the letter of the rule, not the spirit. Unless individuals in sport value the full application of the rules, more and more rules will have to be written and enforced to close the loopholes currently being exploited to someone's advantage.

Given the American addiction for winning at all levels of sport, athletes and coaches spend endless hours developing ways to gain advantages both within and outside the rules. A favorite ploy appears to be trying to see how much one can get away with and not get caught. Rather than matching opponents' talents and strategies, too many games lapse into players and coaches seeking to gain advantages without being penalized. Short of having one official per player and endless whistles, flags, and ejections, can officials, as rule enforcers, prevent increases in violent behaviors?

Should those who write the rules specify the letter of the rule, as well as explain the spirit of the rule? In other words, should the letter of the rules include an explanation of why it was developed and how it applies to fair play? This would lead to officials consistently enforcing these rules, with increased and more severe penalties for infractions and league officials at all levels matching the penalty to the severity of the violation and taking into account prior actions and, possibly, the level of play.

Why Violence Is Condoned

Violence continues because some fans enjoy it, the media glamorizes it, and it helps athletes win. Basketball and ice hockey illustrate how fans condone and even encourage violence. Although rule books at every level of play clearly describe basketball as a noncontact sport, this game allows some contact while penalizing other actions. Some fans want the officials to let the athletes play, advocating that pushing and holding are all part of the game. In ice hockey, many fans thrive on the rough and often violent action displayed on the ice. They make heroes out of players whose primary roles are to hurt opponents.

An unending debate surrounds whether the violence in ice hockey enhances or impedes its growth in popularity. Some claim that the fights heighten the game's appeal, whereas others disdain such violence because it distracts from the skill of the sport. In the past, ice hockey remained content with its image as a violent sport; otherwise, rules preventing some of the violence would have been enforced. Canada's Fair Play Commission, in conjunction with the International Hockey Program of Canada, offers a glimmer of hope. On the basis of concern about moral education and the image of ice hockey, amateur and professional ice hockey programs are beginning to advertise without the use of violence.

Society reinforces violence in sport. For example, Jack Tatum, a former professional defensive back, received praise for describing in *They Call Me Assassin* his injurious exploits as he continuously intimidated and injured wide receivers. Consider the antics of "The Worm," Dennis Rodman, who is a sort of anti-hero because of his violent, successful behavior on and off the court. Or consider the advice of Charles Barkley who advises that athletes are not role models. His antics appear not to affect his marketability or even his intentions to run for political office in his native Alabama. Sport in America rewards the victorious with multimillion-dollar contracts and lucrative endorsements. If violent behaviors help advance an athlete, then these actions will likely be repeated, regardless of who might be harmed in the process.

Do fans condone and thus perpetuate violence in sport by purchasing tickets, watching televised sport, and following their favorite teams in print? Do the electronic and print media glamorize and publicize violence because of its sensationalism? Must fans cease to buy tickets or newspapers to send a clear message that violence is unacceptable? The likelihood of this change remains doubtful because many fans are no more morally educated than most athletes. How can athletes be expected to behave morally when society as a whole fails to do so?

Winning is the chief culprit through which violence continues in sport. With only victories praised and rewarded, too many athletes learn and practice whatever actions, moral or immoral, seem necessary to win. Breaking this cycle will not be easy because sport reflects capitalism and its emphasis on competing to surpass everyone else.

Too often in the professional ranks, sport expectations linked with winning demand that teammates enter the fray in defense of a wronged teammate. Although such behavior may be considered manly, it certainly fails the test of honor. What moral questions arise if an athlete races onto a field or court and swings at people because of team loyalty or team affiliation? Teammates may have no idea who threw the first punch or why; some seem not to care—anything for a good fight. Would these actions stop if management dictated that such actions will no longer be tolerated and, furthermore, will be punished? Competing or striving to perform to the best of one's ability defines sport. However, should an athlete have the right to harm another person or to take an unfair advantage just to win? Many justify such practices, stating that only the winner gets the trophy, the front page picture, and the chance to advance to the next level of competition.

The Impact of Violence on Sport

Violence undermines the values that potentially can be learned through sport and makes a travesty of the meaning of sport. When permitted, violence threatens to drive out fair play, cooperation, and self-discipline. Antithetical to fair play, violent behaviors are used to gain an advantage outside the letter or spirit of the rules. Contrastingly, fair play demands an adherence to the spirit of the rules to ensure equity for all. Cooperation denotes a willingness to work for

the good of the whole, be it the game itself or one's team. Whereas athletes with propensities for violent behaviors primarily care for their personal status and success, the principled player will not inflict injury or harm on an opponent to gain an advantage.

Sport can be defined as games and activities directed toward the play experience in which organization and rules have a significant role. The true meaning of sport requires a fair and just playing field or one on which each opponent has an equitable chance for success. When any individual or team uses violent behaviors, the meaning of sport erodes. For example, is the athlete who holds an opposing player on the line of scrimmage or under the basket cheating and possibly contributing to fisticuffs when this behavior goes unpenalized? Will the values and meaning of sport thrive only when violence and other unethical behaviors are prevented?

RECOMMENDATIONS

Before seeking to control violence, those involved in sport must admit to its pervasiveness. An examination finds parents attacking umpires, other youth players, and coaches; coaches hitting their athletes or verbally abusing them; fans causing riots in the stands and throwing objects at officials or visiting athletes; and athletes intentionally inflicting injuries on opponents (See Box 5–3).

A myriad of controls are needed to eliminate or at least curb violence in sport. In youth sport, league officials and coaches should teach and enforce sport rules and ethical values. No violations by any player or coach should be tolerated; penalties should be swift and appropriate to the behavior. Any adult—coach, parent, or fan—who engages in

THEORY BOX 5–3

PUNITIVE MEASURES AND CONTROL OF MORAL BEHAVIOR

Punitive measures in sport only control the behaviors of those who value the rules. Punitive measures comprise a part of the lowest form of Kohlberg's stages of moral development; that is, do right or you will be punished. The higher levels of moral development are based on the principles of reasoning and thinking. Individuals should want to do right because they value or believe in right. Each person's value and belief system, as emphasized in Chapters 1 and 2, must be cultivated and learned. If sport managers want principled thinking by their coaches and athletes, they must help them gain true reasoning ability based on moral principles.

violent behavior should be banned permanently from the bench or the stands.

Interscholastic sport under the direction of school administrators and coaches should enact similarly stringent rules governing their programs. All sport, league, school, and team rules should be followed and additional ones enacted to prevent violent and unethical behavior. Coaches should be held accountable for teaching these rules and for player development, not for the number of victories they tally. Parents and fans should be held to a code of conduct that requires them to either behave responsibly or forfeit their right to spectate. Players should comply with constitutive, proscriptive, and sportsmanship rules, including those governing the letter and spirit of the sports they play; if they do not, they should be eliminated from their teams.

Similarly, intercollegiate athletes should be expected to adhere to sport rules and team guidelines for conduct. There should be less emphasis on the winning-at-all-costs attitude that too often leads to rule-breaking behaviors. The college, the athletic department, and the coach should consistently emphasize to athletes that their choice to play or their acceptance of grants-in-aid obligates them only to do the best they can within their abilities, to try to win.

Colleges should place restraints on boosters and fans who seem to have an insatiable appetite for

Although these controls may deter some violence in sport, a more effective means for change calls for a comprehensive program in moral education for coaches, athletes, parents, fans, administrators, and the media. This program should focus on values, moral reasoning, universality, and principles. The principles and concepts of moral reasoning would challenge people's values and their commitment to them. As stated in Chapter 2, the moral values that should guide people's actions are justice, honesty, responsibility, and beneficence. The principles based on these values are, respectively—do not be unfair; do not lie, cheat, or steal; do not be irresponsible; and do not be uncivil. Discussions about values and ethics are needed, and everyone in sport must commit to these. Such a moral education program should completely refocus people's attention on the values that can be modeled through sport. Perhaps team captains could affirm the following statement on behalf of everyone:

"We are here today to play each other to the best of our ability. We hope that we are sportspeople enough to play by both the letter and the spirit of the rules. We challenge you to help us in this attempt. We ask that you cheer us on to excellence. And we ask that you neither boo us nor demean our playing in any way. We ask that you help us. Will you be good sports, too?"

SUMMARY

This chapter exposes the ethical problems associated with violence in sport. The evolutionary development of constitutive, proscriptive and sportsmanship rules has paralleled growth in incidences of violence. As winning emerged as the most important aspect of sport, rules expanded in an attempt to control violence and other ethically questionable behaviors.

Six categorical imperatives were suggested as the moral principles upon which sport should exist. An examination of sport shows a pervasiveness of violence that violates these maxims. Possibly understanding why violence exists and is condoned, as well as its impact, will help establish controls to curb or prevent it. Sport managers, officials, coaches, and athletes should re-educate themselves morally if sport is to eliminate violence and replace it with moral behaviors.

winning. This can take place if colleges, rather than independent organizations, govern athletic programs and stipulate that coaches will be evaluated on the basis of players' athletic, academic, and social development, not the number of contests won. In addition, colleges should hold their fans, students, athletic administrators, coaches, and athletes to an ethical code of conduct that prevents violence in and surrounding sport.

Although controls at the professional level are more difficult, they are nonetheless important and possible to implement. Because players' jobs are on the line, league and team management should dictate that violent behavior will not be tolerated and if it occurs will be penalized severely. It may take one or two incidents and harsh penalties to stress the seriousness of the situation, but a clear message will impede the spread of violence. Should an NBA player be permitted to choke his coach and continue to play in the league? A similar approach with coaches should require that they cease encouraging and condoning violence in the name of winning.

Fans can be controlled through the visible use of police officers and through announcements that violators will be removed from the stands. The media should help re-educate fans by ceasing to glamorize and publicize violence in sport. This would be of help at all levels of sport, especially in the popular professional leagues.

ISSUES AND DILEMMAS

CASE 5–1

Peter started playing football when he was eight and had been a linebacker ever since. He loved to make hard tackles and to see the boys he had hit give him looks of respect when they struggled to get up. He always played on championship teams in Pop Warner, junior high, and high school. Coaches loved his aggressive style, which was why he had been recruited to play at the university.

As a freshman, Peter began to learn new techniques for playing his favorite sport. Although in the past his size and strength had enabled him to hit hard, yet cleanly, suddenly everyone vying for a place on the team was at least his six-foot-four and 230 pounds. Peter was coached on how to hold without getting caught, how to fight off blocks using illegal techniques, and how to tackle with the goal of injury, as well as that of stopping an opponent. At first using these maneuvers bothered Peter, but soon he learned that if he did not use them, others who did would get to play, not him. So Peter mastered these and other violent techniques that he could use against opponents to help his team succeed.

The university's team won two major bowl games during Peter's college years, with his play contributing to both victories. It seemed that players at all defensive positions had been taught similar techniques because the Tigers were renowned for their hard hitting, as well as their sometimes unethical techniques. They led the league in penalties but in most defensive categories, too.

1. It could be argued that Peter is a victim of moral callousness brought on by the game itself. If you want to play, you learn to play by the rules (including those that aren't written—you do what you have to do to win). If the nature of the game is about gaining advantage, is there a place for sportsmanship?

2. Should we even consider the ethical ramifications of pushing the rules to the limit? It is often argued that in the real world, the golden rules applies: Those with all the gold make all the rules. Is it naive to think that rules exist to be followed?

3. America is a competitive society in which winning is commended. As Vince Lombardi said, "There is no room for second place. I have finished second twice at Green Bay and I never want to finish second again. There is a second place bowl game but it is a game for losers played by losers. It is and always has been an American goal to be first in anything we do and to win and to win and to win." If Lombardi is right and winning is what competition is all about, how would ethics apply? Or the reverse,

if ethics are important, what happens to winning? Or can one be a winner and be ethical?

◆ ◆ ◆

CASE 5-2

The Memphis Suns, a Triple A baseball team in the Cardinals organization, were perennial favorites in the Southern Conference. Their nemesis for years had been the Little Rock Stars, who were affiliated with the Braves' minor league system. Although players moved up and down from their parent clubs, the Suns and Stars always managed to vie for the conference title come late August, and 1998 was no exception. As the Suns started the final three-game series in Little Rock Memorial Stadium, they were tied for the league lead with the Stars. Two games later, the situation was the same; either the Suns or the Stars would capture the conference championship in the final game of the season.

The Suns' ace, Carroll Lyttle, held the Stars scoreless through six innings, whereas the Suns had managed to push across two runs. In the bottom of the seventh, the Stars opened with a single by Baylor and a double by Ramsey, with John Miller coming to the plate. Miller hit a line drive to right field, sending Ramsey speeding toward home with the tying run. Because of a misplay by the catcher, Lyttle had to cover home. Although the ball arrived long before Ramsey, he never hesitated as he crashed into the pitcher, who was prepared to tag him out. The six-foot, 195-pound Lyttle crumbled under the impact of the six-foot-six, 249-pound Ramsey and dropped the ball. Instantly, both benches cleared, and the brawl began. Several players were injured by the punches thrown before order was restored, but only Lyttle had to be carried off the field with a broken collarbone.

1. If the play worked and the ball was knocked loose, what would the call be? If the umpire ruled the play "fair," was the action acceptable? Why or why not?
2. If taking Lyttle out, helped win the game, was the action acceptable?
3. If an advantage is gained and the practice is the norm, should we question the action?

◆ ◆ ◆

CASE 5-3

Mario started playing organized ice hockey when he was six years old. By the time he was fourteen he was one of the best junior ice hockey players in New England. Coaches eagerly tried to get him to join their age-group teams because they liked his aggressive style of play, yet were not concerned that he spent several minutes each game in the penalty box for using his stick as a weapon and for fighting.

Mario's team, the Sabres, carried its undefeated record into the league championship game against the Blazers, who had lost only one game against the Sabres. In the final period with the score tied 1–1, the Blazers' star player, Stefan, appeared to break away for a clear shot at the goal. Somehow, Mario managed to catch up with Stefan but only by hitting him on the side of his head with his stick—so hard that Stefan's helmet flew off. This flagrant action was compounded when Stefan's head hit the ice with a thud. Attempts to revive Stefan were unsuccessful, and he was pronounced dead on arrival at the local hospital. Due to a wrongful death lawsuit filed by Stefan's parents, Mario was arrested and charged with manslaughter.

1. This unfortunate incident could have been avoided. How?
2. In an aggressive game in which body contact is part of the strategy, how can the aggression be tempered? Some athletes argue that by not playing hard, they are bound to get hurt. If this is so, then what? Can we play an aggressive, contact game and be ethical?
3. It is often argued that contact sports are for the tough. If such is the case, should we realize the nature of these conditions and accept the responsibility? In other words, accidents do occur and aggression is part of the game. In this case, the lawyer for Mario will probably argue that Mario had no intention to "harm," but harm did occur through the very act of the game. Mario then cannot be guilty of anything more than playing the game aggressively. How would you respond to this point of view?

◆ ◆ ◆

CASE 5-4

LaShonda and Ramona, the leading players for their teams, kept up a steady barrage of trash talk throughout each of their Women's National Basketball Association (WNBA) games. As they played offense and defense against each other, they traded verbal assaults. Typically, the officials ignored such trash talk, especially when it occurred between two of the league's stars.

When their teams met in the WNBA Finals, LaShonda and Ramona significantly increased their attempts to "get inside the head" of the other. But, when LaShonda's language became incessantly vulgar, Ramona asked a referee to intervene before she took matters in her own hands. Observing this plea, LaShonda, convinced that she was winning the psychological battle, escalated the insults she was hurling at Ramona. When the officials seemed unwilling to put an end to LaShonda's vulgar taunting, Ramona punched LaShonda in the face several times before being pulled away.

Coaches argue that psychological intimidation is the game or at least a very large part of the game. The tough survive; the weak lose. Coaches, therefore, teach and coach their athletes to be survivors and winners. If such is the case, one could argue that it would be unethical to NOT practice the norm. That is, if everyone else practices intimidation and you don't, your team will probably not be successful. Also, if your team practices the ideal, the team may be in physical jeopardy when everyone else is physically intimidating, psychologically intimidating, and so forth. How does one resolve this issue? To practice or not to practice intimidation is the question.

REFERENCES:

Beller, Jennifer M., and Sharon K. Stoll. 1995. Moral reasoning of high school athletes and general students: An empirical study versus personal testimony. *Journal of Pediatric Exercise:* 352–63.

Kretchmar, R. Scott. 1995. *Practical Philosophy of Sport.* Champaign-Urbana, IL: Human Kinetics.

ADDITIONAL READINGS

Berger, Gilda. 1990. *Violence and sports.* New York: Franklin Watts, Inc.

Jones, J. C. H., K. G. Stewart, and R. Sunderman. 1996. From the arena into the streets: Hockey violence, economic incentives and public policy. *American Journal of Economics & Sociology* 55(2) (April): 231–43.

Lapchick, Richard E., and John B. Slaughter, eds. 1989. *The rules of the game: Ethics in college sport.* Phoenix: Oryx Press.

Leach, Robert E. 1997. Violence and sports. *American Journal of Sports Medicine* 25(5) (September): 595.

Leonard, John. 1998. *Smoke and mirrors: Violence, television and other American cultures.* New York: New Press.

O'Brien, Richard and Kostya Kennedy. 1996. Kids, it's just a game. *Sports Illustrated* 85(22) (November): 24–26.

Trash the trash talk! 1995. *Scholastic Coach & Athletic Director* 64(7) (February): 57.

CHAPTER 6

Eligibility in Sport

- ◆ How do eligibility issues at all levels of sport relate to moral values?
- ◆ Is it ethical to encourage young athletes to pursue professional sports given the small number of athletes who attain this level of performance?
- ◆ Why did the International Olympic Committee eliminate its requirement that Olympic athletes had to be amateurs?
- ◆ Are eligibility rules developed and expanded due to distrust of opponents who might not behave ethically?
- ◆ Why have the number and specificity of eligibility regulations at all competitive levels of sport increased?
- ◆ Can eligibility regulations legislate moral behavior or does sport mirror society by displaying what is most valued?
- ◆ How can the ethical dilemmas regarding eligibility in all levels of sport be resolved?

Eligibility concerns pervade competitive sports. If the nonmoral outcome of winning exceeds in importance playing the game for the game's sake, competitors will be tempted to do and will often succumb to doing whatever is necessary in order to win. Beginning with early Greek competitors, winners have received lucrative rewards and recognition, while nonwinners often are made to feel inferior, as losers. Because athletes vigorously pursue the victors' prizes, eligibility regulations have been and continue to be cleverly and creatively exploited at every level of competitive sport. When seeking to win results in unethical behavior concerning eligibility, the **nonmoral value** of winning supersedes the **moral values** of justice, honesty, responsibility, and beneficence.

This chapter begins by examining the major eligibility issues confronting participants in youth, interscholastic, intercollegiate, and Olympic sport. From historical and sociological perspectives, behaviors manifested by some athletes, coaches, and sport managers indicate that they value winning more than playing fairly, abiding by the rules, and acting responsibly. The reader will be challenged to determine why eligibility rules exist, why they have changed, and how they relate to societal values. Ethical dilemmas associated with these eligibility issues challenge everyone

THE ETHICAL ISSUE ABOUT ELIGIBILITY IN SPORT

The ethical issue about eligibility has to do primarily with the values or principles of **justice, trust,** and **honesty.** The purpose of justice in sport is to set up a level playing field so that all competitors, in theory, have an equal chance of succeeding. Without an equal chance, there would be no logical reason for playing a game. In the ideal sport experience as described in Chapter 2, each competitor contributes to the experience on a supposedly equal footing. Competitors should be able to trust that opponents will adhere to the same standards in being qualified to play. The overall purpose of eligibility rules is to attempt to make the field level, fair, and equal. That is why rules exist. Such rules give everyone an equal chance. If people choose to knowingly change the eligibility rules to their unique advantage, then they are cheating by competing dishonestly and unjustly and with distrust.

involved in sport to establish a moral reasoning process (see Box 6-1).

HISTORICAL PERSPECTIVE

Recreational sports as played by the colonists, rural youth, urban gentlemen, or upper-class socialites of both genders found no need for eligibility rules. Their games welcomed everyone because their purposes included fun, camaraderie, and exercising for health. As winning grew in importance, such as when opponents placed friendly wagers on the outcome, some tried to surreptitiously change the way the game was played.

Amateur baseball in the mid-1800s provides an example of what can happen in sport in the absence of eligibility rules. This sport lacked formalized or consistent rules because these were thought unnecessary for the gentlemen who competed. As winning became more important though, teams began to recruit and pay the best athletes. Although this

did not violate eligibility rules, because there were none, such behavior raised the ire of competitors.

In another example, the Amateur Athletic Union, established in 1888, began sponsoring competition among amateurs who played for fun, not remuneration. Until the late 1970s, this organization controlled many sports—from its age-group events through national championships and Olympic trials—while maintaining an emphasis on amateurism as a prerequisite to eligibility. However, elitist and amateur athletic clubs, in the late 1800s, ceased to sponsor competitions solely between members when these players were replaced by so-called "tramp athletes" who marketed their skills to the highest bidders (Smith 1988). To prevent the appearance of illegitimacy, these lower- and middle-class men were given memberships in these elite clubs in return for their demonstrated prowess. Additionally, they were paid lucrative sums and given various gifts. The justification was winning. Thus, a model for how to circumvent eligibility rules existed long before sport became organized at different levels.

Youth Sport

Organized sport programs for children began in the 1920s when businessmen provided the financial resources to sponsor team sport leagues for boys (Berryman 1975). Although altruistically justified as programs to teach values and to prevent juvenile delinquency, these early sport leagues were characterized by the pervasive advertising of businesses on T-shirts, uniforms, and ballpark signs. As Little League Baseball (1939), Pop Warner Football (1930), and other leagues grew in popularity and participation, parents' and coaches' involvement resulted in the formulation of rules to thwart strategies to gain competitive advantages.

Several eligibility problems gradually began to enter child competitions. These included eligibility issues relative to age, weight, residence, and gender. Today, issues concerning rules against female participation on typically male-dominated youth sport programs have generally been eliminated through court action. Yet issues concerning eligibility and weight, age, and residence still exist. As one way to equalize competition and account for differences that occur due to age and weight, many youth sport leagues separate participants by age. Typically, those of similar age are of similar height and weight, thus helping ensure a more equitable and safe sporting environment. Related to the issue of age and helping to ensure that competitors are equitably matched (avoiding the matching of an 80-pound child against a 110-pound child), many youth sport programs such as football and wrestling set weight limitations.

Issues of eligibility also emerge concerning residency within certain communities or cities. Oftentimes, youth sport programs are sponsored through public recreation departments. The rules of these programs state that those who live within the geographic region financially supporting the program are eligible to participate in the program. Parents sign forms and state that they reside within that particular district, city, or community. The direct rules exist for a couple of reasons: (1) those families who pay taxes in a particular area support the program and (2) there is need to ensure that players of all skill levels make up each team. The first reason for the rule concerns funding and opportunities for youth in that geographic region. The program exists because of family contributions through taxes. The second reason for the rule is based more on the law of averages: varying skill levels will be present throughout all geographic areas, thus allowing for a more equitable competition between teams. The **spirit of the rules,** however, is much broader than the rule(s) per se. Specifically, the spirit implies that if players of varying skill levels are distributed within and between each set of teams, a more fair and equitable competitive playing field should occur.

However, because of the drive to win and be number one, even at the youth sport level, eligibility problems arise. Some parents have falsified birth certificates and lied on participation forms concerning residency and legal guardianship. With a falsified birth certificate or age report, a larger, more skilled player plays against a younger, lesser skilled player. The result is a lopsided competitive arena and sometimes injury to the smaller players. The 1992 Little League World Series is a classic example of parents falsifying birth certificates so that their older, more skilled children could play, increasing the probability of winning the series. Although the 1992 Little League championship team was eventually stripped of its title, over-aged youth still compete—without getting caught.

While programs such as football restrict players to certain weight classes to limit the injury potential of larger, heavier individuals competing against smaller, lighter players, wrestling raises slightly different eligibility rules. Although scales monitor specific weights, ethical and health issues surface concerning how athletes attempt to make lower weight classes. In an attempt to make weight classes, parents, coaches, and others encourage athletes to lose as much weight as possible before the time of weigh-in prior to the actual contest. The quickest ways for children to lose weight in a 12–24 hour period is to reduce caloric intake to low levels, exercise in plastic or rubber suits, and/or take diuretics. In an attempt to reduce the injuries and eliminate deaths in wrestling, on all levels of sport, rules have been implemented against this practice. Despite the rules, the practice still occurs. Considering the potential of serious health problems which might result in death due to dehydration and severe electrolyte imbalance, and considering that these actions violate most sport governing body rules, if wrestling in weight classes is about matched competition, what does this say about how we perceive the spirit of the rules and how we value the individual?

Interscholastic Sport

Interscholastic sport competitions began in the early 1900s, modeled after those in the colleges (Williams and Hughes 1930). Interscholastic sport had as its main purposes to be an educational arm of the school and to develop character to prepare individuals for life. These contests, while initially primarily for boys, became a rallying point for communities. On Friday nights on rural fields and in local gymnasiums, numerous teams and towns vied for bragging rights in football and basketball. Sporadically, abuses crept into school sports when an overemphasis on winning became common place (Coakley 1998; Eitzen and Sage 1997). To curb many of the problems that surfaced concerning in-eligible players, eligibility rules were enacted by state athletic associations affiliated with the National Federation of High School Associations. These rules addressed age, residence, remuneration, and academics.

Eligibility rules have been enacted in inter-scholastic sport for several reasons. First, because interscholastic sport was formed within the auspices of an educational model with goals, such as the development of character, eligibility rules were enacted to help ensure that athletes were enrolled in and making educational progress in classes. Second, eligibility rules existed to help ensure that athletes who resided in a particular geographic area attended schools within the specified region. However, the abuses within the system continued.

Considering that interscholastic sport was developed as an educational model and the education of our youth was deemed imperative to society's future growth, and if, in order to stay eligible, players received credit for courses they did not pass, what did that say about how we viewed the value of education? What did it say about how we valued our young people? And, if athletes were recruited into districts in order to stack teams, what did this say about how we valued the worth of matched competition?

Age requirements stipulate both maximal age limits and the number of years a student can compete. To prevent older and more mature students from continuing to play in interscholastic sport, state organizations typically establish the age limits for athletes. Unfortunately, falsified birth certificates allow a few athletes to play when they are older. Another eligibility rule usually specifies that students can compete for only three years between the tenth and twelfth grades. Even though state associations have enacted this limitation to prevent parents from holding their children back a year (similar to collegiate redshirting whereby athletes are withheld from competition for a year for developmental or medical reasons), at times parents circumvent this rule by forcing a child to repeat a grade before high school for nonacademic reasons.

Most public schools serve a specific geographic area; thus, athletes on school teams must live within

a certain district. However, when another school offers a better opportunity for success, many high school athletes, with their parents' encouragement, have chosen to transfer. Often this is achieved when the legal guardian of the athlete is changed or when the athlete leaves home to live with relatives or friends (sometimes the coach). Because private and public magnet schools offering unique academic programs have district-wide service areas, many coaches of teams at these institutions openly recruit star athletes. Because interscholastic athletes compete on amateur teams, regulations limit the benefits they can receive from sport. Normally, this includes competitive expenses, uniforms, and minimal awards for winning or athletic achievements such as trophies and plaques. When adolescents who compete on school teams during summer competitions receive shoes, warm-ups, bags, and other sport clothing and equipment, they often expect such benefits to continue; or they are influenced to seek out these benefits, which violate interscholastic sport rules. A few outstanding high school athletes accept money and other benefits from sport agents, even though this is in violation of high school and college eligibility rules.

State high school athletic associations regulate the academic eligibility of those youth who represent their schools. One of these regulations, often called *no pass, no play,* helps prevent academic exploitation by requiring that students meet minimal academic standards for eligibility to play on school teams. Under the guise of meeting academic standards, some coaches counsel athletes to take less rigorous technical courses, rather than college preparatory curricula, just to stay eligible for school sports. Some coaches pressure teachers to give athletes unearned good grades. Is academic eligibility that is achieved in these ways fair and honest? What are these coaches teaching their athletes about acting responsibly or beneficently?

Intercollegiate Sport

Recreational interclass activities for male collegians were initiated in the late 1800s to offset the rigors of academic work and the perceived oppression of faculty constraints on students' behaviors (Smith 1988). As intercollegiate sport became more popular and expanded in the 20th century, faculties saw a need to take more institutional control and thus found a means to justify the integration of athletics and education (Williams and Hughes 1930; Smith 1988). Because no regulations or prohibitions existed, collegians enlisted nonstudents, townspeople, alumni, students from other colleges, and even professional athletes to help win. Initially, no student or faculty member considered the need for eligibility standards requiring a minimum time of enrollment at an institution, a certain number of hours taken or passed, or progress toward graduation. As a result, the football eleven or the baseball nine often had a limited relationship to the institution the team supposedly represented. Even though students took no issue with such practices, college presidents and faculty expressed concerns about debasing their institutions' reputations for the sake of victories.

The question of who controlled college sports became a somewhat volatile issue as four groups wanted to govern college sports and hence decide who could play (Smith 1988). First, students argued that athletics belonged to them. However, they agreed to impose minimal eligibility regulations on themselves, primarily to equalize competition between colleges. Second, faculties demanded implementation of strict academic eligibility regulations to prevent the playing and paying of nonstudents, thus threatening their colleges' reputations. Third, university and college administrators, realizing the kinds of revenues and publicity that were being generated through intercollegiate sport, es-

pecially football, thought they should govern athletics. Fourth, graduates wanted to provide continuity and some experienced program administration while focusing on winning games rather than on eligibility issues.

The NCAA, regarded by many as the most powerful sport organization in the United States, started in 1906 as the Intercollegiate Athletic Association of the United States. As it grew to nearly a thousand members representing the larger colleges and universities and their conferences, the NCAA depended on institutional control for most eligibility rules. Not until the start of national championships (1920s) and the initiation of college sports on television (1950s) did the NCAA begin to gain leverage over its members. During the 1950s, colleges increasingly agreed to comply with NCAA eligibility rules that governed recruiting and grants-in-aid as long as their opponents would be required to adhere to the same rules. The pursuit of championships and the sharing of television revenue became the lucrative benefits accruing to institutions that complied with the NCAA's extensive eligibility regulations. Banishment from championships, television, and even competition (the death penalty) represented the punishments for noncompliance.

The *NCAA Manual* (1998) dictates the permitted and the forbidden in amateur sport eligibility in intercollegiate sport programs. Past rule violations by athletic personnel, especially coaches and individuals interested in promoting a college's athletic program, led to the NCAA's voluminous eligibility regulations. That is, more and more rules were written to explicitly ban wrongful actions performed by coaches and others exploiting loopholes in the rules. Essentially, coaches, administrators, athletes, and others regarded ethical conduct as synonymous with only the written rules, meaning that the spirit of the rules did not exist. Specifically, if a particular action was not covered by an explicit rule, it was seemingly acceptable, regardless of whether or not it was ethical.

The eligibility rules broken most often in intercollegiate sport include those governing academic standards, recruiting, and payments to athletes. Falsified transcripts of high school athletes have led to the NCAA rule that prospective student-athletes

THEORY BOX 6-2

ETHICAL DILEMMAS FOR HIGHER EDUCATION ADMINISTRATORS

Sport scholars' research gives rather conclusive proof that if big-time collegiate sport is only about making money, abuses will occur. If coaches' jobs depend on winning, they will be sorely tempted to push all the rules to the limit. Athletic directors could readily stop the cheating process driven by a compulsion to win if they wanted it halted. The steps to eradicate cheating are quite simple.

1. Make an explicit, public statement about the purpose of athletics in higher education.
2. Give a clear pronouncement about the roles and responsibilities of college students who also are athletes.
3. Hire only coaches who have demonstrated commitment to the first two statements.
4. Make it abundantly clear in coaches' contracts that any deviations from the letter and the spirit of the rules provide grounds for contract termination.
5. Make sure all sport managers model the stated rules.
6. Delete any mention of won-lost records in contracts.
7. Set evaluation standards for coaches based on an educational model; for example, athletes' graduation rates and progress toward degrees are most highly valued.
8. Take these action steps to league members; if they cannot or will not accept them for everyone, find a new league with which to affiliate.
9. Encourage and expect athletes to take advantage of their grants-in-aid to grow intellectually.

must be certified by the NCAA Clearinghouse relative to their high school grade-point averages in 13 core subjects and their SAT or ACT scores. The failure of many student-athletes to graduate led the NCAA to require minimum academic loads, progress toward a degree, and declaration of a major before the fifth semester of enrollment.

Academic exploitation, though, continues to characterize some institutions. Some athletes are admitted to colleges even though they are academically unqualified. A few players receive unearned grades, sometimes in courses they never attended. Despite toughened NCAA regulations, some athletes play their four years of eligibility and still find themselves without college degrees because they have performed poorly in their classes or have taken only those courses that will help maintain eligibility. Often, athletes fail academically because they give priority to sport in their use of time and level of commitment.

Several questions arise whenever these academic abuses occur. If a college gives preferential admittance to college athletes, what effect does that have on students without such treatment? What effect does such practice have on fair treatment? What

ethical obligations does a college have to the student-athlete who, on the basis of standard admission criteria, lacks the ability to succeed academically? (See Box 6-2). For example, is a college ethically bound to provide a recruited student-athlete with a structured, supportive environment that leads to academic success? Does institutional control exist when athletes receive unearned good grades or manage to maintain their eligibility while making limited progress toward degrees?

Academic abuses in intercollegiate sport pale in comparison with the rampant violations of recruiting rules, according to various media exposés. Prospective student-athletes who experience impermissible treatment may lose all respect for the integrity of eligibility rules. Most adolescent sport stars know that coaches who offer them financial inducements to sign letters of intent, do so in violation of NCAA rules. Also, by accepting money, sport clothing and equipment, cars, and other financial benefits, athletes become culpable along with these coaches. Individuals representing the sport interests of a college, according to NCAA rules, cannot give gifts or promise money to lure athletes to their favorite institutions. Athletes become ineligible upon receipt of any of these monetary items, even though frequently this does not occur because disclosure often comes years later, as illustrated by Marcus Camby, former University of Massachusetts star, who admitted receiving such benefits while a college athlete.

Many times payments from coaches, fans, and sport agents to athletes continue after enrollment. Many universities have been given NCAA sanctions for this and other violations. Because NCAA rules restrict financial aid to tuition, fees, and room and board, athletes who receive anything beyond this are in violation of eligibility rules. Some athletes in the major football conferences commonly receive benefits that violate NCAA rules. For example, at many NCAA Division I institutions, athletes have been given money, use of cars, clothing, food, and benefits to family members and friends, such as jobs, homes, and college scholarships, by athletic supporters. Such action was one reason why Southern Methodist University received the "death penalty" from the NCAA.

In trying to equalize competition, the NCAA, the National Association of Intercollegiate Athletics (NAIA), and the National Junior College Athletic Association (NJCAA) specify permissible recruiting practices in minute detail. The legalese used in their policy manuals reflects these organizations' intent to project an image of integrity, although the language used in these manuals to specifically prohibit certain actions may actually contribute to widespread circumventions of the rules.

Still, ethical issues relative to eligibility and recruitment in intercollegiate sport remain. If eligibility rules exist to help ensure that athletes have the opportunity to enroll in classes, work toward meaningful degrees, and seek educational attainment, what steps can be taken to reduce eligibility infractions both with the explicit rules and the spirit of the rules? If student athletes know that financial inducements are explicitly against the rules, should they lose eligibility to play? Because most rules violations result in sanctions against the entire team and future teams probably not involved in the violation, what moral issues arise when these teams lose their eligibility for conference and bowl games? If coaches, boosters, and others are involved in eli-

gibility violations both within the explicit rules and the spirit of the rules, what steps can be taken to reduce these types of infractions? And, because many confuse the spirit of eligibility rules with an argument about competition itself ("because everyone else violates eligibility rules, we must too in order to remain competitive"), is anyone morally or ethically bound to follow the rules?

Olympic Sport

Eligibility for athletes in the Olympic Games illustrates ethical dilemmas in elite sport. In 1896, the first Olympians in the modern era had to verify their amateur status before they were allowed to compete. Consistent with the British Amateur Sport Ideal as propagated by Baron Pierre de Coubertin, the founder of the Olympic Games, only gentlemen athletes, who played for the love of sport, were eligible (Lucas 1980).

The International Olympic Committee (IOC), which governs this event, initially prohibited athletes from receiving remuneration and endorsed the ideal that true sportsmen play sport for the game's sake, not for financial gain. However, when athletes received money or other benefits in violation of the amateur rules, the IOC seemed unwilling or unable to enforce its eligibility regulations.

Some national governments, and especially those in the former Soviet and Eastern Bloc, in seeking to promote their ideologies, trained, sponsored, and rewarded Olympic athletes. Under-the-table payments used for training and competitive expenses became commonplace. Some athletes trained for their sports full-time while serving in their nation's military forces. Next came appearance fees as event organizers paid the best athletes to participate in their competitions. Overt commercialization, such as skiers displaying corporate trademarks on their uniforms or track athletes wearing their sponsors' shoes around their necks on the victory stand, abounded in the 1980s but began much earlier. Did the pursuit of gold medals sweep aside ethical concerns about whether athletes met the eligibility regulations for participation?

The Olympic Games have survived numerous barrages directed against their eligibility regulations. Supposedly competitions between amateurs, the Olympic Games have not hosted such idealized events for decades, if ever. While espousing friendship among nations, the Olympic Games grew into opportunities for the promotion of national ideologies. To do so effectively, nations' athletes had to prove their superiority. As a result, the top athletes received funding, preferential treatment, and specialized training to ensure that their national ideology won acclaim. Violations of eligibility regulations, prohibiting athletes from receiving financial rewards for their prowess, continued.

Today, extensive rules specific to each sport specify the monies that Olympic athletes may receive while maintaining their eligibility. For example, Jackie Joyner-Kersee, Olympic gold medalist in track, grossed more than $750,000 in endorsements and stipends in 1992 while being named Amateur Sportswoman of the Year by the Women's Sports Foundation. Most men's and women's basketball Olympians are professionals. Still, some of the Olympic competitions remain among nonprofessional athletes.

SOCIOLOGICAL PERSPECTIVE

Sport mirrors society. Values viewed as important in society are transferred into sport settings as essential outcomes. Rules governing eligibility in sport, regardless of the level, will be followed only if participants respect moral principles. Violations occur because coaches, players, parents, and sport managers esteem the nonmoral value of winning more highly than playing honestly, justly, and responsibly. Eligibility regulations governing youth, school, college, and Olympic sport will be disregarded or violated indiscriminately unless those subject to these rules value them. People who lie, cheat, and deceive to gain competitive advantages do so because they value honesty, justice, responsibility, and beneficence less.

What can lead to an increase in the value of sport rules that govern eligibility? Winning must return to a less dominant place in sport. In the 1950s, for example, sportsmanship characterized intercollegiate sport. Most everyone expected student-athletes to reflect a balance between academics and sports; few recruiting rules existed. Seldom were inducements offered and athletes usually graduated.

Once television revenues, status, and other benefits went to the victorious, some athletes and coaches violated rules to help win. Many argue that NCAA III (nonscholarship), NAIA, NJCAA, and colleges with a Christian mission and focus have kept winning in perspective. Since the financial bonanzas associated with "big time" sport are not present, the need to violate eligibility rules to remain highly competitive does not exist. Such is not the case. Ten years of research in all levels of sport from youth through Olympic levels has found that no matter the level, athletes view winning as most important (Hahm 1989; Beller 1990; Beller and Stoll 1992; Beller and Stoll 1995; Beller and Stoll, Burwell, and Cole 1996; Stoll and Beller 1997). Many value the nonmoral value of winning as more important than the values of honesty and justice about the letter and spirit of the rules.

Youth Sport

Most youth sport programs are loosely organized and rely on voluntary compliance with a philosophy of fun-filled athletic programs for children and adolescents. Yet, the actions of some parents indicate a willingness to do whatever it takes to get and keep their children playing on the best teams. Without a formal enforcement mechanism, usually such actions go unquestioned. Some even praise the craftiness of these individuals. Coaches, like parents seeking ego fulfillment, occasionally violate league rules. Young athletes learn unethical lessons from parents and coaches who irresponsibly demonstrate that eligibility rules are made to be broken rather than followed.

Young athletes are most easily victimized because they often have no choice but to acquiesce to parental dictates whether ethical or not. Seldom are children and adolescents consulted about whether to be held back a grade to give them physical advantages in sport later or about their legal guardian or residence. Even if asked, they probably would agree with actions that could enhance their athletic status, because winning matters the most. Although willing parties in ethically questionable practices at the time, these young athletes later may conclude that they were exploited. Children cannot be expected to act as moral adults or to be responsible for the immoral actions of their parents.

Interscholastic Sport

Two challenges face high school athletic associations with regard to eligibility. First, a failure to thwart an overemphasis on victories, as modeled by intercollegiate and professional sports, can lead to a winning-at-all-costs mentality. Monetary inducements to get students to change schools, payoffs to parents to relinquish legal guardianship of their children, falsification of birth certificates, changing grades, and redshirting are among the ploys used to circumvent eligibility rules in the pursuit of winning. Second, schools are challenged to withstand the pressures to win when only successful teams are televised nationally. Pursuit of much-needed revenues may tempt school administrators to violate eligibility regulations just as they have led to violations in college athletics.

Intercollegiate Sport

The NCAA, NAIA, and NJCAA cannot legislate morality. Rather, these organizations enforce eligibility rules to facilitate equitable competitive opportunities among their member institutions. Small enforcement staffs attempting to investigate compliance by hundreds of coaches, thousands of athletes, and millions of fans can never ensure that everyone plays by the rules. Seldom does an institution self-report a violation and accept the associated penalty. Although many think that if institutions have not been penalized for rule violations they must be in compliance, there remains a good chance that they simply have not been caught.

In a cost-benefit analysis, some coaches may weigh the anticipated results of enticing (through rule-violating actions) the best blue-chip athletes to their institutions against the small likelihood of getting caught and the severity of the possible penalties. The benefits may exceed the low risk of being caught and penalized, such as when a team wins a national championship with illegally recruited players. Many coaches claim that every coach violates some of the rules, as if to justify their immoral actions. This rationalization that "everyone else does it" is **relativism.** As discussed previously, relativism as an ethical argument is inconsistent and irresponsible.

Some coaches emphasize that no college can fully comply with the myriad eligibility rules because many are too nebulous. The fact that the NCAA primarily sanctions those institutions that repeatedly and flagrantly violate the rules, especially those rules that prohibit giving athletes financial inducements while they are being recruited, reinforces this perception. Thus many coaches and sport managers rationalize that if their actions and institutions are not penalized for noncompliance, then they must be honest, just, and fair.

Do colleges and universities exist to provide education or to sponsor sport entertainment? In reality, many institutions of higher education in this country enjoy greater status and prestige for their victorious sport teams than for the numbers of athletes who graduate, Nobel Prize laureates, or Rhodes scholars. Although academics may not have concerned students who initiated intercollegiate sport, the undermining of educational integrity has always distressed faculties. For more than a century, the major ethical issues relative to eligibility in intercollegiate athletics have focused on academic abuses.

Because the NCAA, NAIA, and NJCAA maintain minimal academic standards for eligibility, athletes masquerading as students have vanished. Yet some athletes compete for their institutions during their last seasons of eligibility even though they have stopped attending classes. The one-year enrollment requirement before competition for transfers has virtually eliminated the recruitment of athletes from other teams; simultaneously, this rule binds athletes to institutions, but the coaches who recruited them can leave whenever they choose. Is this an ethical action?

Some coaches play academic games with their athletes' futures. Coaches seldom lose their jobs for low graduation rates; they are fired for failing to win. In the past, college presidents often turned deaf ears to outcries against coaches who recruited unprepared students or who cared about their athletes only as long as they were eligible to compete. What moral responsibilities do coaches owe their athletes?

If a coach promises an education to a recruit, should this educational opportunity be conditional on a student's esteem for the nonmoral values of

PUSHING THE RULES

Many people have good motives and good intentions for helping athletes. Unfortunately, sometimes these result in wrong actions. Athletes and coaches often are so popular that others want to share their limelight. When a high school algebra teacher gives athletes unearned good grades, the message intended may be a desire to help them stay eligible and to befriend the coach who says that an athlete cannot be expected to perform in the classroom and on the field or court. In reality, the message clearly states that algebra is unimportant. Such actions may result in athletes who have been coddled academically all of their lives by well-meaning people. No one does this for evil motives. Rather, all these individuals wanted to help the athletes. Too often the outcome of all this helping is an irresponsible person who does not have the temperament or the preparation to succeed in anything in life except sport.

effort, self-discipline, and hard work? Often, attaining a degree must include attending summer school and time beyond the four years of playing eligibility. Although college programs serve as training grounds for the few athletes making it into the professional ranks, guaranteeing this advancement in lieu of an education could be considered deceitful, with the percentages of college players who become professional athletes less than five percent in football, basketball, and baseball (Coakley 1998).

Athletes are responsible for their actions. Some recruits hear only what they want; others, with visions of professional sport grandeur, make only weak attempts to earn degrees, happily content to "major in eligibility" until they get chances to become professionals. Some athletes refuse to take advantage of tutorial help. A few willingly agree to have substitutes take entrance tests or course examinations. Some colleges hire individuals to walk athletes to class; often even this does not result in athletes taking advantage of their educational opportunities. Treating adult athletes like small children, however, fails to teach moral responsibility (see Box 6-3). Should coaches be expected to instruct their athletes in ethical conduct and to demonstrate such behavior themselves? What are some characteristics of ethical conduct relative to eligibility in intercollegiate athletics?

Olympic Sport

Although the word *amateur* appears nowhere in the IOC rules, the Olympic Games traditionally have been competitions for the world's best amateur athletes. After years of sporadic enforcement of its eligibility regulations, the IOC in the 1980s began to acknowledge that amateurism in Olympic competition simply was an ideal, not a reality. For decades, Olympians while in the military have been paid to train and compete for their countries. No longer would athletes have to perjure themselves by signing an oath of amateurism before competing. Although eligibility regulations vary dramatically by sport, professional athletes are the most acclaimed and successful Olympians in recent years.

ELIGIBILITY AND MORAL REASONING

In order to equalize competition, the essence of sport, eligibility rules govern who can play. At various levels of sport, every athlete desires to compete against opponents who have met the same criteria for playing. Thus eligibility rules govern the age, size, residence, affiliation, academic status, benefits received, and similar qualifications of opponents. Playing fairly, justly, and honestly demands that everyone respects and follows these rules. It also necessitates not cheating or deceiving others.

If winning, success, and money become more important than adhering to eligibility rules, then mistreating others to get these nonmoral rewards becomes paramount. Any person who values winning may yield to the temptation of violating ethical principles. Responding to the questions listed in Theory Box 6-4 provides an opportunity for analyzing what each individual's moral principles are in a sport context. Moral development is learned. Through education and living in a principled environment with honorable role models, individuals learn how to make good decisions. The structure of competitive sport does not always support moral development. For example, when children play on their own they consider cultural variations and differences in ability, without any eligibility rules. Rarely do they argue about who can play. Children understand the meaning of fun. In contrast, when adults make decisions for children, teens, and young adults in sports, does this negatively influence how these young people grow morally?

Recent research (Beller and Stoll 1992, 1995; Beller, Stoll, Burwell, and Cole 1996; Penny and Priest 1990; Krause and Priest 1993; Rudd 1997; Stoll and Beller 1997) with more than 35,000 sport participants, from ninth-graders through university students, found that the longer individuals participate in sport, the more morally calloused they become; that is, the less they respect their opponents and teammates or take into account honesty, justice, and the letter and spirit of the rules. Moral callousness is the antithesis of moral reasoning which challenges individuals to take others' perspectives into consideration when making decisions. The reality of sport today, on analysis of the competitive model, does not support the concept of being responsible, honest, fair, or concerned for others.

Young people seldom have to take responsibility for decisions in highly organized sports because adults make all the moral and competitive judgments. When adults make decisions for children, teens, and young adults in sports, it negatively influences how these young people grow morally and may stunt their developmental processes. This probably occurs as a direct result of the structure of sport programs at all levels. As noted earlier, moral reasoning is learned. Through education and living in a principled environment with honorable role models, individuals learn how to make good decisions. Unfortunately, the structure of competitive sport does not support moral reasoning and, therefore, many individuals do not learn to make good, sound, consistent moral decisions.

Relative to school and college sports, several principles should be considered if moral values are important outcomes of these programs. Should school administrators and coaches make attempts to commercialize interscholastic sport and to thwart associated violations of eligibility rules? Should college presidents, faculties, and athletic administrators control the existing emphasis on entertainment sports, which often leads to the playing of athletes who are quasi-students? Should educational leaders enforce a defensible standard regarding the academic performance for athletes? Should school and college sport programs increase student involvement in the decision-making process to allow them to mature in their ability to reason morally?

ETHICAL DILEMMAS REGARDING ELIGIBILITY

Issues regarding eligibility challenge individuals involved at all levels of sport. Each person can choose whether to adhere to or disregard the principles of honesty, justice, responsibility, and beneficence. When addressing an ethical issue, a person should begin by establishing the underlying value and then find a solution by determining how this action will affect them and others; every person's actions, it is hoped, will demonstrate consistency and impartiality. Theory Box 6-5 presents challenges relative to moral values and eligibility. Select alternatives from the list on the right side of the box, or suggest others. In responding to these questions, note that the ethical principles in Theory Box 6-6 may guide moral reasoning.

THEORY BOX 6-4

QUESTIONS ABOUT ETHICS IN ELIGIBILITY

- Is it ethical to pay an amateur athlete to play sport? If yes, under what circumstances?
- Why were eligibility rules initially standardized?
- Is it honest to play a non-student in an intercollegiate competition?
- When, if ever, does trying to win by any method become dishonest?
- Can morality be legislated through rules?
- Does dishonest, unjust, and irresponsible behavior necessitate the establishment of specific rules and regulations governing eligibility? Do such rules and regulations make people honest, just, and responsible?
- Did faculty mandate eligibility regulations concerning academic issues because students were acting unethically?
- Why do some coaches use financial inducements to recruit players?
- Why do some coaches allow and even encourage their athletes to emphasize sport more than earning diplomas or college degrees?
- Are athletes at all levels responsible for making moral decisions?
- Is the lowering of admissions standards for athletes ethical?
- When, if ever, should an athlete's grade be changed to permit playing eligibility?
- Can an interscholastic sport governing organization legislate morality in its competitions?
- Can an intercollegiate sport governing organization legislate morality in sport?
- Why do eligibility regulations in youth sport exist?
- Why do eligibility regulations in interscholastic sport exist?
- Why do eligibility regulations in intercollegiate sport exist?
- Why do eligibility regulations in Olympic sport exist?

- Do eligibility rules result in more honest or dishonest behavior by coaches and athletes?
- Are more and more eligibility rules necessary to prevent coaches, athletes, and sport managers from using every imaginable tactic to try to win? Why or why not?
- Should there be a moral basis for the conduct of sport competitions at all levels? If so, what should it be? Does it vary by level of sport?
- What role, if any, should the media play in promoting a moral basis for the conduct of sport competitions?
- Is it ethical for a college to receive huge revenues and yet not give spending money to the athletes who help earn these revenues?
- What is the ethical difference, if any, between receiving money for agreeing to attend a particular college or university and receiving money for point-shaving?
- What is the moral justification for holding a child back a year in school to gain an advantage in sport?
- Was the IOC dishonest in not declaring athletes ineligible when they received money while claiming to be amateurs?
- Is it ethical for coaches to use athletes for personal gain?
- Is it ethical for parents to use their children for personal gain?
- Are athletes being told that moral values are important in sport while they observe adults circumventing eligibility regulations?
- Does the absence of a rule and penalty prohibiting a particular action make that action moral?
- What are the determining factors in making an action moral?
- Is winning a nonmoral value? Why or why not?

THEORY BOX 6-5

ETHICAL DILEMMAS: YOU DECIDE

Dilemmas

1. Does the absence of prohibitive rules governing eligibility give moral license to do anything (that is, no rule, no harm)?

2. Are eligibility rules inherently honest?

3. What makes an action such as violating an eligibility rule dishonest?

4. Should youth, school, college, or Olympic athletes who receive money from fans lose their eligibility to compete?

Possible Resolutions

a) Yes, without rules, one has the freedom to do whatever is desired.
b) Actions should be based on personal moral values, not rules.
c) This absence of rules gives license to do whatever it takes to win.

a) The existence of a rule does not necessarily make it honest. Civil disobedience calls for violating a rule if it is unjust.
b) Because a rule exists, it is honest and just.
c) Honesty requires compliance only with the letter of the law, not necessarily with the spirit of the law.
d) If a rule exists and everyone agrees to play by that rule, then everyone is obligated to follow it. If anyone disagrees, that person can refuse to play or initiate a movement to get the rule changed.

a) Dishonesty exists only if punishment or penalties result.
b) A fraudulent or dishonest act is immoral, regardless of whether it is penalized.
c) Every situation and the associated circumstances determine whether an action is honest or dishonest.
d) Dishonesty is wrong only if a person believes in the value of honesty.

a) Yes, receiving money violates a rule.
b) No, rules that prohibit receiving money discriminate against the economically disadvantaged.
c) No, these athletes have earned whatever money they receive on the basis of their athletic achievements.
d) It depends on why the money was accepted; if it is used to fly home to visit a sick parent, it is permissible, but using the money to buy a CD player is not acceptable.
e) Yes, it is immoral to receive money as an amateur athlete.
f) No, athletes are entertainers and should be paid.
g) Yes, these athletes agreed to follow the rules; but, the rules need to be changed.

ETHICAL DILEMMAS: YOU DECIDE—cont'd

Dilemmas

5. Is it ethical to require athletes to achieve at a specified academic level before they are allowed to compete?

6. Are coaches acting honestly when they get athletes promoted or get them unearned good grades in order to maintain eligibility?

Possible Resolutions

a) Yes, competition is a privilege, not a right.
b) Yes, schools and colleges exist for the purpose of education, not athletics.
c) No, academic standards discriminate against the academically disadvantaged.
d) No, the system is basically immoral; sport competition remains a right of every student.

a) Yes, athletes deserve preferential treatment because of their contributions to victories, revenues, and institutional prestige.
b) No, athletes should be held accountable for their academic progress.
c) The emphasis on winning has forced coaches to act in this way. It is dishonest only if the athlete does not want this or if the coach is penalized.
d) No, lying or cheating is never morally acceptable.

THEORY BOX 6-6

ETHICAL PRINCIPLES FOR RESOLVING ELIGIBILITY ISSUES

1. Keep winning in perspective.
2. Educate coaches, athletes, and sport managers about the basic moral values of honesty, justice, responsibility, and beneficence.
3. Inform athletes, parents, coaches, and sport managers about the importance of the rules and the moral spirit of the rules.
4. Develop and publicize codes of ethical conduct for coaches, parents, athletes, and sport managers and require adherence to them.
5. Penalize consistently every dishonest action by an athlete, a coach, or a sport manager who previously has been educated about moral decision making.
6. Question and change sports rules and policies that are unjust, precipitate dishonest actions, or are irresponsible.

7. Guarantee every athlete an opportunity to get an education and help ensure this with proper advising, tutorial assistance, adequate time to complete academic work, financial aid, and career counseling.
8. Hire and retain coaches on the basis of factors other than their won-lost records.
9. Reward coaches who help their athletes achieve academically.
10. Articulate specific eligibility rules for all levels of sport competition and enforce them consistently and impartially.
11. Recognize and reward athletes, coaches, and sport managers who teach and practice the moral values of honesty, justice, responsibility, and beneficence.

SUMMARY

Is moral reasoning a priority in society and in sport? If so, then athletes must be educated about moral responsibility, honesty, justice, and beneficence. Unless those involved with sport value morality, eligibility problems will worsen. Intervention programs that teach athletes how to reason morally are needed because many individuals involved with sport programs do not practice moral reasoning. One teaching method could be discussing sport situations and analyzing how and why athletes would choose to act in certain ways. Through an open forum among teammates assisted by a person who asks probing questions, athletes could begin to question whether their values are being followed or violated in sport. If the latter is found to be the case, then, perhaps change will occur. It takes courage to speak out about one's values and to stand behind them.

In contests between two teams or individuals who previously agreed to conform to established eligibility regulations, when either opponent violates the rules, the equity of the competition is destroyed. Congruency and consistency with the purpose and conditions of sport competitions must exist if fairness counts. Instead of many of the claimed values of sport, lying and other immoral behaviors persist to enhance the chance of winning. When a potentially good sport contest is perverted through unethical actions such as the violation of eligibility rules, the real losers are the athletes.

Ethical conduct is critical to eligibility in sport at all levels. The issues discussed in this chapter can be resolved through moral education, legislation, enforcement, and commitment to playing the game by the letter and the spirit of the rules, not for winning alone. Sport leaders need to (1) establish the value structure, (2) educate people morally, (3) legislate against unfair and dishonest competition, and (4) enforce this legislation.

ISSUES AND DILEMMAS

CASE 6-1

Jerry began wrestling at age eight and quickly developed into a fine athlete in this sport. Wrestling at 55, 64, 70, and 77 pounds, over the years he won or placed high in several local and even state competitions. When he was eleven, he began to gain weight, moving up one weight classification and competing against older boys. For several months thereafter, Jerry failed to do well in competitions, usually losing in his first round matches.

Even though Jerry's weight was average for his age, Coach Miller suggested that he try to lose some weight so that he might wrestle at his previous weight classification of 77 pounds, instead of at 85 pounds. Coach Miller recommended a strict diet with no meats or sweets and daily 2-mile runs in a rubber suit.

Because Jerry loved to wrestle and always tried to do what Coach Miller asked, he strictly followed this training program. Before his next match, Jerry was down to 79, so he still had to wrestle at 85 pounds. Not only did he lose again, but he felt weak during the match.

In the days before the next wrestling event, Jerry ate very little and exercised harder. He believed that all this was worth the effort when he tipped the scales at 77 pounds. At this lower weight classification, Jerry won several matches before losing in the finals.

This near-victory helped motivate Jerry to adhere strictly to his diet and jogging regimen. Although Jerry appeared tired and unenergetic, Coach Miller praised his self-discipline and encouraged him to keep his weight at 77 so he could achieve success, which Jerry did.

1. Is Coach Miller violating any ethical principles by instructing Jerry to wrestle at a weight below that at which he would naturally compete? If so, what principles?
2. Is the motivation to succeed influencing Jerry to violate any ethical principles? If so, what principles?
3. Is Jerry cheating by wrestling at an unnatural weight (for example, a more mature athlete taking advantage of a less mature athlete)? Why or why not?
4. How are Coach Miller and Jerry treating the eligibility rule governing weight classifications to equalize competition?
5. What moral lesson is Coach Miller teaching Jerry?

◆ ◆ ◆

CASE 6-2

Lynn, a high school student, has developed a very good friendship with Jamie, who is a great athlete, probably one of the best in the history of the school. Besides being a great athlete, Jamie is a good student. If it were not for athletics, Jamie would probably be a straight-A student. But because of the demands of practices, games, and related sport activities, Jamie is doing only above-average work in most classes, except in one, Algebra II, which is causing problems. Jamie's lifelong dream has been to go to college, but this will require better grades in Algebra II. In fact, the final grade must be a C for Jamie to meet the NCAA eligibility requirements. Because the majority of the grade in Algebra II comes from the final exam, if Jamie can make a high grade, a C is a possibility.

Lynn and Jamie stop by the principal's office to ask a question but find no one there, even though the door is unlocked. Jamie sees the final exam for Algebra II lying on the secretary's desk awaiting duplication. Jamie picks it up, walks over to the copy machine, and makes a copy. Lynn says nothing as Jamie leaves with the exam.

1. In this situation, considering the opportunity for a grant-in-aid and a college education, would it be acceptable for Jamie to take the exam?
2. What should Lynn do? (Lynn knows that Jamie must pass this test to go to college. There is no way that Jamie could afford to go any other way than on an athletic grant-in-aid. This may be Jamie's only chance.)
3. If Lynn says nothing, is Lynn being dishonest?
4. Does a friendship take precedence over a moral principle? Does Lynn's loyalty to Jamie come before the rule about honesty?
5. Should Lynn ask Jamie to return the exam?

◆ ◆ ◆

CASE 6-3

Mr. McLendon coaches at Albemarle University, an NCAA school. The NCAA requires that he take an examination certifying that he knows and understands the rules, which he has done. One day Marty, who comes from a poor family, stops by his office to talk about strategy for the next game. Marty obviously has a terrible cold. Coach McLendon notices that Marty's coat is too thin for the weather conditions. Marty is not wearing boots. Coach McLendon asks about the coat and boots. Marty replies that there is no money for a better coat or boots. Later that afternoon, weather conditions worsen. On the way home from his office, Coach McLendon passes Marty, who is walking and dripping wet from the sleet. According to NCAA rules, Coach McLendon is not allowed to give Marty a ride or any extra benefits. After picking Marty up, Coach McLendon takes him to a store, where the coach purchases a warm coat and a pair of boots for Marty.

1. Did Coach McLendon knowingly violate a rule?
2. Was Coach McLendon cheating by buying Marty a warm coat and boots?

3. Is it acceptable in this case to violate a rule? Why or why not?
4. If this is an exception, what about the rule? Should the rule be kept or honored if it could violate basic human decency?
5. If you learn about this situation, are you honor-bound to report Coach McLendon's actions to the NCAA?

◆ ◆ ◆

CASE 6-4

After winning several cross-country races and two consecutive NCAA titles, Joan dropped out of college to train for the 2000 Sydney Games. As the United States record holder in the 10,000 meters, she felt confident that one year of concentrated training would help her achieve her lifelong dream of winning a gold medal.

Because her parents were unable to help her financially and her training program left time only for a part-time job, Joan depended on her sport successes for money to pay the bills. Her plan worked during the early part of the European track season, until she was injured. Without the guaranteed appearance money, Joan quickly got into a financial bind.

At this time, a sport agent, Edgar Rogers, contacted Joan. He offered her $10,000 to appear in a commercial promoting several types of wine. The contract specified that this television commercial would not appear until after the 2000 Olympic Games because advertisement of alcoholic beverages by athletes would violate the eligibility rules of the International Amateur Athletic Federation (governing organization for track and field). Joan could, however, accept the fee "under the table" immediately.

1. What ethical principle regarding eligibility, if any, would Joan violate if she appeared in the wine commercial?
2. What ethical principle regarding eligibility, if any, would Joan violate if she accepted the fee for doing the commercial?
3. Under what circumstances, if any, would it be ethical for Joan to accept the fee for doing the commercial?
4. Is an eligibility rule unfair and unjust if it prevents an athlete from receiving money to pay the bills for living expenses?
5. Does the ultimate objective of winning a gold medal justify breaking an eligibility rule?

◆ ◆ ◆

CASE 6-5

Marlene, the 25-point per game, three-time All-American for Southeastern University (SU), was in serious academic difficulty. Facing final exams in her last summer school courses, she knew there was no hope of making the two Bs she needed to remain eligible for her senior year. She realized that, as in most other courses she had taken as a speech communication major, she had put forth little effort. Even though she had been a special admit at SU, she had thus far managed to make minimal progress toward her degree and to achieve the required grade-point average (GPA). But, she had to have Bs in these two courses in her major, or she could not play her senior year.

Coach Harris, who was anticipating his first conference title and NCAA tournament bid, was really upset when he learned that Marlene's ineligibility would probably put these two dreams in serious jeopardy. How could she, he asked himself, seemingly have ruined everything? After all, he had managed to get her admitted even though her high school GPA and SAT score had been significantly below SU's standards. Through a friend, he had helped Marlene's mother get a higher paying job and qualify for a new home loan. Three times Coach Harris had convinced faculty members to give Marlene special exams or assignments in order to help her raise her grades and stay eligible.

Knowing that no one in the Department of Speech Communication would help Marlene to raise her summer grades after they were recorded, Coach Harris decided to talk with Charlie Stafford, Dean of the College of Arts and Sciences. Since Dean Stafford's daughter was a member of the basketball team, Coach Harris thought that maybe he could get Marlene's grades changed by the Dean.

1. Was it ethical for Coach Harris to get Marlene admitted to SU even though she did not meet the minimal academic standards? Why or why not?
2. Was it ethical for Coach Harris' friend to help Marlene's mother with the new job and home loan? Why or why not?
3. Was it ethical for Coach Harris to get professors to provide special exams or assignments in order to help Marlene maintain her eligibility? Why or why not?
4. Was it ethical for Coach Harris to ask Dean Stafford to change Marlene's grades? Why or why not?
5. What ethical values, if any, had Marlene violated?

◆ ◆ ◆

CASE 6-6

When most people think about interscholastic sports, they assume that these teams are comprised of boys and girls who live in the surrounding school district. Historically, high school coaches could be great coaches but never have truly outstanding athletes attend their schools. In today's world of magnet schools, independent or private schools, charter schools, and summer camps, adolescents are seldom restricted to the local school. Recruiting abounds. Coaches of summer teams influence impressionable adolescents to affiliate with the highest bidder, which could be with a cross-town school, with a team sponsored by a shoe company, or with a coach who can provide national exposure in the media.

1. What rules govern what school team an adolescent must play for?
2. What factors have contributed to the recruiting of high-school-age athletes?
3. What athletic benefits can or should an interscholastic athlete receive?
4. What rules govern the recruiting of high school age athletes?
5. What ethical values should govern the eligibility rules in interscholastic sports?

◆ ◆ ◆

CASE 6-7

In the wake of media exposés about the academic woes of many college athletes, the NCAA, in recent years, has significantly tightened its academic eligibility rules. The NCAA mandates completion of 13 core courses and a sliding scale of grade point average (GPA) and SAT/ACT scores in order to qualify through its Clearinghouse for a college grant-in-aid. Once enrolled, a student-athlete must make progress toward a degree and maintain a minimal GPA. While these higher academic standards have been praised by many, concerns have been raised that these new requirements have disproportionately affected minorities. Recent data have verified that a higher percentage of African American youths have failed to qualify for grants-in-aid or have lost their grants due to academic problems.

1. What are the ethical arguments for raising academic standards regardless of who might be affected?
2. What are the ethical arguments against raising academic standards if they discriminate against a minority group?
3. Assuming that the NCAA academic rules are discriminatory, what is the moral basis for changing this situation?

REFERENCES

Beller, Jennifer M. 1990. A moral reasoning intervention program for Division I athletes: Can athletes learn not to cheat? Ph.D. diss., University of Idaho.

Beller, J.M., and Sharon K. Stoll. 1992. A moral reasoning intervention program for student-athletes. *Academic Athletic Journal* (spring): 43–57.

———. 1995. Moral reasoning of high school student-athletes and general students: An empirical study versus personal testimony. *Pediatric Exercise Science,* 7(4):352–63.

Beller, J.M., S.K. Stoll, B. Burwell, and J. Cole. 1996. The relationship of competition and a Christian liberal arts education on moral reasoning of college student athletes. *Research on Christian Higher Education* 3: 99–114.

Berryman, Jack W. 1975. From the cradle to the playing field: America's emphasis on highly organized competitive sports for preadolescent boys, *Journal of Sport History* 2(2):112.

Coakley, Jay J. 1998. *Sport in society: Issues and controversies.* 6th ed. St. Louis: The C.V. Mosby Co.

Eitzen, D. Stanley, and George H. Sage. 1997. *Sociology of North American sport.* 6th ed. New York: WMC/McGraw-Hill.

Hahm, C.H. 1989. Moral reasoning and development among general students, physical education majors, and student athletes. Ph.D. diss., University of Idaho.

Krause, J., and R.F. Priest. 1993. Sport values choices of United States Military Academy cadets—A longitudinal study of the class of 1993. Unpublished manuscript, Office of Institutional Research, United States Military Academy.

Lucas, John A. 1980. *The modern Olympic Games.* New York: A.S. Barnes.

1997–98 NCAA Manual. 1997. Overland Park, KS. National Collegiate Athletic Association.

Penny, B., and R.F. Priest. 1990. Deontological sport values choices of United States Academy cadets and selected other college-aged populations. Unpublished manuscript, Office of Institutional Research, United States Military Academy.

Rudd, A. 1997. Moral callousness as evidenced by trash talking t-shirts. Master's thesis, University of Idaho.

Smith, Ronald A. 1988. *Sports & freedom: The rise of big-time college athletics.* New York: Oxford University Press.

Stoll, S.K. 1993. *Who says this is cheating?* Dubuque, Iowa: Kendall/Hunt.

Stoll, S.K., and J.M. Beller. 1997. (September). Ethical gender issues in sport. Presentation to the annual convention of the International Philosophic Society of Sport, Oslo, Norway.

Williams, Jesse F., and W.L. Hughes. 1930. *Athletics in education.* Philadelphia: W.B. Saunders Co.

ADDITIONAL READINGS

Bailey, Wilford S., and Taylor D. Littleton. 1991. *Athletics and academe: An anatomy of abuses and a prescription for reform.* Phoenix: Oryx Press.

Coakley, Jay J. 1998. *Sport in society: Issues & controversies.* 6th ed. Dubuque, IA: McGraw-Hill.

DeVenzio, Dick. 1986. *Rip-off u.: The annual theft and exploitation of major college revenue-producing student-athletes.* Charlotte, NC: Fool Court Press.

Edwards, Harry. 1969. *The revolt of the black athlete,* New York: Free Press.

Eitzen, D. Stanley, and George H. Sage. 1996. *Sociology of North American sport.* 6th ed. Madison, WI: Brown and Benchmark.

Farrell, Charles S., 1995. Report blasts NCAA test score-based sports eligibility. *Black Issues in Higher Education* 11 (January 12): 26–7.

Greenspan, Emily. 1983. *Little winners: Inside the world of the child sportstar.* Boston: Little, Brown, and Co.

Kirk, Sarah V., Wyatt D. Kirk, and Richard E. Lapchick, Eds. 1993. *Student athletes: Shattering the myths & sharing the realities.* Alexandria, VA: American Counseling Association.

Klatell, David A. and Norman Marcus. 1988. *Sports for sale: Television, money, and the fans.* New York: Oxford University Press.

Lapchick, Richard E. 1986. *Fractured focus: Sport as a reflection of society.* Lexington, MA: Lexington Books.

———. 1991. *Five minutes to midnight: Race & sport in the 1990s.* Lanham: Madison Books.

Lapchick, Richard E., and Jeffrey R. Benedict, Eds. 1995. *Sport in society: Equal opportunity or business as usual?* Thousand Oaks, CA: Sage Publications, Inc.

Leonard, William M. II. 1993. *A sociological perspective of sport.* 4th ed. New York: Macmillan.

Underwood, Clarence. 1984. *The student athlete: Eligibility and academic integrity.* Lansing, MI: Michigan State University Press.

CHAPTER 7

Sport Elimination

- ◆ What are the ethical dilemmas associated with the drop out phenomenon in youth sport?
- ◆ What are the ethical dilemmas associated with the drop out phenomenon in interscholastic sport?
- ◆ Should youth who lack skills be cut from sport teams?
- ◆ How does an overemphasis on the nonmoral value of winning contribute to sport drop out?
- ◆ How is sport drop out an ethical issue at the college level?
- ◆ What are the moral problems associated with drop out for elite and professional athletes who have finished their competitive careers?
- ◆ Why does physical burn out occur, and are there any moral principles violated in this process?
- ◆ What are the ethical issues surrounding psychological burn out?
- ◆ What causes social burn out?
- ◆ How can sport drop out and sport burn out be prevented, ameliorated, or eliminated?

Millions of people in this country annually participate in, watch, and read about sports. They spend billions of dollars on tickets, signature sports equipment, and team-licensed products and clothing. Few question the pervasiveness of sport in the United States; many individuals plan vacations, outings, and social gatherings around the in-season sport.

Not everyone, however, is caught up in this sport mania. Millions of nonsport fans and nonpartici-

pants never read newspaper sport sections and sport magazines, do not own a team sweatshirt or autographed racquet, and prefer a movie or video to any televised or live sporting event. Although much has been written about sports fans and participants, the invisible minority (or is it majority?) remains a perceived anomaly. These folks seem totally innocuous to their self-imposed separation from the most popular coffee club, bar stool, or office topic of conversation—sport. Some of these individuals may have no interest in sport because they dropped out of sport (see Box 7-1).

Competitive Athletics Are Not for Everyone

In American society, it seems that professional athletes with their multi-million dollar contracts, college athletes revelling in their championships and media exposure, and high school athletes with visions of achieving what these two groups have attained have become heroes (occasionally heroines) and role models. As the media creates and publicizes these stars, youngsters aspire to "be like Mike" (Michael Jordan, that is) even though the odds are against them. Less than one percent of athletes will go on to become sport stars.

Sport elimination, unfortunately, probably is an outcome of an overemphasis on competitive athletics. First, not everyone enjoys competition. While competition is valued by the successful, it is avoided by those who do not succeed, in sports and in other activities. The message here is that sports do not have to stress competing against and defeating someone else. Second, athletics, which pit individuals against others and are governed by highly structured rules, do not appeal to or meet the needs of millions. Recreational sports and fitness activities are valued by many for sheer enjoyment, personal development, and social relationships. Sport elimination too often occurs because of a loss of fun, a lack of success, and pressures to win. Thus, when faced with the choice between playing competitive athletics or not, the choice often is something else.

This chapter begins with an examination of the ethical issues associated with the drop out phenomenon in youth, interscholastic, intercollegiate, and professional sport. Next, the factors that lead to sport burn out at these four levels are analyzed to determine whether any ethical standards are being breached. It is suggested that incidents of drop out and burn out in sport are associated with violations of ethical principles, that is, justice and responsibility, at various competitive levels.

FACTORS LEADING TO SPORT DROP OUT

Numerous factors contribute to the phenomenon of athletes choosing to drop out of sport. Many of these are listed in Theory Box 7-2. Sport dropout refers to voluntary or involuntary separation from sport for one or a number of reasons, any of which may be positive or problematic.

Lack of Skills

Children's sports, especially competitive team sports, socialize youth about the cultural values of capitalistic America. Early in life, society encourages boys to engage in sports as a rite of passage and to take pride in their athletic abilities and achievements. Boys learn to link status on the playground with their physical prowess. To a lesser extent, pre-adolescent girls are reinforced for displaying physical skills but usually only in those sports society deems appropriate for them.

Youth Sport

Youngsters embarking on their first organized sport experience bring few preconceived notions to the field or court. They simply want to play. Children prefer playing on losing teams to sitting on the benches of winning teams. Youth believe that their sport participation will help develop their skills, but they quickly learn that their more skillful teammates play the most in games and at their preferred positions while receiving more praise and attention than those not so skilled. This translates into fewer opportunities to play, a primary reason for dropping out (see Box 7-3).

Citing lack of money, coaches, and space, many municipalities and leagues set limits on the number of children who can participate on their teams. Instead of making a place for every interested child, after a few days of tryouts coaches post the names of those girls and boys good enough to play. The devastation of being cut as a small child is probably not fully understood by adults. Parents can console and encourage their children to try again next year, but the feelings of inferiority, helplessness, and loss

THEORY BOX 7-1

VALUES SOUGHT VERSUS VALUES REALIZED

Dropping out of sport is not an ethical issue. It becomes an issue only if and when certain processes and practices violate the ultimate purpose of the activity. That is, if a sport organization's stated purpose is to provide positive, educational experiences, then the organization and the people involved in the organization are bound to follow the stated purpose or change it. Most educational organizations from youth sport through school sport to university athletics are rooted in the assumption that sport supports the educational mission and goal of the institution. Therefore, sport managers and coaches are obligated to follow the tenets and purposes of the educational mission. Because educational experiences in this country are predicated on the assumption of fairness, justice, and responsible action, youth sport through university athletics are obligated to follow these same ethical tenets. Thus, if an athlete drops out of sport because of practices of the organization or the coach that violate the stated purpose, then dropping out becomes an ethical issue. When coaches are irresponsible in following the educational purposes of an organization or unfair in how they treat athletes, then athletes dropping out becomes an ethical issue. If the organization allows practices that are unfair and irresponsible to the stated mission and goal, then that organization is unethical in its practices.

Parents encourage their children to enter sport because it is believed that they will learn teamwork, fair play, cooperation, discipline, sportsmanship, and self-confidence, values that can be transferred to later life. Youth who play sports want to have fun, participate in an exciting game, build new friendships or nurture existing ones, and learn to play better. Dropout at this level occurs when children and adolescents leave sport because it stops being fun, fails to provide positive social interactions with friends, and becomes too stressful. Oftentimes, these negatives occur when adults organize and dominate youth sport programs and lose sight of the stated goals. Instead, adults violate their ethical responsibility.

Proponents of interscholastic sport state that these programs positively impact students academically, teach values, develop physical vigor, generate school spirit, and rally community support. Dissenters argue that sports in the schools subvert educational goals by using limited resources and distracting all students, especially athletes, from their academic work. Dissenters argue further that sports undermine rather than teach moral values. School students usually drop out of sport because they lose the intrinsic motivation to continue, are cut, quit because they do not get to play, want to emphasize academics, or find other interests.

The size of a college or university usually determines whether it sponsors "big-time" athletics or a smaller scale program. The "big-time" sport programs are operated like businesses in which the stated purpose of football and men's basketball teams is to earn revenue. All of these programs, with varying degrees of success, claim to provide extracurricular competitive opportunities while stressing academic achievement. Other espoused goals include fitness training, value development, social and psychological enhancement, and preparation for life. Some of the comparatively few high school athletes who play intercollegiate sport drop out of college sport programs due to the lack of playing time, problems with coaches, conflicts between academics and athletics, inadequate time for social relationships or other interests, and excessive pressures to achieve success in sport.

Because professional sport exists to entertain fans, concern for values and individuals has become secondary to economics. Athletes as employees exist as expendable commodities given this profit orientation. When athletes drop out because of diminishing skills, recurrent injuries, contract disputes, and a lack of the desire to compete, dozens of others are eager to replace them. Frequently, this drop-out is forced when former athletes are released or aspiring ones are cut.

THEORY BOX 7-2

REASONS ATHLETES DROP OUT OF SPORT

Youth Sport

- Lack of skills
- Limited opportunities to play
- Cannot play preferred position
- Team cuts
- Loss of enjoyment
- Lack of control over own games
- Lack of intrinsic motivation
- Changing interests
- Pressures from parents and coaches to win
- Lack of positive reinforcement

Interscholastic Sport

- Lack of skills
- Lack of opportunity due to not enough teams or no team in preferred sport
- Team cuts
- Loss of enjoyment
- Lack of intrinsic motivation
- Lack of time because of job
- Changing interests
- Pressures from parents and coaches to win

- Lack of positive reinforcement
- Conflicts with coaches

Intercollegiate Sport

- Lack of skills
- Lack of opportunity because teams are mainly comprised of recruited grant-in-aid athletes
- Loss of enjoyment
- Lack of intrinsic motivation
- Changing interests
- Academic demands
- Pressures from parents and coaches to win
- Conflicts with coaches

Professional Sport

- Released by team management
- Diminishing skills
- Loss of desire to play
- Nagging injuries
- Pressures from coaches and the media
- Conflicts with coaches and management

THEORY BOX 7-3

WHAT ETHICAL PRINCIPLES ARE BEING VIOLATED?

The purpose of any youth sport program *should be* to foster development of physical skills through a positive social and moral environment. Ethical issues arise when the goals of a program are forgotten or displaced in the urgency to become successful as results become more important than performance. If only talented children play while the less talented warm the bench, coaches are openly stating that they think the purpose and goals of the program are wrong. They are demonstrating through their coaching that what is important is winning. That is, coaches are violating the principles of the program, which they explicitly or implicitly gave their word to

follow, and are behaving unethically by focusing on winning.

If the purpose of the program is for all children to play, then the number of teams should not be limited and coaches should not be allowed to cut players. If money is limited and only a few can play, then the program has a moral responsibility to say so. It is doubtful that any public youth sport program could justify itself if it is only for the physically elite or more physically mature. Rather, each child deserves the opportunity to develop physical skills, have fun, and learn various social skills and moral values through sport.

SCHOOL SPORT FOR ALL OR FOR THE ELITE?

The ethical issue of justice focuses on the purpose of sport within the school experience. Should a school, whose moral purpose is equitable treatment of all, support a system totally based on a meritocratic philosophy? Is the school being fair to all youth and adolescents in the system and responsible to its stated purposes by supporting such a system? Is the school being just and fair to all by having such inequities, that is, one program for the elite and none for the rest? This is not to say that elite programs per se are unethical. It is ethically possible and defensible to have elite programs if the stated purpose of the organization provides only for exceptional experiences. That is, it is perfectly acceptable to offer an honors class in chemistry or advanced music classes for exceptional students. Not everyone is talented enough to pass honors chemistry or to sing opera; not everyone should be expected to, and not everyone should be placed in the program.

If funds are available to support the philosophy of an advanced program, then such programs are justified. However, if programs are developed only for the elite with nothing available for the not-so-elite, then such a philosophy violates equitable treatment for all. It is unacceptable to develop an honors chemistry class for advanced students and have no other chemistry class available. It is unacceptable to develop an advanced opera class with no other music classes. It also is unacceptable to have a varsity athletic program with no other sport experiences available. Do schools have a responsibility to offer intramural or club activities for all students? Should such programs be supported with the same financial fervor and the same level of coaching and advising competencies that exist in the elite program? Should such programs be viewed as just as important as the elite program and be supported in all the same ways?

of confidence may be irreparable, especially if it happens multiple times. Some would argue, though, that failure is an important part of growing and living. Is the purpose of youth sport to initiate the development of professional athletes or to maximize participation? If it is the latter, should communities and sponsoring organizations provide all children opportunities to play their favorite sports?

Some children will diligently work on their skills and make the team when a year older and more mature. Others will forget the sport in which they were rejected and channel their energies and interests into different sports. The persistent ones, through whichever sports they are fortunate enough to get to play, will be more likely to lead healthy, active lives as children.

Unfortunately, though, many children will simply never again submit themselves to the humiliation and hurt of not getting selected for a team. These girls and boys may never again attempt to learn the skills and knowledge needed to achieve the healthful benefits of being active in sports. At an early age, they will join the ranks of those who just do not like sports. Thus, at the youth level, one ethical dilemma is whether children should be cut from teams or whether every child should be guaranteed the opportunity to play.

Interscholastic Sport

Many of the reasons that youngsters opt out of sport also characterize explanations given by teens. Significant among these, though, may be the fact that schools, like many youth sport programs, limit the numbers of girls and boys allowed to participate on their teams with the justification that this ensures better competition for highly skilled players. Again, limitations in money, coaches, and facilities are cited to rationalize the elimination of dozens of girls and boys who try out for one of the coveted team uniforms. Many others who self-assess that they lack the skills do not even bother to try.

One ethical dilemma at the school level is trying to understand how a public educational institution established for all young people can justify a meritocratic sport program (see Box 7-4). Within the school curriculum, all students are placed in classes that meet their academic needs. But in the extracurricular arena, schools provide only for the highly skilled. If values can be learned through sport, do not all students have the right to learn these principles? Interscholastic athletics perpetuate and exacerbate self-elimination from sport.

Many schools have increased support for intramural sports for all interested school students, in addition to providing limited varsity teams for only the best athletes. These educators advocate that a combination of interscholastic sports and intramurals focuses on participation and skill improvement for all students, which are appropriate educational objectives.

Intercollegiate Sport

The elimination process in sport continues in college as thousands of former high school athletes suddenly find their skills inferior to those of their peers. With few exceptions, the awarding of grants-in-aid at most colleges and universities automatically dismisses any thought the nonrecruited student may have about trying to gain a place on the team. Some young men, however, searching for team association and the social status of being an athlete, willingly "walk on" and become practice players who never earn varsity letters or compete in a game; a few women become walk-on athletes as well.

Many former high school athletes become intramural, extramural, and recreational sport participants in college. Others channel their enthusiasm for sport into the spectator role, even though they are seldom active themselves. Some outgrow sport during their college years as interests change and new talents are discovered. They adopt new lifestyles, deciding that they no longer enjoy sport competitions.

As the pyramid narrows at the top, only the highly skilled become intercollegiate athletes. Because most of these individuals are heavily recruited, attending a particular institution primarily because of athletics, the regular college student may question the purpose of college and university sport programs. For many institutions, the answer is that intercollegiate athletics exist primarily for entertainment with its associated revenue and only secondarily as a valued extracurricular activity for students.

Professors argue that universities exist for the purpose of critical inquiry. How, then, can any programs sponsored by universities place entertainment provided by heavily recruited athletes, who often are marginal students, higher in priority than academics? Some would respond that this has occurred because of the lack of institutional control and to appease fans.

If athletics teaches important lessons for life and enhances the collegiate experience, should not every interested student, regardless of skill level, be allowed the opportunity, even encouraged, to participate? However, how can a college or university afford to fund competitive sport opportunities for all who desire them? Student fees usually help accomplish this through intramural and recreational sport programs. Selective systems that separate individuals by ability levels are not inherently wrong. Many claim they are unethical when those students who are cut or self-eliminated have few comparable alternatives.

Professional Sport

The less than one percent of high school athletes who end up playing professionally (Coakley 1998) or reaching the pinnacles of their sport in amateur competition have survived many cuts because of their exceptional sport abilities and dedication (see Box 7-5). Many of these individuals, though, still face the most difficult separation from sport. This final cut traumatizes many athletes because for most of their lives their self-concept has been inextricably linked with sport. That is, many athletes may believe that they are liked, respected, and preferentially treated solely on the basis of their sport achievements; without sport, they will lose the elite status that elevated them above others.

Forced disengagement from sport can be devastating at any age and competitive level, although the longer the personal involvement in sport the harder it may be to cope. Admitting to diminishing skills when compared with the abilities of youthful stars remains difficult for many professional athletes. A career-ending injury abruptly changes one's

THEORY BOX 7-5

THE BUSINESS OF PROFESSIONAL SPORT

Professional sport has quite different ethical dilemmas than does amateur and school sport. The purposes of professional sport are entertainment and profits. The athletes who choose to become a part of such a system must realize that their talents are marketable. When they chose to become a professional athlete, they chose to be marketed. This is not to say that the professional sport does not have to be responsible, fair, and honest in its transactions with the athlete. Sport businesses are obligated by law to hold to the same ethical and legal principles that are necessary for any American business. However, it must be remembered that a purpose of professional sport is to make money. Professional sport does not hold to the same equitable, ideal perspectives about the athletic experience that amateur and school sport do. If an athlete spends three years in the professional arena and then is cut, it is not the professional sport's fault that the athlete is judged to have nothing left to contribute. All athletes must be held accountable and responsible for their actions. Many high school and collegiate athletes dream of making millions just like professional athletes. They want the money and the good life without realizing that huge salaries mean the purpose of the sport experience is no longer fun. The purposes now are entertainment and profits. However, it cannot be forgotten that the organization's purpose has a direct effect on how it views its moral and ethical responsibilities.

life; many injured athletes totally withdraw from anything associated with the sport experiences they can no longer share.

On average, three to five years after signing a professional contract, winning a gold medal, and reigning as number one in the world, the dream ends for athletes. The subsequent and often abrupt disengagement from sport traumatizes many athletes conditioned from an early age to singularly focus on sport. They then suddenly find themselves eliminated from sport, often without an education, career counseling, or coping skills for life without sport.

The media has publicized athletes who squandered their professional earnings and ended up destitute, who attempted ill-fated comebacks when life without sport seemed meaningless, and who committed suicide because of depression and other sport-disengagement problems. Did these events occur because the American sport system exploited these athletes by promising fame and fortune, only to forget them as soon as some more highly skilled individuals came along? Does a belief in the worth of the individual sport participant obligate sport managers to educate athletes pragmatically about managing time and stress, coping with and without fame and fortune, and preparing for life after sport?

Not Fun Anymore
Youth sport

Backyard and playground games, where children make up the rules as they play, have become increasingly hard to find. These spontaneous pastimes ceased to thrive when adults began to impose their rules. Many adults indicate that they organize their children's games because playgrounds have increasingly disappeared as a result of urban sprawl or because crime has made these areas unsafe. Certainly parents want to protect their children, but the question remains, how structured should youth sport be? Because children play sports to have fun and the lack of fun causes many to drop out, should parents provide safe environments and give the games back to the kids? Do youth through sport need to learn how to organize, develop leadership abilities, solve problems, and value fair play?

At the opposite end of the continuum from being cut is the athlete who quits voluntarily. By age twelve, more than half of all youth already will have opted out of the sport programs in which they previously competed. Many of these girls and boys state that sport is not fun anymore, the number one reason for dropping out of sport. Although some may leave sport because of other interests and possibly other sports, what other factors cause early exits from sport?

The most important contributing factor to sports not being fun anymore may be the lack of success. People naturally pursue those activities that provide feelings of accomplishment. Children enjoy receiving praise for their achievements and awards for their physical talents, although adults may have emphasized these extrinsic awards too much. Being successful can be characterized by learning new skills, earning significant playing time, playing a preferred position, achieving status among one's teammates and peers, and avoiding negative reinforcement from parents and coaches. Success does not have to mean being the superstar or the game-winning heroine or hero. However, the lack of positive feedback, whatever the source, can contribute to a young person's conclusion that sport is not fun anymore. Some other use of time might be more enjoyable; so they quit.

A contributing factor to drop-out may be that instead of sport teaching and reinforcing the moral values of justice, honesty, responsibility, and beneficence, it undermines them. Youth may question whether they are receiving fair treatment when they spend more time on the bench than playing, never get to play their preferred positions, and endure disparaging comments from coaches about their lesser skills. By reducing the fun, does an elitist pyramid of sport starting at the youth level cast aside those who do not possess sufficient skills?

Many youth sport athletes lose the fun aspect and drop out because the pressures to specialize in only one sport, train year-round, endure pain while playing with an injury, cheat or circumvent rules, and emphasize athletics over academics become too intense and are perceived negatively. They also may feel that no one cares about them as individuals. Each athlete weighs the pleasures received in sport against the stressors from any one of these pleasures. They continue to participate if sport is personally rewarding.

Interscholastic sport

Athletes who compete for their school teams usually find their extracurricular sport experiences enjoyable. They achieve a certain status as representatives of their schools and in their hometowns, especially in those towns without college and professional teams. Unfortunately, not all interscholastic sport provides positive reinforcement to its participants. Some coaches take the fun out of sport when they drive their athletes unmercifully in the pursuit of improved physical and skill development. A few coaches, seemingly insensitive to the needs of adolescents, cause adolescent athletes to drop out because sport stops being fun socially and psychologically.

Sport may also stop being fun when schools fail to support it adequately. This may take the form of ill-prepared coaches, schedules that provide no challenge or little hope for success, not enough teams for everyone to get a chance to play, no teams in certain sports, poor facilities, and a lack of general support of athletics by the school. As a result, athletes may adopt a similarly apathetic attitude.

Intercollegiate sport

Many college athletes who consider practice to be work and certainly not fun have to endure all types of physical, verbal, and emotional abuse just so they can compete. These individuals suffer through this abuse because they value team affiliation and social outcomes as pleasurable enough to overcome the abuse. Others who do not, drop out.

Individuals who choose to quit their college sport teams, even for academic reasons or because of changing interests, are often stigmatized. Sometimes former teammates deride those who quit. Rather than trying to understand why, ex-teammates often impugn the motives of anyone who does not stick with the sport. The negativism associated with quitting increases at higher levels of sport. Males find this especially difficult because their masculinity may be questioned when they do not persevere.

Sport sponsored by educational institutions claims to teach life-long social, emotional, and ethical values. This societal perception suggests that participation in sport prepares individuals for life in general and specifically for America's capitalistic economy. Because of these firmly held beliefs, those athletes who drop out because they have stopped having fun or for related reasons are thought to be shortchanged and thus disadvantaged.

Professional sport

Professional athletes accustomed to starring at lower levels of sport may experience difficulty in adjusting to being substitutes, seldom playing, or losing. This may wreak havoc on their self-confidence, leading to lessened enjoyment. In response, some athletes will work harder to earn a starting position or to improve their abilities; others will become disgruntled or lose interest in playing.

Diminishing skills frequently contribute to professional athletes' loss of enjoyment in their sport. Many find it hard to cope with the reality of being a step slower or of seeing younger athletes surpass them in ability. Many professional athletes choose to retire from sport when they realize that they have played their best, wanting to leave at the peak of their careers. Others remain as role players as long as they have the desire to play or until management releases them.

Sport managers and coaches at all levels should examine whether structural or operational issues based on moral principles cause athletes not to have fun anymore. Do children, adolescents, and young

---

THEORY BOX 7-6

THE RIGHT, THE GOOD PURPOSE, AND THE WIN

Performance versus results is at the root of the ethical dilemma facing American sport today. If the results that come from winning (feeling important, being number one, and reaping financial perks) are more important than how people are treated or how performances are valued, then ethical dilemmas will occur with every swing of the bat, hike of the ball, or swing of the racket. Why do these ethical dilemmas occur? What is the purpose of sport? If the purpose is only to win, then why be upset when unethical practices occur? If winning is the main objective, then go for it. Kick them in the head, knee them in the groin, intimidate, taunt, whatever it takes . . . these become the ethic of sport. However, if the sport experience is more than winning and a certain ideal standard of what "sport should be" in its performance is valued, then people are obligated to hold to a higher standard of conduct. Behaving ethically means trying to do the right thing. Ethical behavior in sport means that there is a certain standard of right worth attaining. Therefore, the goal of sport should be focused toward the right and the good. In sport, the right and the good purpose lead to valuing the performance and one's opponent more than the win.

---

adults have a right to participate in sport competitions that are fun? Is it morally defensible to focus coaching and playing opportunities primarily on those who mature the earliest or possess the greatest physical talents? Can sport programs allow for strong competition while encouraging the lesser skilled to be physically active? What changes are needed to ensure fun experiences for athletes? What is the purpose of sport? (See Box 7-6).

Dealing with the transition out of sport

Whether an athlete is ten, twenty, or thirty, at some point in time she or he will no longer participate in sports, at least not at the same level. Just as corporations help former employees prepare for alternative careers, athletes often need assistance in making a smooth transition into other activities. For children and adolescents, leaving one sport may lead to entering another sport that is more fun and personally rewarding. It may mean substituting recreational activities or other hobbies for competitive sports. The important issue here is to encourage youth to value physical activity.

Pressures To Win

Youth sport

The most traumatic and indefensible causal factors in sport drop-out include the extreme, sometimes unconscionable, pressures placed on young athletes by some parents, coaches, fans, and the media. Has an emphasis on the nonmoral value of winning emerged as the primary culprit? On manicured fields, with youth-sized uniforms, and in leagues with drafts, play-offs, and championships leading to huge trophies, children and adolescents are coached by individuals who too often mimic the coaches they see on television or read about in the sport pages. As family lives come to revolve around youth league competitions, the importance placed on winning may surmount all else.

Probably most parental involvement with youth sport begins innocently enough as children eagerly choose to join teams. However, some parents burden their children by living vicariously through their offspring. That is, these parents force their children into nonpreferred sports or refuse to let them quit, regardless of the reason. Parental sacrifices of money, time, and team involvement such as coaching or program leadership may entrap the young athlete who really does not want to play, or at least does not want to play under the existing circumstances.

Parents who reward and praise winning, while berating or ignoring losing, send clear messages that they value only one outcome. Early in their sport experiences, youth learn how much emphasis their parents place on their scoring, being the game-winning player, and demonstrating superior sport skills. The child or teen who lacks self-confidence or places significant importance upon parental approval may be driven to use whatever means available in attempting to achieve the extrinsic rewards and status associated with being a winner. Some parents exacerbate these pressures by withholding love from children who do not win. Starting at the youth level, athletes in sport competitions perform under the scrutiny of parents, fans, and the media. Unfortunately, at each advancing level of competition more and more parents, coaches, fans, and teammates begin to expect and even demand victories. Sometimes the child athlete uses pain and injury to escape excessive parental pressures. This pressure to win exists even though most participate in zero-sum games (that is, at least one loser for every winner). Public display of athletes' performances usually intensifies the pressures felt, as does seeking the rewards that primarily accrue to the victorious.

Interscholastic sport

When parents perceive that their children have been blessed with exceptional sport talents, some increase exponentially the pressures to succeed. Youthful pleasures and social relationships often are abandoned in search of greater skill development, often on school teams. Some parents push their children toward professional careers as teenagers or eagerly seek grant-in-aid offers from colleges. Although adolescents may eagerly participate in sport development camps and enjoy specialized coaching, many tire of devoting their lives singularly to one sport. They also grow weary of listening to their parents berate them, their coaches, and the sport officials. When many of these athletes become bored, fatigued, or completely fed up, they drop out of sport.

The sport media in various forms contributes to the drop-out rate in the most popular sports. An outstanding high school sophomore in the 1980s shot himself. His suicide note conveyed the sobering statement that, after leading his football team to the state championship, he simply could not cope with the pressures of being expected to carry his team to the championship for two more years. An age-group tennis champion took her life because she could not handle all the pressures from her parents to keep winning. Certainly other pressures could have played a part in these suicides, but no one will ever know the role played by these pressures to win in sport.

Although parents' and coaches' pressures start subtly, the media and fans impose a social responsibility on the teen sport star. As schools, communities, and states become heavily invested in the sport achievements of young people, these individuals feel increasing pressures to not lose, lest they disappoint their parents, coaches, and fans. Geometric increases in these pressures to win occur as athletes advance up the competitive ladder.

Intercollegiate sport

College coaches who lack a balanced perspective about the role of sport may exert even more pressures on athletes. Winning, the driving force at the college level (and increasingly in the schools), becomes essential for maintaining one's job. The status, lucrative salaries, and other benefits accruing to coaches (such as shoe contracts and country club memberships) accrue only to those who win consistently.

Thus, most college coaches expect their athletes to specialize in one sport, condition and train year-round, obey without question all directives, and sometimes even circumvent game rules in pursuit of victories. Fans cheer for and expect such strategies, and the media praises them.

College coaches exercise control over various academic, social, and psychological aspects of their athletes' lives. Although such domination has been questioned recently, some coaches continue to dehumanize athletes on the premise of getting them to perform better and to win. A few coaches also have been known to teach their athletes to play unfairly and to take drugs known to enhance performance. Do these pressures from coaches violate athletes' rights?

Some behaviors by coaches occur because of ignorance; coaches may suffer an endemic malaise of disbelief in research or scientific data. Overall, coaching education remains woefully inadequate, and programs focusing on moral reasoning are nonexistent. Most coaches are good and decent people who may not know what effects they may be having on their athletes psychologically, physiologically, or morally. Fearing for their jobs or their authority, many are unwilling to admit their lack of education or to rectify this situation.

Professional sport

The pressures to win placed on professional athletes emerge from their roles as entertainers. Fans—through ticket purchases, television viewing, and product purchases pay the salaries and provide the prize money to these athletes, and they expect victories or at least maximal effort. Athletes who intentionally lose or give less than their best efforts can expect boos and derisive comments from the stands and in game coverage by the media.

Conflicts between coaches and athletes can become constant sources of pressure for both. Some conflicts, such as Latrell Sprewell's strangling of Coach P.J. Carlesimo, are condemned as unethical because of the physical abuse. But, is a psychological berating by coaches of players unethical, too?

The media derides, questions, and belittles losers, yet praises and rewards winners in big-time college athletics and especially professional sports. Fans seem happy only with victories; effort does not seem to count. Athletes must respond to the pressures to win in front of huge crowds. No wonder individuals who survive the high drop-out rate from sport and compete professionally are characterized by a need for achievement and psychological endurance.

Pressures to win can become contradictory to the moral principles of justice, honesty, responsibility, and beneficence. Has winning become the only desired outcome of sport? Should the seeking of victories preclude an ethical approach to sport based on moral principles? The development of the whole person—physically, socially, and psychologically—far exceeds winning in importance because it is lasting; winning is transitory. Should parents, coaches, fans, and the media reevaluate the roles they play in overemphasizing the importance placed on winning?

Relationships with teammates and coaches

Within sports, rumors abound about homosexual relations among athletes. For example, the media backlash to Billie Jean King's homosexual affair and to Greg Louganis' announcement that he was homosexual seemed to reinforce these suspicions. Even in a time of liberal acceptance of alternative lifestyles, athletes in the public arena are expected to be heterosexual or to remain "in the closet" regarding their private affairs. Some coaches, especially in women's sports like basketball, seemed to make a point when recruiting young women that allegations about rampant homosexuality were simply untrue. However, some women may have opted out of softball and men out of figure skating because they did not want to be labeled or have people question them.

Another reason why some athletes have dropped out of sport is to escape from promiscuous coaches. Recent exposès about a male coach of a girls' volleyball team having sexual affairs with his players and a youth ice hockey coach forcing his athletes into homosexual relations have frightened many parents and athletes. When a youth sport coach can control the development of girls' or boys' athletic abilities and opportunities, these youngsters are totally vulnerable. The victims of these forced sexual encounters have reported that their unquestioning submission to their coaches had shattered them. Their only choice was to get away from the coach, and hence the sport. Thus, drop-out may occur because of factors not associated directly with sport.

SPORT BURN OUT

Sport burn-out sometimes occurs because of the overwhelming emphasis on results, with a concurrent disregard for performance. For example, if a Division I football team throughout the season refuses to "run up the score" on its opponents, it may drop in its national ranking. This decline in ranking might result in not getting invited to a prestigious post-season bowl game, resulting in the loss of several million dollars. How do these performances that seem to value beneficence and justice count relative to the importance of generating revenue?

So, what is the purpose of sport? To the aspiring athlete, sport should be about skill development and testing oneself, personal growth in areas like cooperation, self-discipline, teamwork, self-control, and intrinsic motivation, and development of social abilities and relationships. Parents who encourage their children to participate in sports seem to believe that these can potentially be outcomes. Ideally, playing sports, regardless of the final score, should have a positive influence on youngsters.

When intercollegiate and professional athletes are questioned, they often respond that they play their sports because they value having fun while displaying their outstanding talents. Upon reflection, they realize that at least half of the time (zero sum game), they will not win. If they cannot find solace in giving maximal effort and in the enjoyment of the sport itself, they will burn out. They will not train hard and deny themselves other pleasures or opportunities if winning is the only thing that counts.

Sport elimination includes both those former athletes who drop out for the reasons just described, as well as those athletes who simply *burn out* (see Box 7-7). This term usually refers to those athletes who demonstrate outstanding sport skills or potential at an early age but drop out of sport before achieving at an elite level. This may occur for physical, psychological, social, or other reasons (see Boxes 7-8 and 7-9), each taking its toll in different ways. Physical burn-out includes the repercussions of overuse, overtraining, and overspecialization. The mental and emotional pressures from demands for improved performances and winning result in psychological burn-out. Manifestations of social burn-out are the absence of a life outside of sport and the adverse effect on the opportunity to spend time with friends.

Physical Burn Out
Youth sport

The overuse syndrome did not occur in youth sports until programs under adult leaders began to mimic collegiate and professional models, including an overemphasis on winning. Children, seeking to become like their favorite athletes, joined competitive leagues that adults organized as miniature versions of professional leagues. The compulsion to develop one's skills was driven by the dream of a professional contract or a gold medal.

Unfortunately, injuries from overuse before maturation plague most children who start their competitive careers early. Many aspiring superstars as youth and teens have had their dreams shattered by injuries related to overuse. Adolescents undertaking prolonged and intensive training programs during their growth spurt become particularly susceptible to skeletal overuse injuries. Youth baseball leagues had to enact limitations on the number of

THEORY BOX 7-7

TOO MUCH, TOO OFTEN, TOO SOON

Burn-out occurs because of too much, too often, and too soon of a supposedly good thing. A parent's purpose is to guide, love, instruct, and care for the child. The coach's purpose is *in locus parentis* ("in place of the parent"). Coaches essentially have the same purpose to act in the child's best interest. The parents' and coaches' moral and ethical principles should support their stated purpose. If their actual motives, intentions, and actions do not, then they are in ethical violation of their principles. Many people argue that sport specialization is in the child's best interest. Unfortunately, research does not support that position. The data are conclusive: too much, too often, and too soon is not in the best interests of a child. It is the duty of the parent and the coach to stay abreast of the latest information as it impacts programs for their children and athletes. The moral dilemma is how much competition is beneficial, and how much is too much? The answer to these questions should focus on the purpose of sport in the child's development.

THEORY BOX 7-8

INFORMED CONSENT

One strategy that can help prevent sport elimination is *informed consent*. In sport, this means that adult athletes and parents of underage athletes must be told the risks involved so they can decide whether to participate or not. For example, when an athlete is injured seriously enough to miss a practice or a game, does a physician determine readiness to return to participation? If some type of medication is to be prescribed and used, have the medical rationales for this treatment as well as any side effects been clearly explained?

Because athletes learn at an early age that winning is rewarded, they may choose to cover up an injury without realizing that permanent damage may be occurring. The throwing of curve balls by pre-adolescent pitchers is a classic example. Informed consent by a parent should state that they expect league rules prohibiting the throwing of curves to be enforced. Informed consent informs parents or athletes that athletic trainers who know emergency procedures for head and neck injuries will be present at all football games and practices. Informed consent by college athletes may indicate their willingness to submit to random drug testing. The lack of informed consent may occur when an Olympic athlete loses a medal when a drug test reveals that a trainer administered a banned drug. The lack of informed consent may occur when a professional athlete is not fully told by a team physician about the severity of an injury, resulting in a permanent disability. So, informed consent may help reduce sport elimination when used properly. Conversely, experiences at all levels of sport may be shortened when athletes are not allowed to choose when to participate, rest, or heal.

innings youngsters could pitch because in coaches' overzealousness to win they were overtaxing young athletes' maturing bodies. Sports medicine physicians have found that children and adolescents who compete in organized sport put themselves at risk for musculoskeletal injuries, especially if they fail to participate actively in flexibility and conditioning programs.

Numerous athletes in figure skating, skiing, tennis, ice hockey, and gymnastics have dropped out of school in order to train with renowned coaches and in locations distant from their families. While Andre Agassi in tennis, Mary Lou Retton in gymnastics, and Michelle Kwan in figure skating have become champions under these circumstances, thousands of other potential stars

THEORY BOX 7-9

REASONS ATHLETES BURN OUT IN SPORT

Youth Sport

- Overuse and fatigue
- Overtraining
- Recurrent injuries
- Overspecialization
- Poorly qualified coaches
- Demand for improved performances
- Overemphasis on winning
- Loss of intrinsic motivation
- Changing interests
- Conflicts in values

Interscholastic Sport

- Overuse and fatigue
- Overtraining
- Recurrent injuries
- Overspecialization
- Poorly qualified coaches
- Demand for improved performances
- Overemphasis on winning
- Loss of intrinsic motivation
- Changing interests
- Conflicts in values

- Desire for freedom and independence
- Loss of friends and social activities

Intercollegiate Sport

- Overuse and fatigue
- Overtraining
- Recurrent injuries
- Demand for improved performances
- Overemphasis on winning
- Loss of intrinsic motivation
- Conflicts in values
- Psychological manipulation by coaches
- Unwillingness to sacrifice physically, psychologically, and academically
- Desire for more social and extracurricular activities with friends

Professional Sport

- Recurrent injuries
- Diminishing skills
- Loss of desire to play
- Desire to spend time with family
- Desire to pursue other personal and business interests

have flamed out as adolescents. Many of these youngsters showed outstanding ability early, yet their competitors matured, developed their skills, and surpassed those who had defeated them earlier in their careers. These early maturing athletes who find themselves no longer winning oftentimes are unable to cope with being second best or not even that. Pressures to win can be psychologically debilitating to these young athletes who are unable to further extend their skills. As their dreams seem to fizzle, many of these adolescents become victims of sport burn out.

Overtraining occurs when athletes fail to listen to their bodies and demand too much, particularly physically immature athletes who may permanently injure themselves. Prepubescent children, for example, who continually throw curve balls may impede the proper maturation of bones. Many youth sport

coaches lack the knowledge to teach sport skills or pace and sequence them properly. As a result, they often expect too much of their young athletes.

Overspecialization in sport relates to overuse and overtraining. Increasingly, youth sport coaches pressure their young athletes to choose to play only one sport so that they can condition and train year-round. Coaches are entrapped by the belief that more training must be better. These coaches too often are ignorant of appropriate teaching techniques and the latest research, including the value of cross-training.

Interscholastic sport

Overuse and overtraining occur in interscholastic sport, although to a lesser degree because state athletic associations limit sport seasons. Multi-sport athletes who never allow their bodies time for rest and recovery may experience fatigue leading to injuries.

Many interscholastic coaches claim that specialization in one sport enhances athletes' skill development and improves their chances of excelling at the next level of sport, including possibly receiving an athletic grant-in-aid. Of course, these more skillful athletes often will help win games for these coaches, too. If later, these athletes become collegiate and professional stars, a few interscholastic coaches enjoy reflected glory and maybe even job advancement.

Parents, too, may encourage their children to focus on one sport. If this sport is chosen by the athlete, no problem exists as long as overtraining and overuse do not occur. But if the parent forces sport specialization, hoping that a grant-in-aid or a lucrative professional career will follow, burn-out often occurs, with the athlete lacking interest in and dedication to the imposed sport.

Too often, overspecialization prematurely ends athletes' sport participation. Year-round practices, strength and conditioning programs, and learning of sport skills before the body is mature enough hasten burn-out while lessening fun and sport enjoyment. Swimmers serve as good examples of this occurrence. In the past, most swimmers, burned out by twice-a-day practices, stopped competing in their late teens rather than continuing their careers until they had swum their fastest times as adults. Today, older swimmers are setting records through tapered training programs and rest that help them avoid burn-out.

Intercollegiate sport

Recruited college athletes are expected to commit themselves fully to achieving their potential. Whatever training regimen coaches impose must be followed without deviation. Team and individual practices, weight training sessions, film reviews, strategy planning times, and team meetings add up to huge demands on time and the body. The NCAA, in attempting to balance the athletic and academic components of college students' lives, has established a weekly twenty-hour limit on the amount of time coaches can involve their athletes in their sport (exclusive of travel time for competitions).

Self-imposed or coach-imposed expectations for improved performances, though, may cause athletes to train excessively without proper recovery time. It remains unknown how many athletes push themselves too hard in trying to please coaches who determine whether and how much athletes get to play and whether they receive grants-in-aid yearly. Whenever a sport-related goal becomes too important, athletes may train when injured, sick, or fatigued. Eventually, the body refuses to tolerate overtraining and breaks down temporarily or permanently.

Athletes are often taught to be tough and to play through injuries, even though pain indicates a physical problem that needs resolution. Athletes should never be asked whether they want to play while injured, because the answer will invariably be yes. Sometimes well-intentioned coaches push athletes, whom they may categorize as not motivated enough, trying to get more out of them, when in reality these athletes are injured. Is it ever defensible for coaches to cajole their athletes into playing when hurt? Is it morally wrong to allow a formerly seriously injured athlete to return to a practice or competition without a physician's clearance?

Professional sport

Professional athletes, because they are paid, are typically expected to play while injured. Yet sometimes these athletes are lied to or deceived about the seriousness of their injuries so they will choose to compete. Professionals are encouraged to use pain-blocking drugs. Sometimes these athletes become dependent on them—as did Green Bay Packer quarterback Brett Favre—even though this practice can result in even more serious injuries. Physicians, not athletes or coaches, should decide whether these athletes compete, given the possibility of permanent damage to injured areas. Many professional athletes retire, tired of the pain or refusing to risk more severe damage.

Psychological Burn Out
Youth sport

Many young athletes are pressured to improve on their past performances and to win. As these children grow and mature, times run or swum pale in comparison to new expectations placed on them by parents, coaches, fans, and the media. Last year's points per game or batting average seemingly must be surpassed or the athlete is not training, dedicated, or psyched-up enough. Education could help coaches understand and appreciate that more training is not always better. Is attaining and using such knowledge of appropriate training practices a moral obligation?

The appetite for athletes' continual improvement appears insatiable for some youth sport managers. So, when successive years fail to bring superior performances, athletes are questioned, berated, punished, and pressured. Similarly, athletes and teams who do not finish first are treated with scorn or ignored but seldom praised for their efforts. Too often, such treatment causes athletes to lose their self-confidence, resulting in a downward spiral in athletic accomplishments. A greater realization of the physical and social consequences of intensive training and competition also contribute to psychological burn-out.

Interscholastic sport

Psychological pressures to win may increase when adolescents start representing their schools. Now entire communities, rather than an age-group team and family members, take notice of game results. Sometimes coaches increase the pressure on their athletes because their jobs and status depend on victories. As these pressures compound, some athletes succumb to mental fatigue. When their emotional reserves deplete completely, they become victims of psychological burn out from sport.

Adult-imposed pressures to win and for improved performances can cause teenage athletes to respond in other ways, too. They may replace their intrinsic motivation to compete and train with other, less threatening activities. When adults demand sport involvement, adolescents may seek complete freedom and independence for themselves without any participation in sport.

Intercollegiate sport

College athletes face increasing pressures to perform at the peak of their abilities; they are recruited and subsidized to do this. "Big-time" sport especially places pressure on athletes because of the fans, media, and money associated with successful programs. These athletes realize that missed free throws, tackles, or pitches may cost their institutions thousands of dollars because the institutions fail to qualify for bowl games or advancement into the next round of tournaments.

Many universities have hired sport psychologists to assist athletes in handling the mental aspects of their sports and, most importantly, to enhance performance. For example, the sport psychologist helps the field-goal kicker attain the proper level of arousal to help prevent a game-winning attempt from sailing wide right. Other colleges depend on coaches to artfully provide the appropriate mix of positive feedback and psyching up to prevent psychological burn-out from impeding performances.

Professional sport

Many professional athletes for physical and psychological reasons lose their desires or abilities to play. Upon forced or voluntary retirement, however, some fail to cope with life without sport. Many suffer from health problems such as the aftermath of injuries or heart difficulties associated with weight fluctuations. Many former elite athletes lack the self-discipline to change their eating and activity habits when their careers end, leading to premature death or disability. This leads to the question of whether the cost of shortened lives or impaired quality of life for former stars is too costly just to fulfill Americans' desire for sport spectating.

Disengagement from sport for individuals who have lived sport-centered lives traumatizes many former athletes because their self-image for years has been inextricably linked with sport. Often, younger and better athletes cast aside the once athletic stars. In the absence of coping strategies, too many of these athletes may react negatively to the mental and emotional realities of not being special.

Social Burn Out
Youth sport

Early in life, sport plays a minor role in one's life. Weekly practices and competitions consume few hours and seldom detract from schoolwork, family routines, and just being a kid. This all changes whenever children's skills elevate them into the elite leagues or identify them as potentially world class. The social organization of high-performance sport may constrain adolescents' identity development and prevent them from having meaningful control over their lives. The domination of world-class tennis players Venus and Serena Williams' father over their lives and tennis development provides a graphic illustration of these social and psychological pressures.

When sport stops being a pastime and becomes a passion, social burn-out often occurs. Many athletes squeeze schoolwork between two-session-a-day training programs. In some sports, athletes such as teen gold medalist Tara Lipinski must leave home or the family must move in order to obtain top-level coaching. Private coaches spend endless hours perfecting the skills of future gold medalists or number one players. Sport skill development at this level leaves little time for friends and youthful activities and experiences. Social activities are sacrificed for the prospect of future fame and fortune.

Interscholastic sport

Interscholastic sport stars seldom leave home and must schedule their sport involvement around regular school days. Still, they can eat, sleep, and breathe sport by training and competing in one or several sports. A few become so focused on sport that they abandon their friends, and they practice instead of participating in social activities.

While missing many aspects of the growing-up process, youth and interscholastic stars are honing their skills for competing as intercollegiate athletes or professionals. Besides being teens with few if any peer-group friends, these aspiring superstars must cope with the mental and emotional pressures of trying to win. Some handle these pressures well; others do not and burn out. Social isolation traumatizes many young athletes; some quit sport so that they can live like others their ages. The question is whether young athletes should specialize to such an extent that they impede their own social development.

Intercollegiate sport

Many criticize intercollegiate sport for placing so many athletic demands on players that they have no time left to participate in the extracurricular activities available to other students. These critics claim that because such experiences enrich the college years, all students should be allowed the opportunity to participate in activities such as student government and special-interest groups.

Intercollegiate athletes, because of their athletic and academic schedules, enjoy few free hours to interact socially, other than with teammates. Some individuals concerned about the emphasis on college sport advocate that freshmen should be ineligible so these students may have time to stabilize themselves academically, socially, and extracurricularly before adding athletics to their schedules.

Sometimes intercollegiate athletes refuse to continue their commitment to their sports because of a desire to participate in more social and extracurricular activities. They determine that these experiences provide more intrinsic rewards than does competing in sports.

Professional sport

Professional athletes' lives revolve around their training, practice, and competitive schedules. Holiday celebrations, family events such as births and birthdays, and vacations must be arranged around their careers, rescheduled, or missed. When athletes tire of having less control over their lives than desired, many quit. Often, professional athletes cite the desire to spend more time with their families as a primary reason for ending their playing careers. Others add that they want to pursue other personal and business interests not permitted due to their sport careers.

If winning were not so prominent in sports, do you think there would be less burn-out? Has the pursuit of handsomely rewarded victories caused an erosion of values? Overuse, overtraining, overspecialization, excessive demands for improved performances and for winning, and overemphasis on sport to the exclusion of a social life threatens the well-being of athletes while displacing the potential for value development.

If coaches and sport managers are behaving responsibly, should they pursue excellence, and even winning, as long as moral values are not compromised? Does honesty demand that athletes have choices not compulsions? Does justice implore sport managers to treat each athlete fairly so as to not direct him or her along a pathway leading to burn-out?

SUMMARY

The drop out and burn out issues raise many questions; resolving these dilemmas may be difficult. Taxpayers' dollars should not be used to support elite competitions until all children have a chance to play sports at the appropriate skill level. Athletes at all levels should be prepared for and provided coping skills for dealing with sport disengagement. Having fun, learning skills, and trying hard should be reinstated as the goals in youth and school programs. Parental, coach, fan, and media pressures to win should be reduced. Performing to one's potential should replace winning as the top priority, even if this means changing the sport rules, banning adults, and losing corporate sponsorships.

Overspecialization has no place in the lives of children; rather, they should be free to play whatever sports they enjoy. Only sport managers can ensure that overuse injuries will not occur and that athletes will not be allowed or expected to play while injured or to use pain-blocking drugs. Both drop out and burn out are avoidable. Instead of contributing to these, parents, coaches, and sport managers should recognize and prevent the potential harm, teach and reinforce values, and ensure enjoyable sport experiences for athletes of all ages.

ISSUES AND DILEMMAS

CASE 7-1

Shadu loved soccer. Since he was six years old, he has played on a youth league team. Although he was never the best or the biggest player, no one played with as much desire and enthusiasm as he did. His parents attended most of his games, encouraging but never pushing him.

Shadu's father sometimes kicked the ball around with him in the yard but did not really have the knowledge to coach him. Each summer, though, Shadu's parents sent him to a soccer camp at State University. There, he was in sheer bliss as he played soccer for hours without ever tiring of the drills and games.

After ten years of youth soccer, Shadu was confident that he could earn a spot on his high school team as a sophomore. During the three days of tryouts, he tried his hardest and executed all the drills to the best of his ability. It became readily evident, though, that the competition would be tough, with nearly sixty boys trying out for only twenty-two uniforms. This was not like the youth program where everyone who wanted to play could.

On Thursday morning when the squad list was posted, Shadu scanned the sheet over and over but did not find his name; he had not made the team. He was devastated. How, for the first time in ten years, could he survive without soccer? It hurt badly that effort and determination seemingly meant nothing as the bigger and more highly skilled boys were selected. When Shadu asked why he was cut, the coach replied that Shadu just was not good enough to play high school soccer.

1. Should high school coaches cut athletes? Is this ethical or unethical? Why or why not?
2. Should schools provide multiple (varsity, junior varsity, A, and B) teams for all interested students who want to compete? Why or why not?
3. What are the financial and moral ramifications of sponsoring multiple school teams of various skill levels?
4. What are Shadu's options now?
5. How should Shadu's parents deal with their son in this situation?
6. Did Shadu learn anything about values through this experience?

◆ ◆ ◆

CASE 7-2

Jane Maxwell began taking gymnastics lessons when she was eight years old. Immediately, her teacher realized that she had the potential to become world-class. So after only one year, during which Jane progressed remarkably in her skills, she changed programs. Her new instructor helped her develop her skills so well that she became a state all-around champion at age ten.

Now Jane and her parents faced a monumental decision. The best way to ensure that Jane continued to progress was for her to move to Dallas and train in the private gym of Coach Symanski, the national coach. There, she would live with three other gymnasts and a housemother. Between two-hour morning and afternoon workouts, Jane would attend school. The annual cost for this program was $30,000.

Jane's parents could afford to pay for Jane's training in Dallas and urged her to take advantage of this special opportunity to possibly become the top gymnast in the world. Although Jane enjoyed gymnastics because she had always been successful, she was less sure that she wanted to leave her parents and one brother to live and train with strangers. This all seemed so frightening to Jane.

Mr. and Mrs. Maxwell stressed to Jane how fortunate she was to have been given so much talent. They promised to visit her every month. Of course, they would attend all of her competitions. With this urging, Jane agreed.

Coach Symanski was a rigid taskmaster, demanding more and more from his young athletes each day. His practices could be called brutal; he pushed his youthful stars hard. As long as Jane progressed, all went well. But when Jane failed to achieve up to his level of expectations, he chastised her, questioning her commitment and talent. Initially, these mind games motivated Jane, but gradually she began to resent his relentless tirades.

In her second year with Coach Symanski, Jane's maturing body began to restrict some of her former skills, and nagging problems became significant injuries. She hid as many of these problems as she could from Coach Symanski because she was afraid that he would harass her about making excuses for not winning. Gymnastics was becoming work instead of being fun.

Besides all this, Jane had become increasingly homesick. She missed her parents, younger brother, and former friends. Although always around people, she felt lonely.

By the time she reached fourteen, after four years as an elite gymnast, Jane burned out. The physical, psychological, and social stressors had become too burdensome. With great trepidation, she called her parents and said that she was quitting and wanted to come home.

1. What are the ethical issues, if any, associated with starting a highly competitive sport at a young age?
2. Did Mr. and Mrs. Maxwell pressure Jane unduly? If so, why?
3. What are the pros and cons of the sport skills development program operated by Coach Symanski?
4. What types of pressures contributed to Jane's burn out?
5. What ethical dilemmas does this case present for Jane, Mr. and Mrs. Maxwell, and Coach Symanski?

6. If you were Jane's parents would you support her wanting to quit, considering the money invested and the opportunities Jane had to become the best gymnast in the world?

◆ ◆ ◆

CASE 7-3

Virginia Sanborn, although a high school basketball player, was not skilled enough to play for Midwestern State University. Volunteering to serve as manager, Virginia spent four years observing one of the best coaches in the nation. Not only had Coach Turner taken her team to four consecutive NCAA tournaments, but, during Virginia's junior year, the team had advanced into the finals before losing.

Coach Turner stressed fundamentals, teamwork, and never giving up—essentials, in Virginia's opinion, of a quality program. However, Virginia questioned to herself some of Coach Turner's other practices. The coach demanded that team members spend endless hours practicing, even though in excess of the maximum allowed by the NCAA. She seemed to care only that her players stayed academically eligible, never taking an interest in their classes or allowing them to miss practices for academic reasons. She also taught her players how to intentionally violate game rules for their advantage. Coach Turner's methods, to Virginia, emphasized winning as the only important thing.

Virginia was determined to model Coach Turner's positive, and not negative, coaching practices in her first job at Surry High School. Virginia was excited about getting a 4A (competitive division for the largest schools) team to coach, one that had a history of excellent records. She was confident that her emphasis on fundamentals, teamwork, and never giving up would maintain the team's success.

Coach Sanborn quickly earned the respect of her players when they realized that she knew basketball and could teach the skills well. They also really liked her because she seemed to care about them as individuals. Coach Sanborn encouraged them in their classwork, helping if she could or getting them assistance from other teachers if it was needed. Because she always seemed to understand, the players valued her as a confidant whenever they were experiencing family, relationship, or emotional difficulties. The players also learned that Coach Sanborn demonstrated—by her actions, words, and the way she coached—values that emphasized justice, honesty, and civility. She would never allow anyone to be mistreated or a sport rule to be misapplied unfairly in her team's favor.

There was a problem, however. Surry High School's girls' basketball team was not winning most of its games. For two consecutive years, the team finished with about as many wins as losses and did not qualify for the state playoffs—the only times in two decades. Although the girls would have preferred to win, they felt that they were doing their best and certainly were benefiting from their sport experiences.

Shortly after the end of Coach Sanborn's second season, the athletic director, Mr. Ethridge, and the principal, Mr. Farmer, asked her to meet with them. Because Coach Sanborn had developed a good working relationship with both of these individuals, their comments were totally unexpected. Mr. Ethridge commended her on her skill instruction, rapport with the players, and emphasis on academics. But, he said her coaching record was unacceptable at Surry High School. Parents and other fans expected the girls' and the boys' basketball teams to win, not to break even. Mr. Farmer then stated that she had one year to produce a winning girls' team or she would lose her job.

1. Did Virginia Sanborn learn any unethical coaching practices from Coach Turner?
2. Did it take the combination of all of Coach Turner's coaching methods, both ethical and unethical, to build a winning team at Midwestern State University?
3. What were the moral values upheld by Virginia Sanborn as she coached the girls' basketball team and lived her life?
4. How and why did Coach Sanborn earn the respect of her players?
5. Were Mr. Ethridge and Mr. Farmer violating any ethical principles in issuing the ultimatum to Coach Sanborn?
6. What ethical choices does Coach Sanborn have?
7. What would you do if you were in the situation facing Coach Sanborn?
8. Would you quit before sacrificing your principles or would you adopt a different coaching style? Would your answer be different if you were the sole provider for a child?

◆ ◆ ◆

CASE 7-4

Emmitt Larkin was a gifted athlete. In youth sport leagues, junior high school, and high school, he was always the most successful running back and defensive back on his team. He led his teams to numerous championships, including state titles in his junior and senior years. Recruited by every top-ranked Division I university, he chose the University of Michigan, because it was not too far from his hometown of Chicago.

Emmitt was barely eligible for an athletic grant-in-aid, having just qualified with his SAT scores and high school grades. This narrow margin did not concern Emmitt because he had no intention of becoming a serious student. He planned to do the minimal to remain eligible for two seasons of football and then to declare himself eligible for the National Football League (NFL) draft.

Emmitt's phenomenal freshman season seemed to confirm his plans. After his All-American season, however, he did have to attend summer school in order to retain his academic eligibility for his sophomore season. He was even touted as a possible Heisman Trophy candidate in all pre-season publications.

Disaster struck in the first game when Emmitt suffered a career-ending injury. While the paralysis slowly dissipated so that he eventually learned to walk again, he would never play football again.

1. Why was Emmitt banking his future on a multi-million dollar future in the NFL? Was this realistic?
2. What ethical responsibility did Emmitt's coaches have to him relative to academics?
3. What preparation does Emmitt have for life?
4. What should be done to help athletes prepare for an abrupt elimination from sport?
5. How would you describe what Emmitt valued prior to his injury?

◆ ◆ ◆

CASE 7-5

Lonnie Young had been a Division II baseball player and graduated with a physical education degree. He was hired into a teaching and coaching position at Fulton High School after his first interview for a job. The principal was impressed with the young man's values and his strong letters of reference. While Lonnie might have been able to play minor league baseball, he never seriously considered this, because he wanted to work with adolescents.

In his physical education classes, Lonnie stressed having fun in various sport and fitness activities. He never allowed the lesser-skilled boy or girl to be left out or eliminated. He matched students based on their skill levels to ensure that everyone had the opportunity to feel successful and to enjoy their movement experiences.

Coach Young's baseball team reflected the values by which he lived his life. He cared about each player regardless of his skill level. He mandated that everyone be treated with respect and fairly, including opponents and umpires. While striving to win based on extensive conditioning, drills, and strategies, Coach Young placed winning in perspective for his athletes. He gave a uniform to any boy who wanted a spot on the team. While every boy did not play in every game, every player did in most games. Coach Young required all of his athletes to take their studies seriously. They had to make at least average marks in all of their courses. He provided help to any athlete who was struggling academically.

It took awhile for the boys in this urban school to meet Coach Young's expectations, but over the years they continually returned to Fulton High to thank the coach who had taught them how to work hard and enjoy sports. They always told Coach Young that he had helped them become principled athletes and men.

1. Can a coach stress winning and simultaneously teach moral values? If so, how can this be accomplished?

2. Why was cutting a boy who wanted to play baseball not an option for Coach Young?

3. To what, do you think, did these boys attribute their continued love of sport?

4. How do you think Coach Young would have handled a "star athlete" disgruntled when he was replaced by a lesser-skilled teammate?

5. How do you think Coach Young would have handled an athlete who cheated, violated a team rule, or displayed unsportsmanlike conduct?

6. How do you think Coach Young would have handled an athlete who did not achieve academically?

REFERENCE

Coakley, Jay J. 1998. *Sport in society: Issues & controversies.* 6th ed. Dubuque, IA: McGraw-Hill.

ADDITIONAL READINGS

Raedeke, Thomas D. 1997. Is athlete burnout more than just stress? A sport commitment perspective. *Journal of Sport & Exercise Psychology* 19(4) (December): 396–417.

Rotella, Robert J., Tom Hanson, and Richard H. Coop. 1991. Burnout in youth sports. *Elementary School Journal* 91(5) (May): 421–28.

Sandfort, James A., and Gerald Linneman. 1992. Athletic values as the value of athletics. *NASSP Bulletin* 76(546) (October): 101–03.

Udry, Eileen, Daniel Gould, Dana Bridges, and Suzie Tuffey. 1997. People helping people? Examining the social ties of athletes coping with burnout and injury stress. *Journal of Sport & Exercise Psychology* 19(4) (December): 368–95.

Wolff, Rick. 1996. *Good sports: A parent's guide to competitive youth sports.* Champaign IL: Sagamore Publishing, Inc.

Ergogenic Aids for Sport Performance

◆ What are the effects on athletes' performance of the use of stimulants in sport?

◆ What are the effects on athletes' performance of the use of depressants in sport?

◆ What are the effects on athletes' performance of the use of anabolic steroids in sport?

◆ What is blood doping, and why are athletes in the Olympic Games banned from using it?

◆ Should the use of legal drugs be allowed in sport?

◆ Should sport governing organizations or the legal system be responsible for penalizing the use in sport of illegally obtained drugs?

◆ What are the legal and moral issues surrounding drug testing?

Most people in sport enjoy competition; they strive to win. Competition is an integral part of our market-driven, capitalistic economy and society. We seek to outperform the store next door in sales, a company across the country in product line, and an international corporation in our market niche. We strive to graduate at the top of our class, own the biggest house in the neighborhood, and join the most prestigious social club or organization. Seemingly, our self-concept or status in society is based on these numerous extrinsic achievements.

Similarly, sport in America has been heavily influenced by this motive to succeed, to get ahead of everyone else, and to attain status and prestige. The result in sport has been a disproportionate emphasis on outcome or the nonmoral value of winning, rather than on developing skill and having fun. Because of fame and fortune, or at least hero and heroine status and special benefits, athletes realize early in their sport experiences that only winners receive multi-million dollar contracts, endorsements, grants-in-aid, and free sports equipment and clothing. Hence, the drive to win often dominates. When the importance placed on winning supersedes all else, athletes may take drugs to enhance their performances and gain unfair advantages over their opponents.

This chapter provides an examination of how the use of ergogenic aids raises ethical issues for athletes and sport in general. It is suggested that the use of stimulants, depressants, anabolic steroids, and non-drug artificial substances is morally questionable

THE ETHICAL QUESTIONS OF DRUG USE

"To use or not to use drugs" is a question often asked, especially when in many sports one seemingly cannot compete without drugs. That is, everybody else in a particular sport uses drugs; therefore, to be competitive other athletes must also. This argument, however, rests on the premise that ethical principles are guided by what others do. A parallel perspective would be that rules must be followed only if others comply. Chapter 1 showed that ethical rules should be valued without regard to others because these moral principles are inherently right. The first ethical question emerging is: (1) Should an athlete justify the use of drugs because everyone else uses them?

A second ethical dilemma is the question of promise keeping. When people enter contests, they give their word whether explicitly or implicitly that they will follow the constitutive, proscriptive, and sportsmanship rules governing the sport. Therefore, the second ethical question emerges: (2) Do athletes have an obligation to keep their promises?

Third is the question of responsibility. As members of a team, athletes must accept the responsibility of following game rules that will benefit all competitors. Considering that ergogenic aids place individuals in physical jeopardy, the question becomes: (3) Do athletes have the responsibility to not intentionally harm their bodies?

because it provides the user with unfair physical advantages (see Box 8-1). The legal and moral issues surrounding drug testing challenge the reader to determine whether such tests should be banned, optional, or mandated. Questions also will be raised about the appropriateness of legislating morality through sanctions associated with drug use in sport. This chapter, however, does not suggest that legitimate performance enhancements are unethical. For example, athletes who replace lost fluids during competition or eat balanced and nutritious diets positively impact their performance. Gaining advantage through non-drug-assisted weight training, aerobic conditioning, taking vitamin supplements, and using various rehabilitation techniques are permissible within sport rules and not questionable ethically.

USE OF ERGOGENIC AIDS

Increasingly, athletes appear to seek ways to gain competitive advantages, often because obtaining the rewards of winning becomes paramount. One way is through the use of *ergogenic aids,* any aid, supplement, or ingested material that is prohibited by the letter or the spirit of the rules but is used to garner an advantage in the sport experience. Depending on the drug, substance, or means chosen, enhanced endurance, strength, skill, and self-confidence actually may result. In other cases, ergogenic aids alter athletes' perceptions so that they see themselves competing at superior levels, when in reality their performances erode.

Besides the real and perceived improvement in performance that may lead athletes to use drugs, there remains the drive to win, sometimes at all costs. Because winners are rewarded so highly in our society, athletes may succumb to the temptation to use artificial means to gain advantages. Many sport governing organizations and many athletes classify the use of ergogenic aids as cheating. Cheating refers to fraudulent or deceptive behavior. Cheating through the use of ergogenic aids happens more frequently when the likelihood of it going undetected exists and when athletes value winning more than honesty, responsibility, justice, and integrity.

Stimulants

Central nervous system stimulants include amphetamines (speed), ephedrine (found in cold medications and nasal sprays), cocaine, nicotine, and caffeine. These drugs generally cause physiological

and psychological responses such as increased alertness, reduced fatigue, heightened hostility and competitiveness, lessened fear and apprehension, and enhanced concentration, attention, arousal, drive, excitability, motivation, and self-confidence. Because these ergogenic aids affect the body so dramatically, the International Olympic Committee (IOC) bans more than forty different types.

Physiologically, stimulants chemically induce the release of epinephrine, an adrenaline-like substance, into the bloodstream along with stress hormones. Amphetamines stimulate the release of epinephrine and norepinephrine from the adrenal glands and nervous system thus increasing muscle tension, heart rate, and blood pressure. Athletes who take large amounts of stimulants may become overly hostile and aggressive because of their elevated moods, experience a reduction of fear, and demonstrate increased pain tolerance. Psychologically, athletes' perception and alertness are not as good as they think.

Increased blood flow from the heart to the muscles produces more free fatty acids and makes glucose more available. This may help the body use fats for energy instead of muscle glycogen, which may have a sparing effect on valuable body stores. For a long time, endurance athletes have used caffeine and other stimulants to increase their performance levels. Gymnasts and wrestlers often choose amphetamines to help them lose weight because of initial appetite-suppressing effects.

A few athletes have become dependent on legally and illegally obtained dexedrine, ben-zedrine, and methedrine that they believe will help their performance. These drugs mask fatigue, giving the perception of endless energy. Cyclists, runners, and other endurance athletes have died of exhaustion because their bodies, under the influence of stimulants, were unable to naturally signal being overtaxed.

The IOC stripped Rick deMont of his gold medal in the 1976 Olympic Games because he tested positive for a stimulant taken through his asthma inhaler. Because of this and related incidents, the IOC allows the use of certain drugs, if approved in advance, for specific medical conditions. The ethical dilemma here, though, is not the taking of a banned drug but the intentional taking of stimulants to gain advantages after pledging to follow the rules. This makes the issue one of honor and responsibility rather than justice.

Cocaine, another stimulant drug, has become the drug of choice of some professional athletes and others. From the federal drug-trafficking trials that implicated players from several Major League Baseball teams in the 1980s to the highly publicized death of basketball star Len Bias, sports fans have learned of the popularity of cocaine with some athletes. (Because of their salaries and star status, professional athletes can easily obtain cocaine, an expensive, illegal drug.) As an illegal substance, can cocaine be condoned if one agrees to obey the law? Does its use violate moral principles if it gives the athlete a perceived or real competitive advantage? Gary McLain, who led Villanova University to the NCAA basketball championship in 1984, played most games his senior year on a cocaine high, obtaining this drug illegally and playing without being penalized.

The ethical questions associated with the use of stimulants relate to whether drugs that enhance performance through various physiological parameters, reduce or mask fatigue, or provide psychological advantages, are morally defensible. If it is agreed that athletes competing against athletes is the essence of sport, is it honest or just to create an imbalance artificially by ingesting one of these stimulants? Because several sport organizations have banned the use of many stimulants, existing rules make the use of prohibited drugs unethical.

What is the moral reasoning process that an athlete uses to decide to use or not to use banned drugs? If an athlete chooses to use a prohibited stimulant, is this action fair or beneficent? Is an athlete who must compete against an opponent who takes stimulants justified in using a similar drug to level the playing field? What penalty, if any, should be assessed against the athlete who takes stimulants?

Depressants

Although the practice is contradictory to enhanced performance, athletes often use depressants with alcohol as a drug of choice. Professional athletes openly consume postgame alcoholic drinks during interviews with representatives from the media. These athletes and many younger ones relax with their favorite alcoholic drinks as they recover from the intense pressures and adrenaline flow brought on by competition. Some athletes have become dependent on drugs to cope with their demanding lifestyles. For example, a professional football player may drink several bottles of beer in the postgame celebration or drown his sorrows after a tough loss. This may be followed by a few more drinks at a restaurant during dinner or at home with friends as he seeks to unwind from the game or to numb his aches and pains. A sleeping pill or tranquilizer may also be needed to permit him to rest. The combination of these depressants and tough practices may leave him tired by midweek. So, in preparation for Sunday's game, he begins to take stimulants to offset the effect of the downers. By kickoff time, he may be so pumped up with uppers that all he wants to do is hit somebody aggressively, even viciously. This cycle may repeat itself throughout the season. What moral responsibilities do athletic leagues and organizations have relative to issues such as drug use and drug dependency in sport?

Depressants typically are taken to calm feelings and to dull one's sense of problems, but continued use may lead to rapid psychological and physiological addiction. Not only does the mind crave these drugs in increasing amounts, but so does the body. What ethical issues are associated with the use of depressants by athletes?

Anabolic Steroids

The male hormone testosterone contributes to the development of secondary sex characteristics, including muscular strength. Many athletes ingest synthetic varieties of testosterone called *anabolic steroids*. When taken in large dosages before an intensive weight-training program, such artificial hormones cause males and females to achieve significant muscular strength and bulk gains. Not only are there appearance changes, but performance improvements linked directly to the extent of drug usage have been documented. Ben Johnson's muscular definition and his remarkable speed in the 1988 Olympic Games illustrated this vividly. His appearance and athleticism, however, did not prevent the IOC from stripping Johnson of his gold medal in the 100-meter dash because he tested positive for a banned anabolic steroid.

Even though anabolic steroids can lead to increases in muscular bulk and strength, numerous adverse side effects accompany their excessive use. Some individuals who take 50 to 100 times the clinical dosage (as many athletes do) experience life-threatening problems such as extreme psychoses, heart disease, liver and kidney damage, and cancer. Female users risk masculinization and abnormal menstrual cycles. Adolescents using anabolic steroids experience severe facial and body acne and premature closure of the growth centers in the long bones, causing stunted growth.

Many trace the introduction of anabolic steroids in sport to the Soviets, who discovered that Nazi storm troopers had taken these drugs to heighten their aggression. Subsequently, medal-winning performances by Eastern Bloc athletes led to a proliferation in the popularity of anabolic steroid use. Coaches, trainers, and athletes have mixed different types of anabolic steroids to enhance their effectiveness. Others ingeniously discovered alternative ways to use these drugs, such as ingesting equine or rhesus monkey testosterone to gain performance advantages. Some use epitestosterone to mask the addition of these nonnatural hormones, despite associated kidney and heart problems.

Even corticosteroids, medically used to reduce inflammatory conditions and pain, must be regu-

Human Growth Hormone

When sport governing organizations banned the use of anabolic steroids, some physicians, pharmacologists, trainers, and athletes searched for new drugs that would not be detected in drug tests. They found that the naturally occurring human growth hormone (HGH) affects the body in a manner similar to testosterone. The body produces a limited quantity of HGH and since there are so many demands for it medically, it can be obtained only by prescription.

Serious side effects occur from the use of HGH; most destructive are those associated with acromegalia (enlargement of the peripheral body appendages), gigantism (larger physical stature), and organomegaly, which can cause an increase in heart size leading to congestive heart failure. These irreversible changes may result in premature death, even though athletes have been led to believe that use of HGH causes no side effects. Should an athlete take a drug to grow bigger and stronger even if it is not banned? What moral issues exist when athletic accomplishments become more important than personal health?

Blood Doping

Blood doping involves reinfusing one's own red blood cells, which carry oxygen, just before a competition. Athletes who practice blood doping have previously had blood withdrawn (six to eight weeks before the competition). The reinfusion of red blood cells, sometimes called *blood packing,* increases the number of red blood cells per volume of fluid, thereby delivering more oxygen. Some athletes have injected erythropoietin, the glucoprotein hormone produced by the kidney that stimulates the bone marrow to produce more red blood cells. Athletes believe that the reintroduction of packed cells plus their own increased production improves their endurance and, hence, performance. This procedure leads to high risk, however, because if the percentage of red blood cells (hematocrit) overshoots what is physiologically tolerable, heart failure, pulmonary edema, and even death may result.

lated because athletes have attempted to enhance performance through their use. The IOC, for example, bans orally, rectally, intramuscularly, or intravenously administered corticosteroids but permits physicians to prescribe them topically, through inhalation therapy, or intra-articularly.

Weight lifters, track and field athletes, football players, bodybuilders, swimmers, and other athletes of all ages have swallowed or injected increasing amounts of anabolic steroids. With the perception that "if a little is good, a lot must be better," many athletes have taken megadoses, thus increasing their risks. For most athletes, performance improves until some of the side effects develop. What are the moral issues surrounding the use of performance-enhancing anabolic steroids in sport? Is it ethical to become bigger, stronger, and more aggressive through artificial drugs? What moral issues surface when athletes risk everything, including their lives and health, for winning and its associated fame and fortune?

QUESTIONS REGARDING THE USE OF BANNED ERGOGENIC AIDS IN SPORT

1. Should athletes ever be allowed to use a drug obtained illegally to gain an advantage in sport?
2. If an athlete becomes stronger, faster, or more skilled in any way through the use of an ergogenic aid, should the drug, the athlete, or both be banned?
3. If an athlete gains a psychological advantage by using a drug, is there cause for banning its use?
4. Should athletes be allowed to use drugs to relieve the pressures and demands of their sports?
5. Does the risk of negative side effects impact whether athletes should be allowed to use a drug?
6. Should the rules governing drug use vary depending on the level—youth, school, college, elite amateur, or professional—of competition?
7. Should the use of human growth hormone, blood doping, or beta-blockers be permitted in sport? Why or why not?
8. Is the statement, "It's my own body, and what I take is my own business," morally suspect? Why or why not?
9. What are the legal and moral issues surrounding drug testing?

Although not a drug, blood doping has been used to gain a competitive advantage, which led to the IOC and the United States Olympic Committee prohibiting it. Is blood doping or blood packing unethical? Should it be? Why did the IOC ban this practice?

Beta-Blockers

Beta-blockers dilate the blood vessels, resulting in relaxation of the nonvascular smooth muscle of the bronchioles and the intestinal track. Beta-1 receptors affect the heart, kidneys, and adipose tissue, whereas beta-2 receptors specifically influence the arteries, liver, and bronchi. By blocking a specific type of receptor, a beta-blocker can decrease anxiety, heart rate, nervousness, and tachycardia. Beta-blockers have been used by athletes in biathlon, bobsled, luge, ski jumping, archery, diving, equestrian events, fencing, gymnastics, modern pentathlon, sailing, and shooting. The use of banned ergogenic aids in sport raises questions such as those in Theory Box 8-2.

The use of stimulants, depressants, anabolic steroids, human growth hormones, blood doping, and beta-blockers have led sport governing organizations to legislate against these. Rules have been enacted to prevent athletes from gaining physiological and psychological advantages. To ensure that athletes complied with rules prohibiting the use of banned ergogenic aids, drug testing began.

THE DILEMMAS OF DRUG TESTING

As athletes increasingly pursue peak levels of performance and the nonmoral value of winning, they frequently turn to ergogenic aids in search of a competitive edge. Some elite amateur, professional, intercollegiate competitors, and even younger athletes use stimulants, depressants, anabolic steroids, or other substances that they believe will improve their performances in pursuit of victories. Contrastingly, sport leaders suggest that the use of drugs undermines the equity of athletic competitions.

Drug testing was enacted to thwart the development of supernatural bodies or performances in order that these not dominate sport. Drug testing gives college coaches greater control over their athletes and helps ensure good public relations with fans. The IOC, international and national sport governing bodies, intercollegiate athletic organizations, and high school sport associations have banned performance-enhancing ergogenic aids and often mandated drug tests of winners and randomly selected competitors.

Opposition to Drug Testing

Many student-athletes have opposed mandatory drug testing on the basis of constitutional law. Under the equal-protection guarantee of the Fourteenth Amendment of the United States Constitution, athletes argue that they are being singled out for drug testing from among the general student body, whose members do not have to be tested for drug use. A college, if challenged in court for its mandatory drug testing program, must establish a rational basis or compelling state interest for testing (for example, using equity in competition and protection of athletes from harmful side effects as a defense).

On the basis of the Fourth Amendment, which secures the rights of individuals against unreasonable searches, others claim that taking an athlete's urine constitutes a search. Again, the institution or sport governing organization, if challenged, must show a compelling state interest for the search. Usually, athletes are asked to consent to a search as a prerequisite to competing, thus waiving their Fourth Amendment protection.

A third justification for resisting drug testing involves the issue of invasion of privacy. Some question the degree of intrusiveness that occurs when the urine sample is obtained. Because most expect personal privacy during urination, this right must be balanced against the importance of securing a sample from the competing athlete, not a substitute's urine.

Do athletes believe that mandatory drug testing violates their moral values? Do the procedures used humiliate athletes, impugn their motives, or show disrespect for their human dignity? For example, athletes are often dehydrated from their competitions and may not be able to urinate on demand. After hours of consuming fluids and then finally producing the required sample, these athletes may have lost the opportunity to celebrate their victories with teammates and others. Because a few deviant drug users have substituted others' urine through creative methods or diluted their samples, sport governing organizations usually require that athletes be watched when they urinate.

Many individuals resent being assumed guilty because of their status as athletes and strongly disagree with the indignities associated with the drug testing process. They also state that drug testing largely remains an ineffective deterrent without drug education. Still, most athletes readily relinquish their constitutional rights because they want to compete.

Thwarting Drug Testing

Drug tests are able to detect only the specific, banned chemical compounds sought. To avoid being caught, ingenious athletes know how to cycle on and off banned substances without being detected. Even heavy drug users can taper off before competitions and not test positive. Some athletes have learned to take drugs that mask banned ergogenic aids known to enhance performance. By the time these drugs have been identified, banned, and tested for, athletes have started taking other ergogenic aids. So, even though drug testing has been touted as the way to impose moral behavior on athletes (that is, to prevent them from gaining unfair performance advantages), reality indicates that drug testing may deter only those athletes not smart enough to cycle-off or mask banned drugs before getting caught. Is drug testing the way to teach moral principles, or does it perpetuate cheating and a failure to educate about moral reasoning?

Justifications for Drug Testing

Some individuals justify drug testing on the basis of the harm principle. The *harm principle,* a form of paternalism, states that the organization or authority, because of its knowledge, good will, and good intentions, knows what is best for others and for society. These organizations say banned drugs undoubtedly place athletes at risk presently or in the future. Since athletes can be pressured by social conditions to make poor choices, especially when young, the sport leader has an obligation and a moral responsibility to make good decisions for the athlete. Thus, drug testing removes the burden from athletes of having to choose whether or not to use drugs. Therefore, when using the harm principle to justify drug testing, society obligates the authority to keep athletes from harming themselves.

Another justification for drug testing is to equalize competition. This rationale assumes that only by banning ergogenic aids will competitions match athletes versus each other on a level playing field. Does this imposition of a rule eliminate the use of moral reasoning by athletes to decide whether or not it is ethical to use ergogenic aids in sport? Is drug testing a violation of an athlete's ethical prerogatives?

Educating Against Drug Use in Sport

Moral education may provide the key to a fair and just playing field as athletes, coaches, and others discuss what is good and bad. People involved in sport should examine their beliefs and values through cognitive dissonance. Just talking about the physiological and psychological side effects fails to preclude drug use because young people believe in their invincibility and will readily take risks. Many elite athletes would respond in the affirmative, as they did in the 1980s, to this question: "Would you take a drug known to cause cancer or a terminal disease if it would help you win a gold medal?"

Education potentially can convince athletes about the reality of the health risks associated with drug use. However, it should be noted that some athletes with medical conditions, such as allergies, must use prescription drugs whether or not they are athletes. Is it fair and just for the IOC to ban an athlete from the Olympic Games for taking allergy medicine prescribed by a physician? Are athletes who use drugs for medical purposes cheating? Are athletes who use ergogenic aids to enhance performance cheating? Should society reward the use of performance-enhancing drugs?

SUMMARY

The use of ergogenic aids threatens equity, or the concept of a fair and just playing field in sport. Because athletes believe that they can become bigger, stronger, faster, and more skilled, and then relax and recover from aggressive highs and the pressures of competition, many elect to use banned drugs or abuse legally obtained drugs. In search of ever-improving performances and victories accompanied by media attention, awards, and monetary rewards, athletes may risk their current and future health. Drug testing and the risk of losing competitive opportunities have deterred some athletes from using banned drugs. Yet, many question the legal and moral basis for drug testing. Athletes, coaches, and trainers need to examine their personal beliefs and values and determine what actions are fair, just, honest, and beneficent. Making drug testing mandatory should be the final, not the initial, step in a responsible educational system. Sport leaders have the obligation to educate themselves and athletes morally and not to abdicate this responsibility to a governing body that may only mandate drug testing, not educate morally. The use of ergogenic aids then remains a question of responsibility and honor, rather than only justice.

ISSUES AND DILEMMAS

CASE 8-1

Carlos began swimming at the local club at age ten. After beginner lessons, he joined the local swimming team and started competing in club meets, first in the summer and then year-round. For the first few years, he never won a race, even though he entered more events than most boys because he liked all the strokes.

The summer he turned sixteen, Carlos began to question whether he wanted to keep swimming. Although he had always been the skinniest kid on the team, it never bothered him until his teammates, six most noticeably, seemed to grow bigger and stronger remarkably fast. When Carlos questioned them, they invited him to lift weights with the guys at the gym. Because he never enjoyed this activity, Carlos had always declined. This time, however, he accepted so he could see whether weight training would increase his commitment to and success in swimming.

Carlos pledged to work hard in the weight room all summer. Although he saw some strength gains after three months, he seemed to be falling farther behind his teammates and opponents in swimming races.

When Carlos asked why his efforts did not appear to result in as much size, bulk, and strength improvements as his six teammates achieved, the initial answer given was that he was not working hard enough. Carlos refused to accept this because he knew he was training as hard as his teammates. Later, Carlos cornered one of these teammates and begged to know their secret. Tim refused to tell him unless Carlos promised to join the program; Carlos agreed immediately. Tim informed Carlos that for months, the six team members had been taking Dianabol, an anabolic steroid. They were convinced that this drug, combined with their training, had improved their physiques and swimming performances. Tim explained how and where the guys bought the Dianabol tablets. Tim told Carlos where to meet the guys the next day to make a purchase.

1. Why was Carlos interested in weight training and possibly taking anabolic steroids?
2. What are the moral dilemmas facing Carlos?
3. Are there any legal issues or interpersonal relationship ramifications in this situation?
4. Were Carlos' teammates gaining unfair advantages through the use of these drugs, and what would others think if they found out about the use of the anabolic steroids?
5. If no rules prohibit the use of anabolic steroids in age group or interscholastic sports, is their use ethical? Why or why not?

6. What are the potential physiological side effects of adolescents using anabolic steroids?

◆ ◆ ◆

CASE 8-2

Titusville State College had a long history of successful women's volleyball teams, having won two National Association of Intercollegiate Athletics championships and the Western Conference title seven of the last nine years. Coach Whitehead was a successful yet demanding coach. His players respected, but also feared, him.

Cathy Carter, a powerful hitter from the local high school, was eager to become the next star for the Bears. Although Cathy was excited about volleyball and practiced her hardest, she also was concerned about her academic work. An average student in school, she realized that she would have to study long and hard to remain eligible in college.

The one thing she had not anticipated when she joined the team was Coach Whitehead's fixation with his players' weights. He demanded that his team look trim and attractive in their uniforms. This meant that Cathy and three teammates had to lose between ten and twenty pounds, or they would not get to suit up with the team.

Teammates recommended that these four players take diuretics. Cathy, more so than the others, took them frequently, especially when she found that their stimulant qualities enhanced her on-the-court performance. Cathy also found that the antidoze pills she took to help her stay awake to study, when combined with diuretics, really gave her an adrenaline high. The second time she combined these drugs, her spikes were unstoppable and her serves fierce. Coach Whitehead complimented her improved aggressiveness and performance. Even after Cathy lost the required weight and earned a starting position, she continued to use a combination of diuretics and antidoze pills to psyche herself up for matches. After her matches, though, Cathy had to sleep a lot, was somewhat depressed, or popped another duo.

1. What outside pressures contributed to Cathy's decision to use stimulants?
2. Because the drugs Cathy used were obtained legally, should their use be allowed in sport?
3. What are the health risks, if any, associated with Cathy's use of these drugs?
4. How did Coach Whitehead's demands contribute to Cathy's use of drugs? Were his demands morally sound?
5. Are there any moral justifications for what Cathy did? Are there any moral justifications for Coach Whitehead's demands? Why or why not?

◆ ◆ ◆

CASE 8-3

The image of professional sports has been marred by numerous cases of athletes using drugs. From the death of All-American Len Bias from crack cocaine to suspensions of athletes such as Dallas Cowboy Leon Lett for repeated violations of the drug policy, the professional leagues have attempted to use fines, suspensions, and banishment to rid their ranks of athletes who used banned drugs. In 1998, however, questions have been raised about whether the National Basketball Association (NBA) should add marijuana to its list of forbidden drugs, with penalties levied against players who use it. At issue is whether this illegal drug should be treated like other illegal drugs, such as cocaine and heroin. In the National Hockey League, controversy surrounds a legal drug, Sudafed, that is being abused by athletes because of its stimulating effects on the central nervous system. Some controversy exists about Mark McGwire's use of androstenedione, a natural substance that raises a man's testosterone level.

1. Should the use of marijuana be added to the NBA's list of banned drugs? Why or why not?
2. Should the use of all illegal drugs be banned by the professional leagues? Why or why not?
3. What drugs should professional athletes be allowed to use?
4. What drugs should professional athletes be banned from using?
5. What is the responsibility of professional sport league rules regarding drug use in their competitions?
6. What is the responsibility of each professional athlete relative to drug use in his or her sport?

◆ ◆ ◆

CASE 8-4

Kisha often dreamed of being an outstanding runner and jumper as she stared at the life-size poster of Jackie Joyner-Kersee. By her senior year in high school, Kisha had already won numerous races and long jump events and had been called the "little Jackie" by the media. Everyone predicted that she would make the next Olympic team. As she read the hundreds of recruiting letters from college coaches who praised her athletic talents as well as her 3.5 GPA, she was troubled by a new drug testing program that Middlebrook High School (MHS) had just started. Even though she had never used or even considered using anabolic steroids or amphetamines, she knew of some girls on opposing teams who had. She was upset because two boys on the football team had been caught using these drugs and now the integrity of every MHS athlete was being questioned.

Since Kisha believed that mandatory drug testing was an invasion of privacy and a violation of her rights, she felt that she could not agree to a drug test. As her father patiently explained to her, if she refused to be tested, then she could not compete during her senior year. This would jeopardize her getting an athletic grant-in-aid at a major university. Even if she was fortunate enough to get recruited, she would face drug testing at that institution or in a NCAA tournament.

1. What are the pros and cons of mandatory drug testing?
2. Should drug testing be mandatory at any level of sport? Why or why not?
3. Is mandatory drug testing legal or illegal in high school, college, and professional sports?
4. Does mandatory drug testing violate any moral principles? If so, which ones?
5. What recourse would Kisha have if she refused to take a drug test?

ADDITIONAL READINGS

Black, Terry, and Amelia Pape. 1997. The ban on drugs in sports: The solution or the problem? *Journal of Sport & Social Issues* 21(1) (February): 83–92.

Catlin, Don H., and Thomas H. Murray. 1996. Performance-enhancing drugs, fair competition, and Olympic sport. *JAMA: The Journal of the American Medical Association* 276(3) (July 17): 231–37.

Eichner, E. Randy. 1997. What athletes are using—and why. *Physician & Sportsmedicine.* 25(4) (April): 70–83.

Hough, David. 1990. Anabolic steroids and ergogenic aids. *American Family Physician* 41(4) (April): 1157–64.

Maron, Barry J., Robert William Brown, and Christopher A. McGrew. 1994. Ethical, legal, and practical considerations impacting medical decision-making in competitive athletes. *Medicine and Science in Sports and Exercise* 26 Supplement. (October): S230-7.

Pipe, Andrew L. 1993. Sport, science, and society: Ethics in sports medicine. *Medicine and Science in Sports and Exercise* 25 (August): 888–900.

Voy, Robert O. 1991. *Drugs, sports, & politics.* Champaign, IL: Human Kinetics Publishers.

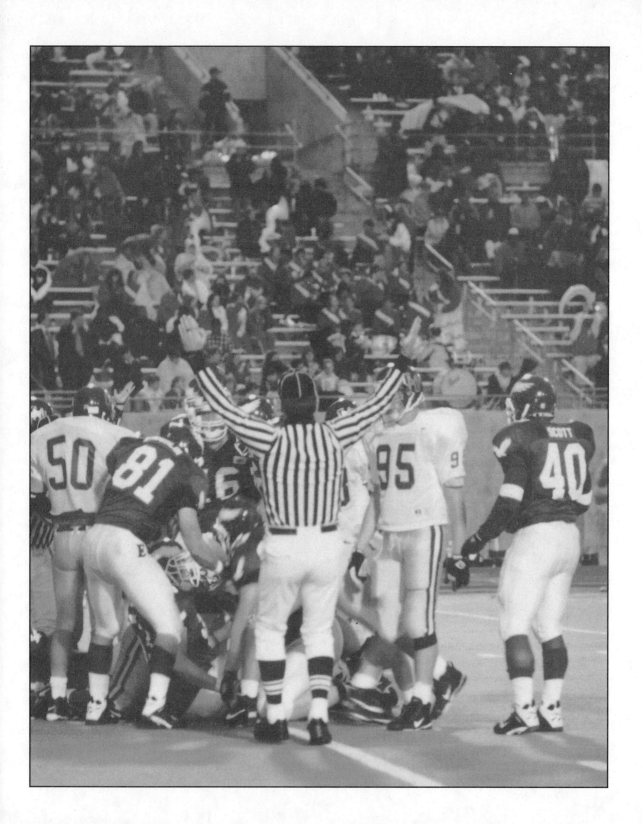

CHAPTER 9

Commercialized Sport

- ◆ What ethical issues have emerged due to the increasing commercialization in sport?
- ◆ What are the ethical issues associated with the use of youth, interscholastic, college, and professional sport in public relations and promotions?
- ◆ How has commercialized sport exploited athletes at various levels of competition?
- ◆ What moral dilemmas have arisen when sport has been used as entertainment?
- ◆ Has sport been used to promulgate economic values to the detriment of ethical values?
- ◆ What steps could be taken to rectify any erosion of moral values in commercialized sport at all levels of competition?

Sport in the United States supposedly transmits values. Most sports receive praise for promoting **character** development, dedication, self-control, discipline, fair play, and other social and personal virtues. As a result, public officials and school and college administrators have for decades accepted an idyllic image of sport, content to allow sports to regulate themselves, thus remaining relatively free from prescriptive laws and statutes. However, potential revenues (such as from shoe companies), internal conflicts, labor-management disputes, and excessive pressures on coaches and players to win, have tainted the purity of this image. Restrictive policies and rules have been scrutinized, overtly and covertly violated, and sporadically enforced—all because of the tremendous

financial and social benefits accruing to winners in many sports. Cheating at all levels of sport is often associated with this compulsion to win or the chance to claim number one status.

Commercialized sport (see Box 9-1) and the associated pressures to win usually affect moral values, often negatively. When sport participants harm opponents physically or psychologically, or ethically to gain competitive advantages, moral values are sacrificed. This chapter presents an ethical analysis of commercialized sport from the following four perspectives: (1) sport for public relations and promotions; (2) sport as a business; (3) sport as entertainment; and (4) sport as a transmitter of economic values. Each will be examined from the vantage point of various competitive levels.

THEORY BOX 9-1

SHOULD SPORT BE COMMERCIALIZED?

Making money is not immoral; commercialization is not immoral. When sport becomes overly commercialized though, athletes, coaches, and sport managers may be tempted to let a nonmoral value like money, success, or fame influence moral decisions. If these values become the primary foci, will immoral actions result, actions such as cheating and a disregard for the welfare of opponents? What may pervade sport is a sense that money controls actions. Then what happens to honesty, justice, responsibility, and civility?

To discuss ethical sport issues in relation to money always raises the question of whether participants and administrators of amateur sport (that is, youth, school, and collegiate) should market their products (the games) as commercial enterprises. Idealists would say that the purpose of sport at these levels is to develop character traits, such as dedication, sacrifice, responsibility, and *esprit de corps* (group spirit). If this is true, then commercialization may corrupt the sport experience. As commercialization expands, the purpose of the game becomes selling or marketing the game rather than supporting individual and team spirit. With the addition of money, morals may evaporate. Realists suggest that youth, school, and collegiate sport develops positive character traits and the public is highly interested in these games, so why

not capitalize on this interest? Charging admission, selling advertisements, and broadcasting competitions on television and radio defray the costs of these programs. Realists argue that neither money nor commercialization is immoral.

The two divergent premises of the idealist and realist are (1) the purpose of amateur sport is the experience; money corrupts; and (2) there is no reason why amateur sport cannot be commercialized, because neither commercialization nor money is inherently evil. Both premises are somewhat true and somewhat false. In statement one, the second part is false; people corrupt, not money. In statement two, the first part is false; there may be reasons known and unknown to limit commercialization. The true ethical dilemma in commercialization is not the money or the promotion but what occurs in moral decision-making when money and the product become more important than the athletes involved. What occurs is that making more money becomes the goal and athletes suffer. Sport can be commercial *and* moral, but sport managers are morally challenged to develop a set of principles and rules to follow when making business decisions. In large athletic departments, the task gets trickier because everyone, including athletes, coaches, and boosters, must accept the same set of principles and rules.

SPORT FOR PUBLIC RELATIONS AND PROMOTIONS

Sport has been used for decades to promote cities, businesses, schools, regions of the country, colleges, and products. Because of their visibility, entertainment value, and association with educational institutions, several sports have historically and socially been publicized as wholesome, worthwhile activities. Affiliation with sport leagues allowed sponsoring groups to gain stature and generate fan interest for their teams, as well as for businesses' services and products. A symbiotic relationship has linked the most popular sports with the print and electronic media. Newspapers and television have promoted

sports, and sports in turn have helped sell newspapers, advertisements, and products.

Youth Sport

When towns and businesses began to sponsor youth sport teams in the 1920s, one of the desired outcomes was promotion. That is, while helping youth, businesses could serve their own economic interests, too. At that time, no one questioned this symbiotic relationship; it was small scale. The extent to which it has grown is phenomenal.

Originally, businessmen furnished equipment, facilities, and T-shirts with the sponsor's name on the back for the boys' teams they subsidized. Minimal adult involvement in these sport leagues led to the claim that these leagues encouraged play and valued sport skills development rather than winning. Gradually, though, youth sport programs changed as sponsors sought the publicity associated with winning championships. This resulted in the provision of equipment, facilities, and uniforms modeled after professional leagues, as sponsors tried to outdo competitors.

Today, coaches for many teams sponsored by businesses and towns, in their zeal for success, bid for the best young players in major league-like drafts. Children are traded, benched, berated, and pushed, seemingly unmercifully, to achieve victories. Perhaps city leaders, in attempting to put their towns on the map, and entrepreneurs, in trying to gain a promotional edge for their products, have used children, perhaps unwittingly, for commercial purposes. Techniques frequently implemented include recruiting players from other towns and teams, playing overage youths by falsifying birth certificates, and giving financial inducements such as athletic shoes and clothing to players and their families. Particularly vulnerable are youth from poorer families.

Shoe companies sponsor summer leagues in basketball for youths as young as twelve and feature all-star teams that compete nationally. Many of the top players are enticed to change leagues, and thus name brands, with the lure of more free shoes, warm-ups, T-shirts, bags, and all-expense-paid trips to competitions where they can showcase their talents before ever-present college recruiters. Are these young athletes paid performers who already have internalized that success (winning) is most important? Or are these youths rightfully benefiting from their athletic talents?

Fun, socialization, and the development of moral values start to erode as young athletes learn that winning-at-all-costs in some leagues is a reality rather than a myth. Outfitted like professional athletes, many young sport participants model the commercialized behavior they view on television or read about in newspapers and magazines. These children grow to expect media coverage and the rewards received by the victorious (for example, playing in the Little League World Series or a Pop Warner National Championship). They also realize that those who do not win receive few benefits. Children also watch as many school, college, and professional athletes successfully exploit sport rules and enjoy winners' awards and acclaim. In what instances, if any, is it acceptable to violate the values of justice, honesty, and responsibility in the name of winning? What instances, if any, exist in which the ends justify the means?

Interscholastic Sport

School administrators increasingly face the quandry about whether sport participation at this level is a right or a privilege. If it is a right, then teams must be school-financed and available to all, regardless of gender, race, or skill level. Federal human rights legislation requires that girls and boys and students of all racial, religious, and ethnic backgrounds deserve equal access to school athletics. Do the highly-skilled, those with average talent, and the differently-abled warrant the opportunity to play their favorite sports wearing the uniforms of their schools? Educational administrators and school board members face the challenge of financing all these teams. No longer will support given only to boys with the highest athletic skills comply with federal laws and equity standards. The question is where to find the money to pay for coaching, uniforms, travel, officiating, facilities, and equipment.

Some schools, in addressing this issue, have redefined the opportunity to play interscholastic sports as a privilege rather than a right. With this change has emerged the concept of *pay to play*. The popularity of this trend increases as schools expect each athlete to pay a fee to defray the cost of personal equipment, the team uniform, and individual travel expenses. Many have supported this alternative in lieu of eliminating varsity teams because of shortfalls in state educational funding. Unfortunately, the economically disadvantaged student may be eliminated from competition because pay to play is possibly an inequitable and unjust standard. In some instances, schools make provisions for these students through funds raised by boosters. For schools that do not, what moral problems surface when students are excluded from play if they cannot pay?

THEORY BOX 9-2

SHOULD A DONATION BUY INFLUENCE?

The perennial ethical problem for any organization in accepting outside donations is the conflict of interest that may occur. For example, if Mr. Reynolds donates $10,000 to his favorite team, he might believe that he has a right to give his opinion on any facet of the program from coaching to recruiting. When individuals donate money, does that give them license to mandate policy? If the organization is a tax-funded entity, such as a public high school or state-supported institution of higher education, should a donor get extra privileges?

THEORY BOX 9-3

SHOULD ALL ADVERTISEMENTS BE ACCEPTED?

The ethical issue in deciding whether to use advertisements for companies promoting tobacco and alcohol products rests in the question of what the purpose of education is. If the answer involves the importance of health and wellness or social responsibility, then the school or university has a responsibility to follow tenets that support good health practices. Tobacco use is a known health detriment, alcohol in the hands of children is unacceptable, and misuse of alcohol is illegal. If a school accepts the advertisement of a beer company, it could be argued that the school endorses the use of alcohol. Therefore, the ethical question becomes—is that school being ethically and socially responsible to its mission and purpose?

Another method that schools have used to finance interscholastic sport is through booster clubs. Individuals in local communities donate private and business monies and conduct fund-raising activities to help pay the increasing costs of sponsoring athletic teams. Because of their contributions, some boosters may seek to influence decisions (such as who should coach the teams) and to demand winning teams (see Box 9-2). When schools were paying the bills, school administrators, including athletic directors, seldom experienced interference from outside groups. Now, however, dependent on varying degrees of external revenue sources, educational decision-makers often struggle to retain an academic, not commercial, focus for their sport programs. Plus, national pride, economic supremacy, and accountability have contributed to the clamor for educational improvement and reform in schools. By comparison, the sponsorship of sport teams appears limited in importance.

The potential for corporate sponsorships and television revenue may be viewed as the panacea for the financial woes of schools. In the struggle to support increased sport opportunities for students, however, schools are faced with difficult decisions. Commercial sponsors, including those selling alcohol, tobacco, and non-nutritional food products, are eager to place advertisements in game pro-

grams, on sport facility scoreboards and walls, and on team uniforms (see Box 9-3). Some sporting goods companies gladly furnish shoes and uniforms to successful teams and pay their coaches. Some boosters and sport agents try to reward the athletic achievements of local stars, despite regulations that prohibit giving these benefits. Who, if anyone, is culpable when these payouts occur? Does acceptance of these monies violate any ethical principle?

Because such bonanzas accrue only to the most successful teams and athletes, some coaches may be tempted to use various questionable tactics, such as conducting practices outside of the allowable season for a sport, recruiting players from outside a school district, lying about players' ages, giving athletes unearned good grades to maintain their eligibility, and teaching game techniques for circumventing the rules to achieve victory. What ethical principles may be violated when these tactics are used? In addition, school-aged athletes are occasionally treated as disposable commodities, of value only in helping improve coaches' and schools' won-lost records. Even at the interscholastic level, commercialization of sport in the quest for revenue may displace educational outcomes, such as the teaching of teamwork, sportsmanship, cooperation, and self-discipline and lead to unethical actions like cheating.

Intercollegiate Sport

As early as the 1890s, college presidents realized that the popularity of successful football teams could enhance the prestige and external images of their institutions. A century later, numerous universities find that admissions applications grow dramatically after consistent rankings in the top ten in football or basketball or the winning of national championships. Most fans can name universities that are nationally acclaimed for winning football and basketball championships rather than for graduating future Rhodes scholars.

University presidents, who are ultimately responsible for the proper conduct of all programs in their institutions, are often willing to emphasize athletics as the most visible public relations tool at their disposal. Frequently, university administrators nurture alumni involvement through athletic-related social events. It is assumed that alumni and many sport fans who never attended their favorite colleges will donate money both for sports and academic programs; in reality, most contributions from non-alumni fans flow into the athletic coffers. When a university is recognized more for sport achievements than for the quality of its educational programs, is the high visibility of its commercialized athletic program detrimental to its academic mission (see Box 9-4)?

Commercialization Related to Ethical Issues

Colleges and universities face ethical challenges relative to commercialization in sport. The four most promising areas for increased income include individual donations, ticket sales, commercial sponsorships, and television guarantees. Obviously, all are integrally linked with public relations and promotions. People enjoy reflected fame when they affiliate themselves with winning teams. Fans are more likely to give money to teams that win league, conference, and national championships. Joining a booster club named for one's preferred team be-

---

THEORY BOX 9-4

DO THE PURPOSES OF ATHLETICS AND EDUCATION AGREE?

Being a football power may have ethical implications if in the process of becoming a football power an institution's coaches, athletes, or supporters violate the mission and goals of the college. What is the purpose of a college? How does athletics fit into that stated purpose? If it can be shown that athletics contributes to the accomplishment of the mission and goals of the educational program, then athletics belong within academics. Conversely, if any program, including athletics, violates or does not meet the mission and goals, then that program should not be continued.

THEORY BOX 9-5

THE ETHICAL ISSUE OF ATHLETIC BOOSTERS

The place and purpose of athletic boosters is not an ethical problem if they follow the expressed purpose and goals of higher education. However, the question of athletic boosters becomes an ethical dilemma if the boosters violate the goal of athletics within the university. If boosters become a power unto themselves with their own agendas (thus violating the tenets of the university or the NCAA, which the university has pledged to follow), then control of the boosters or even their existence, if they cannot be controlled, becomes an ethical dilemma. No allied organization or group can be justified if it violates and does not support the mission and goals of the primary entity. Boosters can positively support an athletic program and the university only if they hold to the same set of moral values as the institution and its programs.

---

comes a status symbol, along with the associated seating, parking, and social perks.

College booster clubs (see Box 9-5) raise substantial amounts of money, millions of dollars at many

NCAA Division I universities. Although most of these monies fund athletic grants-in-aid, some are also used to build or expand athletic facilities and to give performance bonuses to coaches.

Ticket sales often reflect the success of an athletic team. At small colleges, this may mean that only a few dozen, hundred, or thousand attend. Still, taking in these revenues remains critical to the financial viability of many teams. Although "big-time" universities may attract 50,000 to 100,000 fans to their football stadiums and more than 10,000 spectators to their basketball arenas, oftentimes the size of the crowd does not change the expectation that the number of victories must exceed the number of losses to maintain fan support. Every college and university athletic director will acknowledge that *winning = fans = money = winning = fans = money.* This perpetual cycle brings in much-needed revenue, yet this money usually is reinvested to produce more victories. While commercialization predominately affects the revenue-producing sports, commercialization and fund-raising in the so-called non-revenue producing sports may replicate the problems often associated with the revenue-producing sports. Specifically, if gate receipts are generated or marketing techniques employed successfully, a heightened pressure to "win at all costs" may follow with the potential of compromising educational aims. Are any values violated when the need to make money and gain victories becomes the most important incentive for an athletic department?

Few sport programs could exist without private and commercial sponsorships. Business advertisements in game programs, on scoreboards, and on uniforms are pervasive. Should an athletic administrator accept the thousands of dollars offered by a beer distributor or a tobacco company for one of these advertisements? Should an athletic department sign an exclusive contract with a soft drink company that dictates the only type of products sold on a college campus? If provided sports equipment and clothing and large financial payments, should a university sign an exclusive contract with a company? What if this shoe company had a record of exploiting child laborers internationally? Do colleges need to establish ethical limits for what components of their sport programs they will market to the highest bidder? Capitalism, which is neither ethical nor unethical, includes social responsibility tenets such as fair competition and social welfare. Does becoming somewhat subservient to the corporate bottom line lead to compromises in the ethical values of fair play, honesty, and justice?

Television may lead to an erosion in moral values because of the huge potential revenues associated with telecasts. Because of the large sums of money that the national, regional, and cable networks wield, many colleges and universities will say "yes" to most requests. The day of the week, the time of day, the place, and the opponent often are dictated by television through the promise of more money for the cooperating institutions (and, of course, the network).

Professional Sport

Professional teams have become extremely important for businesses' public relations. According to many, no city can claim "major league" status unless it serves as home for at least one professional franchise. Witness the willingness of city leaders and entrepreneurs in Orlando, Charlotte, Miami, and Denver to pay more than $100,000,000 each to entice professional leagues to place expansion franchises in their cities.

A vivid example of the tremendous desire to keep a professional team in town was New York City's willingness to refurbish Yankee Stadium at a cost of millions of tax dollars when the city's budget was in deficit. In Louisiana, generations will be repaying the debt for construction of the Superdome. Many cities, through public funding, have built massive stadiums and arenas and then rented them for practically nothing to entice and keep professional teams in their cities. The justification focuses on the economic impact on jobs, taxes, and business profits resulting from the presence of these teams. When municipal revenues go to subsidize professional sports, however, social services may be underfunded, possibly contributing to inner cities being plagued by crime, drug abuse, and deplorable living conditions. When this occurs, what moral values are undermined?

Daily Effect of Commercialization of Sport on the Public

The media's continuous coverage of professional, college, school, and even youth teams places sport in the forefront of our lives. Office conversations, game-viewing parties at sport bars, and the popularity of the *USA Today* sports section are three examples illustrating the pervasiveness of sport in our society. Children mimic their favorite sport heroes and heroines. They also imitate the behaviors of antiheroes, resulting in violent behavior, unsportsmanlike conduct, drug abuse, and cheating. Regardless of whether professional athletes want to be role models, they are.

Youth, school, and college stars dream of achieving the fame and fortune enjoyed by many professional athletes; shown and discussed during prime time, or twenty-four hours a day, by corporate sponsors who pay the stars millions of dollars to endorse their products. Companies exploit the popularity of athletes to sell their shoes, food, beverages, pain medicine, and other products (see Box 9-6). Is honesty an issue when these athletes promote a product for money even though their endorsements about personal usage are fabrications?

Sport permeates the lives of many people. Besides discussing, reading about, and viewing sports, many people promote their favorite teams by proudly wearing licensed merchandise. Professional franchise owners and colleges collect millions of dollars annually from the sale of clothing and team memorabilia. To a lesser extent, youth and school teams garner revenue from the sale of logo sweatshirts, banners, and caps.

In our capitalistic society, the commercialization of sport remains inescapable. If sponsors pay enough money, they can now rename football bowl games (for example, Tostitos Fiesta Bowl). Television inserts "brought to you by . . ." provide game statistics and replay scoring plays or races; and outstanding player recognitions and championship trophies carry the names of sponsors. Has sport sold out to the highest bidder? Another example of the influence of money can be seen when media representatives from newspapers, magazines, radio, and

THEORY BOX 9-6

TRUTH IN ADVERTISING

In America, people may mistakenly believe that business is amoral. Anything goes in competition. Everybody else does it. People must lie and cheat if they want to get ahead. Because some individuals value money, many athletes make business decisions to advertise various products. Many idolize celebrities because of who they are and how much money they make. Advertising firms and corporations realize this basic truth: Some people will buy a product because a celebrity promotes it. Celebrities justify selling products they really do not use or endorse because they get paid. Have individuals lost sight of some fundamental moral insights?

television receive special perks leading to favorable coverage, an essential for fan appeal. Is investigative reporting the exception—for example, the Louisville *Herald Leader's* Pulitzer Prize-winning exposé on recruiting and academic abuses in the University of Kentucky basketball program?

COMMERCIALIZED SPORT AS A BUSINESS

The sport industry is a multi-billion dollar business when its competitive and recreational components are combined. Although recreational sports through their focus on participation may contribute to the development of values such as fair play, self-discipline, and cooperation, the potential to reap financial benefits has changed competitive sport, even at the youngest levels.

The physiological and psychological well-being and personal improvement of each athlete competing in highly structured leagues often are viewed as inferior to an emphasis on winning and on achieving the recognition and rewards given to winners. Most of the increased financing for and commercialization of sport comes from businesses and corporations seeking profits, directly or indirectly, through associations with youth, school, college, and professional teams. Athletic commercialization starts early, for example through advertising on Little League uniforms and the provision of free shoes and athletic clothing to teens.

Youth Sport and Interscholastic Sport

Athletes in youth leagues and on school teams are less likely to experience sport as a business, but at times they do. Early in some of their sport careers, athletes are given lucrative prizes, athletic shoes, clothing, and equipment, even though these young people are amateur competitors. High school athletic associations specify allowable remuneration for students, yet independently organized youth competitions may have no such restrictions. One unfortunate example occurred in 1993. Several male high school basketball players lost their eligibility, were suspended from a few games, or were otherwise penalized when they played in a Nike-sponsored event in violation of state interscholastic sport rules. Using collegiate and professional models, some corporations and youth sport organizations may sponsor competitions without regard for eligibility rules of the athletes in other settings.

Young athletes, as early as four years old, learn that the rewards of victory, such as huge trophies, newspaper publicity, popularity among peers, and preferential treatment, outweigh the few pats on the back for optimal effort in games lost. As these youthful stars mature, become more knowledgeable about the increased value of awards, and experience the stress associated with seeking to gain these lucrative benefits, the pressures to win may lead to ethical dilemmas and unethical actions such as taking performance-enhancing drugs, lying about one's age, and accepting money.

Schools, through the actions of coaches and parents, may overemphasize winning for the sake of ego fulfillment. Children's sport successes may enhance parents' status in the community. Stardom in the sport arena also may lead to financial inducements flowing to parents, who it is hoped will persuade their child to attend a certain college. Some youth sport or interscholastic coaches may seek to advance their personal careers through their athletes' achievements.

THEORY BOX 9-7

ATHLETIC GRANTS-IN-AID: A BUSINESS CONTRACT OR AN EDUCATIONAL OPPORTUNITY?

Perception of right and wrong may become murky for some college coaches and athletic directors. A few athletic directors, coaches, and other sport managers sometimes lose sight of moral values when faced with ethical dilemmas. One ethical issue revolves around whether the purpose of an athletic grant-in-aid is to help an athlete earn a college education. If the answer is yes, then the athletic portion of the experience is secondary to the educational experience. If the answer is no, then the educational experience becomes secondary.

Ethical dilemmas occur when actions do not match the stated motive and intention. The usual justification for unethical actions when faced with ethical issues and dilemmas is a form of palliative comparison, using business as the backdrop. "Everyone else puts athletics before academics, so we have to do it to stay competitive." For example, if people measure the rightness or wrongness of what they do by what others do, no integrity exists except in relation to the social expectation. Situational ethics becomes the moral norm.

Intercollegiate Sport

In commercialized intercollegiate athletics (primarily in Division I of the NCAA), there may be many exploited athletes. The greatest travesty ever perpetuated upon this group of people, and especially upon academically marginal students, has been the myth that receiving an athletic grant-in-aid leads to a college degree (see Box 9-7). Most athletes have fulfilled their part of the agreement in giving maximally to their sports. Too many colleges, even small-time programs, have failed to adhere to this bargain by withholding financial aid after a year of competition if an athlete does not achieve the expected level of performance or by not helping athletes succeed in the classroom. Many freshman football and basketball players enter college with the belief that they will earn college degrees, but by the end of their first year, they become more realistic about their meager chances of combining athletics and academics.

Educational exploitation in colleges may take many forms. Lowering admissions standards to allow academically unprepared students into college may set them up for failure. Tutoring, close monitoring of progress, personal advising, and minimal course schedules filled with nonrigorous classes may not bridge the gap for marginally prepared student athletes. Despite such help, to prevent failure, these students may be tempted to cheat on tests, let others write their papers, or expect good grades to be given because they are athletes. Others may "major in eligibility," with or without their coaches' encouragement, doing whatever it takes to stay eligible to play. In contrast, many athletes take full advantage of educational opportunities made possible through their athletic prowess by earning their degrees.

Although the NCAA limits the number of hours in a week that student-athletes can spend practicing and competing in their sports, the time demands on college athletes are extensive. Because compliance with maximal competition and practice time rules is based solely on a program's or coach's integrity to document all hours spent in athletics, many hours go unreported. In some programs, athletes sign blank forms weeks in advance and allow coaches to fill in the maximum allowable times, even though the athletes regularly exceed these hours for practices and competitions. If this rule can be circumvented, can others, too? Athletic commitments also detract from the opportunities for student-athletes to enlarge their social contacts and participate in other college organizations and activities. Proponents for the ineligibility of freshmen cite the importance of achieving academic success and participating in social and extracurricular activities before allowing athletic competition.

Psychological pressures may exceed the academic and social demands. Because most NCAA Division I athletes receive grants-in-aid, they are expected to perform at high levels. Pressures to win, exerted by coaches, fans, teammates, and personally if allowed to become excessive may hamper performance. Overemphasis on one's sport may lead to a reduc-

tion in social development because nothing and nobody are as important as winning. Other areas of psychological exploitation include pressures to maintain coach-imposed weights (leading to eating disorders) and the underdevelopment of athletes' decision-making skills and responsibility because of coach domination.

On the financial side, many say that some college athletes in Division I programs also are exploited. In exchange for grants-in-aid worth between $3,000 and $30,000, depending on the institution, some athletes may help their universities collect millions of dollars in gate receipts and television-rights fees. The NCAA regulations prohibit paying athletes. Athletes can accept an athletic grant-in-aid only if they choose to play college sports.

The NCAA also regulates the mobility and duration of college sport careers, pools and distributes profits (to and from its members), and polices its members by levying penalties as it deems appropriate. For example, if an athlete signs a letter of intent with a particular college and later decides to transfer to another institution for academic or athletic reasons, the athlete is not allowed to compete for one year at the new institution. In contrast, a coach can drop or reduce an athlete's grant-in-aid at will with no due process accorded the athlete. Moreover, coaches can break their contracts and move to colleges offering more lucrative benefit packages without penalty. Are these different rules for athletes and coaches justifiable?

Professional Sport

Professional athletes realize that they are paid to entertain. Yet they question whether they must endure physical exploitation. Playing while injured may be the standard in the professional leagues, but is coercing athletes to endanger their postcareer well-being defensible? Some athletes have been subjected to improper treatments for injuries and incomplete diagnoses resulting in chronic and career-ending disabilities. One example of a continuing controversy focuses on whether playing on artificial turf, which is more cost-effective for stadium owners, actually causes many athletes to suffer debilitating injuries. Lowered life expectancies and mobility limitations are among the realities facing many former pros.

Regardless of the level of sport, exploitation occurs when winning surpasses more important outcomes such as obtaining an education and value development. Exploitation is felt when athletes are manipulated and used for others' benefits, usually with no regard for the welfare of those integrally involved. What is the moral effect on sport when winning and gaining financial benefit become all-important?

SPORT AS ENTERTAINMENT

One moral dilemma of sport as entertainment centers around whether this role of sport threatens the educational mission of schools and colleges. Educational institutions exist to provide instruction, preparing students for life experiences and making contributions to society. Universities seek to expand and disseminate knowledge. Critical thinking, learning, and the pursuit of excellence and the truth are the goals of education. Can sport as entertainment coexist with these purposes? Have moral dilemmas become commonplace because the concept of sport as entertainment within educational institutions is inherently contradictory?

Youth and Interscholastic Sport

Although modeled after college and professional programs, sport for young athletes remains somewhat insulated from the seamier side of entertainment. Lesser-skill athletes attract fewer spectators and problems. Still, though, supportive parents and enthusiastic local fans may expect or even demand adult-level entertainment from children and adolescents. A classic example was the Philippines' team that initially won the 1992 Little League World Series. Pressures to succeed led this team to use overage players and boys who resided outside district limits to defeat the Long Beach, California, team that competed within the rules.

A handful or a few hundred may boo and berate adolescent athletes who do not win championships. Other adults may heap bountiful recognition and rewards on the winners. Family, school, and town

pride may rest on the narrow shoulders of teens who feel heavy burdens both to entertain and to emerge victorious. When the pressures become too strong, youthful athletes may cheat and violate rules to win games, praise, and awards. If sport spectators pay, do they expect to be entertained, even when the athletes are in miniature? No doubt the higher the skill level, the greater the expectation for entertainment. Failure to perform up to the standard demanded may lead to disparaging comments and abandonment of support.

Intercollegiate Sport

The president of the University of San Francisco eliminated the men's basketball program in the 1980s because of NCAA sanctions for abuses. He questioned how educational institutions could allow their principles, integrity, and students to be prostituted for the purposes of winning and achieving ill-gotten recognition and income. Does sport as entertainment cause newspapers to print point spreads used by gamblers? Do the huge amounts bet on college sports contribute to athletes' accepting money to intentionally lose games or "cover the spread." Universities today face an ethical quandary

are conducted honestly, justly, responsibly, and beneficently depends on the ethical values of those in charge and on their application of these moral principles.

Although presidential and institutional control are pivotal factors that can lead to reforms in intercollegiate athletics, the fact that major universities put few of their own dollars into athletics threatens this control. Athletic departments' multimillion dollar budgets are primarily financed by gate receipts, television appearance guarantees, and conference sharing agreements (from bowl games and television packages). Many university presidents have found out the hard way that controlling the policies, personnel decisions, and actions of those administering athletics on their campuses is difficult. One question often asked is whether integrity is compatible with sports as entertainment.

The NCAA and its Division I member institutions are in the entertainment business. Fans value, as indicated by their willingness to purchase tickets, the entertainment provided by college athletes. The fact that these athletes are students is secondary in importance, if relevant at all. The coach has one primary responsibility—to provide the most enjoyable entertainment possible, which is usually defined to include winning.

Professional Sport

Athletes in the professional leagues realize that they are expendable commodities in a continual process of providing entertainment while making money. Players are bought, sold, and traded either to enhance chances of winning or to save money. In a time when a World Series title could be bought (like the 1997 Florida Marlins) or a championship team sold (again, the 1997-1998 Florida Marlins), fan loyalty to identifiable players on their favorite teams was eroded as free agency blossomed.

Professional athletes with their multimillion dollar contracts are the beneficiaries of huge television revenues and high ticket prices because fans are willing to pay to be entertained. They revere Cal Ripken who will sign autographs endlessly. They will wait for hours to have Joe Montana sign a football and proudly wear a John Elway jersey because

of trying to preserve their academic credibility when their highly visible athletic programs are multimillion dollar entertainment businesses. The tough question remains: Should universities and colleges sponsor athletic teams? Does the fact that these programs have existed for decades automatically exclude them from scrutiny?

The extent to which coaches, sport managers, and even presidents may use sport as entertainment to promote themselves, their universities, and their teams may yet be unknown. The monetary stakes are huge. Perhaps no ethical boundaries exist for sport used as entertainment, at least not as long as sanctions are ineffective deterrents. This is even more true when we realize that many interpret the rules to their institutions' benefit and push the rules to the limit. Whether athletic programs the electronic media has shown their heroics time and again. While having heroes is positive, should most children name sports stars, rather than parents, teachers, and community or national leaders, as their heroes? What is being valued in these choices?

SPORT AS A TRANSMITTER OF ECONOMIC VALUES

Early in an athlete's career, economic values exceed ethical values because the former are rewarded while the latter may be faintly praised. Financial benefits are so important that most people have redefined sportsmanship as "pushing the rules to the limit without getting caught." For example, athletes of all ages too often are rewarded for throwing at a batter's head, taking out a player with an illegal block, or holding an opponent on a rebound attempt. It is difficult for athletes to see the difference (is there one?) between shaving points in basketball games and receiving money as enducements to get them to attend particular universities.

Economic Concerns and Rule Violations

Sport competitions require rules and participants' respect for them. A direct result of the importance of economic values occurs when the "spirit of the rules" dies. Constitutive rules (see Chapter 5) give boundaries to sport. If a player commits an act outside these boundaries, then a violation has occurred. Sometimes players violate rules unwittingly; other times they do so intentionally to help win and attain the associated benefits. Two kinds of intentional violations are frequently observed. First, a player may consciously violate a rule expecting to be caught, yet willingly accept the penalty in order to attain some tactical advantage that the violation affords. Second, a player may intentionally violate a rule, hoping to avoid getting caught.

Penalties for intentional fouls are stated in basketball rules since players have violated rules to gain advantages. Faking an injury in football to stop the clock and thus allowing the field goal kicker onto the field may be within the letter of the rules, but some would argue that it violates the spirit of the rules. Do these rule violations or circumventions occur because the economic rewards for winning outweigh ethical behavior such as honesty and development of values such as sportsmanship?

Youth Sport

In some situations, youth ice hockey teaches and rewards rule infractions. In fact, instead of being taught formally and systematically the normative rules of the game, some are taught how to perform illegitimate acts and how to avoid detection. Since the use of illegitimate tactics is considered strategically important by some coaches, players may believe that disobedience to game rules is important to the coach. That is, rules should be violated if this helps win. These same behaviors also characterize some in youth football; players are coached how to hold without getting caught. In youth volleyball players are coached not to say they touched balls tipped out of bounds.

Intercollegiate Sport

Some common myths surround the economics of "big-time" college sports. Box 9-8 lists some of these myths and the realities in some programs. At times, media exposés claim that the college athletic system is morally bankrupt. Some sportswriters argue that the NCAA and many of its member institutions value economic, not ethical, outcomes. For example, coaches and sport managers apparently feel no ethical trepidation about pocketing annual salaries in excess of $100,000 while some of their athletes have no spending money due to the limits placed on grants-in-aid.

A more realistic argument places the responsibility for the commercialization of intercollegiate athletes on the shoulders of college administrators and coaches. Each university votes to enact the regulations that make the NCAA heavily reliant on voluminous rules. Often, these rules have been legislated as knee-jerk responses to the behaviors, usually perceived as unethical, of NCAA members. Member institutions of the NCAA have perpetuated economic (not ethical) outcomes and only they can change this spiral of moral bankruptcy.

THEORY BOX 9-8

MYTHS AND REALITIES IN COMMERCIALIZED INTERCOLLEGIATE SPORT

Myth	Reality
1. College sports are part of the educational mission of all American colleges and universities.	1. The main purpose of NCAA Division I sports is commercialized entertainment.
2. The alumni demand having large and successful college sports programs—more than academic programs—in their alma maters.	2. Many alumni contribute to the academic units of their colleges and universities. Other research indicates that many major donors to athletic programs actually are boosters, people who never attended the school, who give money to the athletic department only in proportion to its team's success on the field or court, and who do not contribute to the institution's academic programs.
3. College sports are incredibly profitable, earning huge sums of money for American colleges and universities.	3. Most college sport programs expend more money than they earn in revenues.
4. Universities receive millions of dollars when their teams play in football bowl games.	4. After expenses and conference sharing, many participating universities seldom make money and may even run a deficit.
5. The money earned from college sports helps other parts of the university.	5. Because athletic department expenses usually exceed revenues, most money earned by college sport teams stays in the athletic department. There are, however, notable examples of athletic departments using revenues for non-athletic scholarships, library support, or other university-wide purposes.
6. College coaches deserve high annual incomes because they generate huge profits for their athletic programs.	6. The vast majority of coaches direct programs that lose money for their institutions. Market factors and past winning records lead to high salaries.
7. College athletic programs provide a wonderful opportunity for black coaches.	7. White athletic directors mostly hire individuals who look like them.
8. College athletic programs provide a wonderful opportunity for women coaches.	8. The percentage of women coaches has decreased significantly and steadily in the past twenty-five years.
9. College sports provides an excellent opportunity for black youngsters to get out of the ghetto, earn a degree, and contribute to American society.	9. Some athletic programs recruit black athletes primarily to play sports, even though they are ill-prepared for the academic demands of college.
10. For college athletes, the opportunity for a university education is as important as playing intercollegiate sports.	10. Many college athletes in "big time" programs hope to play their sports at the professional or Olympic level and regard college as their pathway to the pros or the national team.

Gambling (see Box 9-9) provides a graphic example of how sport can be used and abused economically. Sport and gambling, although inseparable in the minds of many, continue to tarnish the image of sport as a builder of values. To heighten interest, thousands of people wager millions of dollars annually on college and professional sport. Although such gambling is illegal, except in a few locations such as Nevada, newspapers persist in publishing point spreads that encourage sport betting. Point-shaving scandals in the past fifty years, especially in college basketball, and certainly millions of dollars of friendly wagers, may have been fostered by these printed point spreads. Some players have

IS GAMBLING AN ETHICAL ISSUE IN SPORT?

Gambling may or may not be a moral issue. Gambling can be defined as one person placing a wager (stakes) on whether a future event will occur. The ethical dilemma of gambling occurs when individual principles such as honesty, responsibility, and justice are violated and others suffer because of the act. The dilemma really exists outside of the issue of legality because in most states government-supported gambling, such as a lottery, flourishes. Legally, gambling may be judged moral because governmental agencies benefit. However, even legalized gambling may become a moral issue if the gambling violates responsible decision making. In the case of sport gambling, the gambling is not the issue; rather the issue is the effect of the gambling on the individual and the integrity of the game. Because people are highly affected by the power of money, and gambling usually uses money as the stakes, gambling becomes questionable moral behavior. Most sport leagues do not permit gambling by their athletes.

justified shaving points because of the money they received as long as the outcome was not affected, especially because newspapers indirectly abetted in breaking the law. Is sport gambling unethical? Should athletes be allowed to place bets on their teams?

Sport potentially can teach teamwork, yet many young athletes injure themselves through overuse while their teammates languish on the bench. Sport potentially can teach self-control; still, basketball coaches and players are cited for technical fouls, abusive language, and on-the-court fighting. Sport potentially can teach discipline; however, college and professional athletes are repeatedly arrested for driving while intoxicated, using illegal drugs, and assault. Sometimes, coaches and sport managers disregard these behaviors as frivolous or mischievous; sometimes, these athletes are aided in avoiding arrest and punishment for their actions. Sport potentially can teach fair play, but athletes are often

taught how to obey the letter of the (sport) law but not the spirit. Sport potentially can teach that the athlete's well-being as a person is foremost, but many coaches treat athletes as expendable commodities. Has the pursuit of profits resulted in a widespread erosion of ethical values? Are sport actions and behaviors influenced by how they will benefit a team or individual, regardless of right and wrong, or potential harm to others? Have economic values replaced ethical values?

ETHICAL DILEMMAS RELATIVE TO COMMERCIALIZATION

Commercialization affects sport at all levels, although the ethical issues vary. Each athlete, coach, and sport manager must choose repeatedly whether public relations, entertainment, and economic values supersede an emphasis on the ethical values of justice, honesty, responsibility, and beneficence. Theory Box 9-10 uses questions to challenge one's thinking about the ethical dilemmas associated with commercialization. Alternatives are suggested, although anyone may have a better resolution.

SUMMARY

Corporate athleticism exists today. The abuses in intercollegiate athletics prevalent in previous years have only expanded, spreading downward into youth programs and pervading the professional leagues. Through televised sport, a college or city can promote itself, but such exposure continues only for those who win. The cycle of *winning* = *fans* = *money* = *winning* = *fans* = *money* perpetuates itself. Exploitation occurs when what is best for the athlete physically, educationally, and psychologically is replaced by what has to be done to win. Too many seem to believe that it is permissible to break any rule necessary to ensure victory. Winning and money are not the villains; the actions of people are suspect. Sport participants can win and still be moral. The challenge is how to subordinate winning and gaining lucrative benefits while treating others morally and playing fairly.

Athletes learn early in their careers that they are entertainers. Professional athletes openly acknowl-

ETHICAL DILEMMAS IN COMMERCIALIZED SPORT

Dilemma	Alternative Resolutions
1. Is a primary purpose of sport the promotion of a city, educational institution, or product?	a) Yes, this is acceptable whenever any of these entities provides funding for sport. b) No, cities large or small should not use sport to "put themselves on the map." c) Sport is an extracurricular activity, not the reason why educational institutions should exist. d) Because corporations pay so much to fund sporting activities, they deserve any and all associated promotional benefits.
2. Should sport be used for public relations purposes?	a) No, educational institutions should build their reputations and images on academic, not athletic, programs. b) Yes, educational institutions should seek to benefit from the popularity and success of their sport teams. c) Yes, having a professional team franchise makes a city "big league."
3. Does the winning-at-all-costs mentality in sport lead to the exploitation of athletes?	a) Yes, but it is permissible to cheat as long as no one is hurt. b) Yes, it is permissible to cheat as long as one does not get caught. c) Yes, it is acceptable to put maintaining eligibility ahead of rule adherence to win. d) Yes, coaches have the right to use their athletes in any way necessary to help win (and possibly save their jobs). e) No, winning is never more important than the physical, psychological, emotional, social, and academic well-being of athletes. f) Yes, often athletes are exploited and ethical principles violated under the guise of winning.
4. When should sports exist for the entertainment of fans?	a) Never for youth sports because the purposes should be fun and sport skill development. b) Not in interscholastic sports because these should be extracurricular activities that teach educational values. c) Most intercollegiate athletic programs provide competitive activities that enrich the collegiate experiences of participants. d) Because football and men's basketball teams at many universities attract huge crowds, these programs should be in the entertainment business. e) Professional sports exist for the purpose of entertainment.

Continued.

ETHICAL DILEMMAS IN COMMERCIALIZED SPORT—cont'd

Dilemma	Alternative Resolutions
5. Do economic values and ethical values conflict in sport?	a) Yes, when money and other financial inducements become paramount, ethical values often are violated.
	b) Young athletes never have to choose between these (that is, no conflict exists).
	c) Seldom are high school athletes lured by money or other benefits to break sport rules.
	d) Only males in the major football and basketball programs are faced with ethical dilemmas with regard to economic issues.
	e) No conflicts between money and moral principles exist in professional sports.
6. How has increasing commercialization impacted sport?	a) Positively, because athletes at all levels are treated better through higher salaries, more grants-in-aid, better facilities, and increased media coverage.
	b) Negatively, because money influences so much that happens in sport such as when, where, and who to play.
	c) Positively, because sport has become more important in the lives of most Americans.
	d) Negatively, because getting more money has replaced the teaching and reinforcing of values as the primary outcome.

edge this, while the colleges still hide behind the myth of the student-athlete. For younger athletes, the higher they climb on the elite sport ladder, the more they realize that they may become pawns used for promotions and the entertainment of others. As a result, sport at many levels has become a business and a transmitter of economic, not ethical, values.

Although sport can teach values, such as loyalty, dedication, sacrifice, and teamwork, moral values such as justice, honesty, responsibility, and beneficence are often compromised when people value more highly making money through sport. Today, commercialized sport has become a tremendous force permeating all competitive levels.

ISSUES AND DILEMMAS

CASE 9-1

Midwest State University (MSU) annually hosts Parents' Day on a fall weekend that includes a home football game. Morning lectures, exhibitions, and social activities scheduled months in advance allow parents and their children to spend an educational and enjoyable time together on campus. Early in the week before Parents' Day, the national television network planning to broadcast the MSU football game contacted the athletic director asking to change the starting time for the game from 1 PM to 11 AM. A larger viewing audience and an additional revenue of $500,000 was promised to both the host university and the opposing institution, which was ranked in the top five nationally. Each member of the host institution's conference would also receive $100,000 if the game time were changed.

1. Are there any ethical issues involved? If so, what are they and how should they be addressed?
2. Should the athletic director consult with anyone before making a decision?
3. Should MSU change the starting time of the football game?
4. What would be the justification for changing the starting time? For not changing it?
5. What is the purpose of college athletics in relation to the rest of the institution?

◆ ◆ ◆

CASE 9-2

Lamont Adair is a talented age-group tennis champion, having already won the United States Tennis Association's twelve-and-under and fourteen-and-under titles twice each. Lamont's parents provide their precocious child with private tennis lessons daily with one of the best pros in the country. By age fifteen, Lamont is entering and winning an average of thirty local, state, regional, national, and international tennis tournaments annually. Because Lamont, an only child, misses so many classes while traveling to tennis tournaments, his mother has started home-schooling him. Lamont's father handles all tournament arrangements, serves as hitting partner before competitions, and acts as coach during events.

Lamont has won many professional qualifying tournaments and progressed into the late rounds of several tour events. Because of his potential, a sports agent has contacted the family about a variety of endorsement opportunities when Lamont becomes a professional.

Lamont is considering becoming a professional soon, and Mr. Adair debates whether to quit his job to manage Lamont's professional career.

1. What are the moral and ethical issues in this case?
2. What are the advantages of a sixteen year old becoming a professional tennis player? Do any of these involve ethical issues?
3. What are the disadvantages of a sixteen year old becoming a professional tennis player? Do any of these involve ethical issues?
4. What are the moral dilemmas, if any, associated with teens dropping out of high school in pursuit of professional tennis careers?
5. Are Mr. and Mrs. Adair acting responsibly if they decide to let their sixteen-year-old son support the family financially? Why or why not?
6. What are the pressures placed on Lamont? Should a sixteen year old have such pressure to succeed?

◆ ◆ ◆

CASE 9-3

Tim Washington's outstanding performances as the freshman center for the University of Western California (UWC) Cougars carried his team to its first Sweet Sixteen appearance in the NCAA Division I men's basketball tournament. As a sophomore, Tim led the nation in scoring (26.2 points) and rebounding (15.5) while helping the Cougars make it to the Final Four. Although his team did not win, everyone knew that Tim's next court appearance would be in the pros.

Even when he was a schoolboy star, Tim and his family had benefited from his All-American status. Tim's room overflowed with basketball shoes, athletic clothing, and sport bags as he profited from switching summer league teams each of his last three years of play. His father got a higher-paying job, and the family moved into a bigger house through the help of friends of the various teams on which Tim starred. Other influential friends made sure that Tim received passing grades in classes that he seldom attended, provided him with a car and spending money, and intervened on his behalf when he had problems with the police for traffic violations, an assault charge, and marijuana use.

When the college recruiting wars intensified, the Washingtons simply stated their price and waited for someone to pay it. While most institutions refused, UWC agreed to the $100,000 payout, which was cleverly deferred until after Tim signed with the Miami Heat. The following year UWC was placed on probation by the NCAA, but UWC Coach Charlie Wilson and Tim Washington had already advanced their careers at the expense of the university.

As a collegian, Tim experienced additional academic and legal problems. He allowed athletic personnel to arrange his classes and grades as long as they maintained his eligibility. Charges of driving while under the influence of alcohol, for assault and battery, and of rape were kept out of the media by powerful UWC supporters. Tim never faced the consequences of his actions because of his "big man on campus" status; he believed that enough money could fix any problem. As a professional, Tim openly marketed his remarkable talent, his dashing good looks, and his charismatic smile. His 12-year, $150 million contract soon paled in comparison to the endorsement deals he signed with 20 corporate sponsors. Within a year, he surged into the top ten in non-sport endorsement income.

Tim's on-the-court performances and likable personality added to his popularity with the fans. Affectionately lauded as "King Tim," he began to rule the "paint" in NBA battles against HaKeem Olajuwon, Patrick Ewing, Tim Duncan, Alonzo Mourning, and David Robinson. Not only was he named NBA Rookie of the Year; he also captured Player of the Year honors in his first year as a pro.

Tim had a reckless lifestyle that included fast cars, plenty of alcohol, occasional drug use, and women whenever he wanted them. He bought everything his heart desired and believed that money could prevent any legal problems. A similar attitude also characterized Tim's play as he expected (and often received) preferential treatment from the officials. Seemingly, they allowed him to hold, push, and play more physically than the other athletes because of his premier status.

1. What ethical values, if any, did Tim violate in summer league play?
2. What ethical values, if any, did Tim violate in his high school years?
3. What ethical values, if any, did Tim violate as a collegiate athlete?
4. What ethical values, if any, did Tim violate as a professional athlete?
5. Are the moral principles applicable to sport always the same, or should they vary by level of competition?
6. How did the economic values learned in his earlier years affect Tim's behaviors as a professional athlete?

◆ ◆ ◆

CASE 9-4

Voters in San Jose would soon decide the fate of professional sports in their city possibly for decades to come. The fate of the funding for the proposed football stadium rested with individuals who had been exposed to a barrage from print and electronic media that sought to win advocates for or against the bond referendum. Proponents argued that the only way that San Jose could become a "big-league" city was to have a team that played in the National Football League (NFL) or the National Basketball Association (NBA) or was a major league baseball team. As the National Hockey League's Sharks had attempted to show, San Jose's economy would benefit as would its national stature by having professional sports teams. Opponents argued that only the wealthy would benefit from hotel and restaurant revenues, purchases from other businesses, and corporate executives who could afford to use luxury suites for business purposes. Due to skyrocketing ticket prices in all professional sports, it also was argued that most people in San Jose would not be able to afford to attend a NFL game.

1. What are the ethical issues, if any, associated with the vote on the bond referendum to publicly fund the football stadium?
2. Should all citizens pay for a football stadium? Why or why not?
3. Is it unethical for a city to build a football stadium so that a team owner can profit from its use? Why or why not?
4. What are the ethical issues, if any, when the revenues from a professional team go mostly to the wealthy?
5. What are the ethical issues, if any, associated with the increased cost of ticket prices for professional sport events?

CASE 9-5

Southwestern University was facing a budget crisis. For the past three years, its NCAA Division I football and men's basketball teams had lost more games than they had won. Even though the university had received over $2 million from the Mid-South Conference due to the successes of other teams, it still faced a $1.5 million deficit. Given the fact that Southwestern had to increase funding for its women's programs because of a pending lawsuit claiming that the university was in violation of Title IX, Athletic Director Andrew Fleming knew that his program was in dire straits and needed a miracle.

The phone call from Michael Zemski appeared to be just such a miracle. After months of negotiation, Zemski confirmed that his chain of chicken restaurants would pay the Southwestern Athletic Department $1 million immediately and another $1 million annually for twenty years if the university would do the following:

◆ Name its football stadium in honor of Zemski's father.
◆ Place patches with his corporate logo and name on team uniforms.
◆ Paint his corporate logo and name on the floor of the basketball arena.
◆ Appoint him permanently to the Board of Directors of the Athletic Foundation.

1. What ethical issues, if any, were presented regarding Southwestern University's budget deficit?
2. Is violating Title IX unethical? If so, why?
3. Who should decide whether or not to accept Zemski's offer with its conditions as stated or after additional negotiations?
4. What would have been the ethical issues, if any, if Zemski's corporation were in the alcohol or tobacco business?

5. Would there have been any ethical dilemmas if Zemski had stated publicly that as soon as he became a member of the Board of Directors of the Athletic Foundation that he would lead the effort to fire John Lewis, the football coach?
6. What are the major ethical issues facing Division I sport programs that seem to be in the entertainment rather than educational business?

ADDITIONAL READINGS

Aaseng, Nathan. 1993. *The locker room mirror: How sports reflect society*. New York: Walker and Company.

Coakley, Jay J. 1998. *Sport in society: Issues & controversies*. 6th ed. Dubuque, IA: McGraw-Hill.

Eitzen, D. Stanley, and George H. Sage. 1996. *Sociology of North American sport*. 6th ed. Madison, WI: Brown & Benchmark.

Kirk, Sarah V., Wyatt D. Kirk, and Richard E. Lapchick, eds. *Student athletes: Shattering the myths & sharing the realities*. Alexandra, VA: American Counseling Association.

Making the assets sweat. 1992. *Economist*, 324(7769) (July 25): S9–S12.

Sack, Allen L., and Ellen J. Staurowsky. 1998. *College athletes for hire: The evolution and legacy of the NCAA's amateur myth*. Westport, CT: Greenwood Publishing Group, Inc.

CHAPTER 10

Racial Equity:
African Americans in Sport

◆ What effects has school integration had on African American athletes and coaches? Were all of these effects ethical?

◆ Have African Americans been exploited academically?

◆ What is "stacking," and how has it affected African Americans?

◆ What has been the media's portrayal of African American athletes? Why?

◆ What are the myth and reality about upward mobility through sport for African American athletes?

◆ Why are African Americans largely excluded from the power positions in sport?

◆ What are the ethical and moral issues associated with racial equity in sport for African Americans?

◆ How can the ethical and moral issues associated with racial equity in sport for African Americans be ameliorated?

Sport fans as recently as a few decades ago would have seen only white male athletes performing, and most print media publicized their sport achievements to the virtual exclusion of reporting on African Americans. Discriminatory practices and unwritten agreements prevented African Americans from competing against and with the supposed dominant Caucasian race. White males dominated sport because of moral ignorance supported by racist educational and social systems. The exclusion of African Americans continued because many whites truly believed that their attitudes, beliefs, and values were proper.

The predominance accorded whites in sport reflected the power and control positions they held in government, education, business, and religion since the founding of this country. Such dominance signaled a lack of justice, honesty, responsibility, and beneficence toward all other groups. For example, the privilege of voting was not extended to African Americans by constitutional amendment until 1865 and, in actual practice, not until much later. Whites governed at all levels, dominated education (although separate but unequal schools and colleges existed for African Americans), managed almost all commercial enterprises, and perpetuated the status quo through social mores proclaimed from pulpits. Firmly entrenched in positions of power, most whites accepted and acted upon the belief that everyone else was inherently inferior and undeserving of equitable treatment. Educational, job, and social discrimination was perceived as morally defensible on the basis of one's heritage. Reflecting white males' dominant place in society, sport included both *de jure* (legal) and *de facto* (existing) segregation.

Ethical concerns emerged because of discriminatory treatment based on preconceived ideas, unfounded **prejudices,** and widespread **biases.** Some athletes claimed physical and intellectual superiority over African Americans, Hispanics, Jews, Irish, and Italians. Lest this superiority be disproved, most white sport leaders and athletes simply refused to allow African Americans, and sometimes other minorities, to join their leagues. When a few tried to break this barrier, they were verbally and physically assaulted. Without the economic power to challenge such exclusion, African Americans formed separate teams and competed among themselves, usually under austere conditions. For example, Negro League stars like Josh Gibson, Cool Papa Bell, and John Henry Lloyd were never allowed to compete in Major League Baseball, although their talents equaled or surpassed the talents of their contemporaries like Babe Ruth, Ty Cobb, and Rogers Hornsby.

Discriminatory practices and segregation in sport set the stage for an examination of the many inequities endured by African American athletes. Historical, organizational, and societal events and perspectives in this chapter describe how such treatment has violated ethical principles. Although the situation has been ameliorated somewhat to yield something approximating equity, several recommendations for improvement are provided.

HISTORICAL PERSPECTIVE OF RACIAL INEQUITY IN SPORT

Before the middle of the twentieth century, African Americans seldom attained economic power; most suffered the ignominy of slavery or the remnants of this subservience. Enduring separate housing, menial labor, and often inferior schools, African Americans were forced by society to accept such discriminatory treatment. A few challenged the status quo, usually with harsh repercussions. Did the exclusion of African Americans from all levels of sport violate any of the three tenets of **moral reasoning:** moral knowing, moral valuing, moral acting? Was it lack of tools to reason otherwise that caused whites to relegate others to a secondary status?

School Segregation Gives Way to Integration

Within their segregated world, African Americans managed to offer their children limited sport opportunities, albeit with few of the amenities enjoyed by the more economically blessed. In all-black schools, judged by the Supreme Court in the 1954 case *Brown v Board of Education* as unequal, African American boys competed in football, basketball, baseball, and track. Although segregated schooling became illegal and civil rights legislation starting in the 1960s guaranteed everyone's rights, only gradually did educational integration occur. Subsequently, school consolidation and court-ordered busing forever changed the face of public education.

A significant consequence of integration was the closing of many former African American schools. Would a more reasoned approach have been to promote cultural diversity by placing students of all races in both former all-white and all-black schools, rather than usually uprooting African American students? As a result of consolidation and the closing of many formerly all-black schools, numerous African American coaches lost their jobs; almost all white coaches at the traditionally all-white schools retained their coaching jobs. Court-ordered busing sought to adjust the racial mix in schools, thus affecting athletic teams. Sometimes, African American males were not chosen for sport teams or not given the playing time they deserved by white coaches, though most coaches put racial biases aside and simply played the athletes who could help win. Through support for football, basketball, and baseball in these integrated schools, many African American students enjoyed better facilities, equipment, and competitive opportunities than they had previously.

As competition for places on baseball, football, and basketball teams increased, fewer white athletes saw these teams as their only sport options because their family circumstances allowed them to pursue sports such as swimming, tennis, and golf that were often associated with private lessons and facilities. As a result of increased numbers of African Americans in team sports and some whites selecting other (individual) sports, many school teams began to separate largely on color, depending on the sport. What are the ethical issues associated with this phenomenon, which has been called *negative discrimination?*

Integration of Intercollegiate Sport

In segregated colleges, African American men proved that they possessed the physical and intellectual abilities to become top athletes and play all positions. Although a few earned spots on Olympic teams, primarily in track, seldom did this Olympic competition, or even Olympic victories, change their plight back home. Jesse Owens, winner of four gold medals in the 1936 Berlin Olympics, personified this fate. Occasionally, when African Americans did get to play on a northern college's athletic team, they suffered mistreatment from teammates, had to sleep and eat in segregated facilities, endured physical and verbal abuse from opponents and fans, and often did not get to play when teams from the South refused to compete against them. Did coaches' or athletes' discriminatory practices retard their moral development?

Colleges began to recruit African American athletes to help win, even though these individuals formerly were barred from admission and remained nonrepresentative of the student body. The classic example of this shift in recruiting strategy occurred after the all-white University of Kentucky basketball team lost to the predominantly African American Texas Western at El Paso team in the 1966 NCAA championship game.

African American men traditionally have been expected to be star players; otherwise, they would not have received grants-in-aid. They were not to date white women, even though few African American women were to be found on campus; they were to accept without retaliation or comment racial slurs and segregated living and travel accommodations. Seldom did anyone assist them if they were not developmentally prepared for their academic work. Did college coaches care more about these athletes' physical talents than about them personally? Did coaches, teammates, and fans, reflecting their value systems, show empathy for the plight of these African American athletes?

While traditional white colleges enjoyed the contributions of these African American athletes, historically black colleges saw their best talent lured away by the larger, supposedly prestigious, colleges that promised glamour, media exposure, and potential professional contracts. Usually, these historically black colleges did not have the grant-in-aid budgets, facilities, and other amenities to compete in recruiting the best African American athletes.

For years, no African Americans were hired to coach by the all-white athletic directors in the NCAA Division I level, despite the fact that the percentage of African American athletes far exceeded the number of coaches of their race. The few African American head and assistant coaches today have at least overcome some of the discriminatory hiring practices of the past (see Table 10-1). Because their

TABLE 10–1

Dearth of Black Coaches

	Black (%)
NCAA Division I	
Men's Basketball Players	61
Men's Head Basketball Coaches	17.3
Football Players	52
Head Football Coaches	4.7
NCAA Overall	
All Coaches of Men's Teams	4.2
All Coaches of Women's Teams	7.1
Athletic Directors	10.1
Assistant Coaches in Men's Sports	12.6
Assistant Coaches in Women's Sports	9.6

Source: Center for the Study of Sport in Society. 1997. *Racial Report Card.* Compiled by Richard E. Lapchick. Boston: Northeastern University.

numbers remain low, many of these individuals serving as assistant coaches on otherwise all-white staffs are viewed as tokens hired primarily to recruit African American athletes. In the aftermath of racist statements or actions by coaches or racial turmoil on campus, some institutions have used the hiring of African American coaches to show that they do not discriminate.

Professional Sport

Although Jackie Robinson is credited with opening the door for African Americans in professional sport in modern times (1947), he was preceded without significant notice by Kenny Washington, Woody Strode, Bill Willis, and Marion Motley in the NFL in 1946. Yet only slowly did prejudicial attitudes and behaviors dissipate and change, even though the professional leagues in football and baseball today comprise approximately 67 percent and 17 percent African Americans, respectively (see Table 10–2). Although superstar African Americans like Shaquille O'Neal, Deion Sanders, and Ken Griffey, Jr., have signed huge professional contracts, many African Americans receive lower salaries than comparably skilled white athletes; proportionately fewer substitutes of color ride the bench. Some have conjectured that the presence of white substitutes helps appease predominantly white fans, especially in basketball, where color is so visible.

In the early years of integration in the professional leagues, African Americans (as notable as Willie Mays) often lived, slept, and ate together, so-

TABLE 10–2

Percentages of African Americans in the National Football League and in Major League Baseball

Professional League	Position	Black (%)
National Football League (1995-1996)	Quarterback	9
	Running back	91
	Wide receiver	91
	Offensive center	16
	Offensive guard	35
	Tight end	54
	Offensive tackle	52
	Cornerback	100
	Safety	87
	Linebacker	74
	Defensive end	78
	Defensive tackle	64
	Total	67
Major League Baseball (1996)	Pitcher	7
	Catcher	1
	First baseman	21
	Second baseman	11
	Third baseman	13
	Shortstop	17
	Outfielder	54
	Total	17

Source: Center for Study of Sport in Society, 1996. *Racial Report Card.* Compiled by Richard E. Lapchick. Boston: Northeastern University.

cially segregated from their white teammates. Like Jackie Robinson, they were told to passively endure physical and verbal abuse from opponents and fans if they wanted to keep their jobs. They were told to not expect teammates or management to intervene on their behalf. Until recently, no African American, not even stars like Hank Aaron, Julius Erving, and Jim Brown, could expect to earn endorsement and appearance income to match that available to the star white athletes.

For decades, African Americans knew better than to expect to be hired as coaches and front-office administrators in professional sport. To date, only a small number of African Americans have been hired in these positions. Also, seldom have they been rehired by another team if they were fired, although whites are. Biases have led those hiring to secretly profess or demonstrate by their practices that African Americans are not intellectually capable of coaching or administering a sport. Although Al Campanis lost his job as vice president for player personnel for the Los Angeles Dodgers because of his racist statement reflecting this perspective, African Americans have achieved few advances into professional sport management positions.

Does injustice characterize the differential status of African Americans and whites? Although fewer inequities occur today than in earlier times, differences in treatment still exist. Sport managers must be very careful in arguing that all is well because things have gotten a little better. For example, a typical administrative argument for the present status is that although African Americans do not hold many positions of authority, things are getting better and will continue to improve. A serious flaw pervades this argument, often called a classical *straw-man* reasoning fallacy. A straw man focuses on the positive nature of an activity while generally ignoring the racist atmosphere. This brings to mind the classical ethical straw-man racial question: "Which was better: a good, kind slave owner or a mean-spirited slave owner?" The straw man attempts to justify unacceptable behavior by comparing it with something that appears even worse.

Racism, like any form of negative discrimination, is usually defended on the basis of one of the following forms of moral justification: (1) palliative comparison, which is like the straw-man example in that one action is better or no worse than another action; (2) displacement of responsibility, in which an action is justified because the people in charge are doing it; (3) diffusion of responsibility, in which one justifies an action by saying that everyone does it; (4) dehumanization, in which one justifies a racist action by stating, "It is okay, because those people are different;" and (5) disregard for consequences, in which one justifies an action by not accepting the brutal truth of what was done to another person.

Those in control of programs at all levels are increasingly being held responsible for treating all athletes alike, regardless of color. Can whites honestly hide behind their prejudices and biases? Does beneficence call for administrators, coaches, teammates, opponents, and fans to treat all athletes equitably? How can moral knowing and moral valuing bring about greater equity in sport for African Americans?

SOCIETAL ATTITUDES

Individual and group attitudes are difficult to alter because society has reinforced maintenance of the status quo. Racial discrimination, once a way of life in this country, has resisted elimination. Many have lauded sport as a leader in integration of the races; in reality, sport reflects society. Most of the first African Americans in sport, law, medicine, business, and education suffered through harsh name-calling, physical abuse, and psychological badgering. Only gradually, and in the face of grudging changes in attitudes, did African Americans achieve more equal status in these and other careers.

Although some individuals from other races gained acceptance because they did not disclose their heritage, skin color stereotyped most African Americans regardless of their abilities. Because of a few courageous forebearers, federal laws, and the desire to win and make more money, today, athletic talent counts more than race, nationality, or any other personal characteristic. In an increasingly diverse culture, acceptance slowly is being based on a belief in equality of all, rather than on some externally mandated opinion.

The key to equity is education. Today, societal leaders urge everyone to accept cultural diversity on the moral principle that learning about different cultures will lead to greater appreciation and acceptance. Can people value different cultures, sharing commonalities such as respect for self, respect for others, and respect for private property while accepting varying perspectives? Establishing mutual values appears to be an appropriate framework in which to work for the elimination of injustices, but this framework may be doomed without an educational program to support these values. Also, people need to develop principles and rules to live by and the ability to critique what they have established.

ARE ORGANIZATIONAL POLICIES AFFECTING AFRICAN AMERICANS DISPROPORTIONATELY?

The NCAA, NAIA, NJCAA, and National Federation of State High School Associations (NFSHSA) did not overtly discriminate against African Americans. Although their rules and regulations were established to facilitate competitions among their members, they failed to prevent or remove harm. Thus, it could be argued that the application of these policies has differentially disadvantaged African Americans, primarily in the area of academics.

Most states require minimal academic achievement for continued participation on school teams. These *no pass, no play* directives have disqualified more African Americans than whites, more as a result of socioeconomic than racial factors. That is, students raised in disadvantaged circumstances often do not have educational encouragement and learning materials such as books and computers. These circumstances can retard students' readiness academically and cause them to fall farther behind each year. When athletes, including many African Americans, subsequently are given unearned good grades for the sake of maintaining eligibility, are they being deprived of an education? Are they being taught to value athletics more than academics? Worst of all, are they being taught dishonesty?

The best high school athletes dream of earning college grants-in-aid, although meeting admissions criteria required by the governing collegiate associations makes this dream an illusion for many. For example, the NCAA currently mandates that a prospective student-athlete must score at least 820 on the SAT or 68 on the ACT with a high school grade-point average of 2.5 in 13 specific core courses. A sliding scale allows a student to be eligible for intercollegiate competition by raising either the test score or the grade-point average to compensate for a lower score on the other.

Some African American coaches have protested that this academic standard discriminates against people of color, limiting the number of African American athletes qualifying for grants-in-aid. Some African American leaders have argued that academic standards remain too low, suggesting that if requirements were raised, athletes would meet them. Although a higher percentage of African Americans have been denied grants-in-aid and eligibility to compete for NCAA member institutions because of these academic eligibility requirements, college presidents and athletic administrators claim that higher standards have been enacted to improve the image and integrity of intercollegiate athletics, not to discriminate against African Americans.

ROLE MODELS

African American culture disproportionately rewards the athletic prowess of its sport heroes and heroines, who are more likely to be role models than are doctors, lawyers, or business executives. African American males may practice their sport skills more diligently because they are rewarded with status and because they see sport as a ticket to a better way of life. The dream of a sport career resoundingly affects 99 percent of high school athletes of all races who never sign professional contracts. Those, however, who do achieve their dream, on average three to five years later, find themselves out of jobs and, too often, poorly educated.

The importance of having role models starts at a young age. Adults encourage or discourage children in almost self-fulfilling prophecies as they are overtly or subtly told about their opportunities in life. Boys growing up in families without fathers at home may seek male role models at school, most frequently coaches. The bond that develops between the coach, usually white, and the athlete, often African American, may lead to a singular emphasis on sport, unless the coach encourages a balance between academics and athletics. The athlete may want to become a coach, but more often the goal is to earn a college grant-in-aid and then play in the pros.

During their school years, students choose heroes and heroines, usually of the same race, in their preferred sports. These individuals serve as powerful role models of behavior, both moral and immoral. Also, each person assimilates the values of the group with which the most time is spent. Although parents and families may teach and model morally acceptable behavior, coaches or teammates might not. It is often the latter whom the athletes imitate. Does the nonmoral value of winning ever displace moral actions because those involved with sport fail to address the issues facing them in moral terms?

Modeling also occurs in position selection in sport. Do few African American boys aspire to become quarterbacks because they subconsciously believe that this is traditionally a white man's position? Have coaches urged African Americans, even though they possessed the requisite skills and leadership for quarterback, to play other positions? Often athletes self-select by modeling their heroes who have historically played in positions requiring speed and reaction time rather than decision making and centrality to the action. This phenomenon has been called *stacking*.

STACKING AND A QUOTA SYSTEM

Position allocation, or stacking, refers to a disproportionate concentration of African Americans in specific positions. African American athletes still predominate in certain positions but seldom play in others (see Table 10-1). There are several possible explanations for stacking: (1) racist stereotypes about the physical, social, and personality attributes of athletes; (2) racial discrimination that keeps some athletes from leadership, responsibility, and authority roles; (3) an economic assumption that athletes of color from lower socioeconomic groups do not have access to training and facilities needed to develop certain position-related skills; (4) self-selection by athletes of color into positions in which they perceive they have the greatest chance to achieve success; (5) the possibility that athletes of color choose to emulate those of their race, who have historically played only in certain positions; and (6) the prejudice that African Americans excel only at reactive positions. Due to one or more of these circumstances, African Americans have often competed against themselves, not against whites, for some positions and opportunities to play.

Historically a *quota system,* whereby only a limited number of minorities could play at one time, has also restricted sport opportunities for African Americans at school, college, and professional levels. Additionally, school and college African American athletes acknowledge that the odds of retaining a place on the roster with only average talent tip heavily in favor of whites. The injustices endured by African Americans serve as a chronicle of the discriminatory practices of coaches and sport managers. Has the idolizing of men of their race who have become pros led many African Americans down a dead-end road? Has accepting position shifts and enduring quota systems damaged African American athletes' self-esteem and limited their options? Have coaches treated these athletes dishonestly? Does ethical behavior demand that team selection, opportunities to play any position, and hiring be based on documented abilities, not the color of one's skin?

AFRICAN AMERICAN ATHLETES AS PORTRAYED IN THE MEDIA

Until recently, the media condoned and perpetuated a second-class status for African Americans in sport. The African American press proclaimed the achievements of Buck Leonard and Ora Washington, but most whites knew little about these outstanding athletes. The white print media praised Joe Louis, who fit its image of a modest champion, while detesting Jack Johnson, who refused to behave demurely, flaunting his wealth earned as the heavyweight title holder. When Hank Aaron became the greatest home-run hitter of all time, many in the media refused to lavish upon him superstar status.

In sport, African Americans were conditioned to passively take orders from white coaches as the media praised those who "knew their place." Boston Celtics star and one-time NBA coach Bill Russell suffered verbal attacks and criticism at the hands of sportswriters and broadcasters because he outspokenly lambasted prejudicial attitudes and behaviors.

Has the media perpetuated prejudice against and stereotyping of African Americans? What values have been reinforced by how the media has portrayed African American athletes? Can the media help make an athlete a star or preclude this based on the amount and type of exposure it provides? Does the media influence whether athletes attain celebrity status, which often translates into endorsement and appearance income? Does race influence how athletes are portrayed by the media? Is there a lack of equity in sport reporting?

DISPELLING MYTHS

Society has perpetuated several racial myths that need to be examined and dispelled before sport will equitably accept African Americans.

Myth 1: *African Americans are physiologically superior (that is, they can run faster and jump higher).* In reality, the research is inconclusive. Questions have been raised about the appropriateness of statistical design, validity, and sampling techniques in some studies that seem to indicate such superiority. Knowledgeable people continue to disagree about whether genetics gives African Americans physical advantages in sport. Are the high numbers of African Americans in public school football, basketball, baseball, and track programs related more to opportunities than to genetics? Contrastingly, do few African Americans participate and excel in golf, tennis, swimming, figure skating, and gymnastics because the cost of private lessons, club memberships, and expensive equipment and facilities bars those from lower socioeconomic levels? Although certain bodily measures have shown differences between black and white athletes in areas such as mesomorphy and vital lung capacity, it has not been proved that these variations directly affect athletic performance.

Myth 2: *African Americans are intellectually inferior and thus not qualified for coaching or team management positions.* In reality, could it be that the "good old boys' " network leads to the hiring of coaches, scouts, general managers, and sport officials who are also white? Maybe those in the power positions feel better about hiring someone known, someone like themselves, rather than an unknown person who is different. If athletic managers use objective criteria and open job searches, will qualified African Americans continue to mostly be excluded? Are there any ethical issues or moral values involved in traditional hiring practices?

Myth 3: *African American athletes use sport as a vehicle for upward mobility.* In reality, African Americans and whites on the playground have about a one-in-a-million chance of becoming a professional athlete, with an average career of less than five years. While chasing the elusive media image of the superstar, too many youths squander educational opportunities. Due to differential socioeconomic opportunities, however, the African American seems disproportionately affected.

Coach Joe Paterno, former tennis champion Arthur Ashe, and many others have argued that the myth of upward mobility for African Americans has channeled these youths into viewing a sport career as the only goal worth pursuing, even though most do not achieve it. Without a professional contract or a degree, the stark reality of a limited future hits abruptly and harshly. Parents and coaches should emphasize education to youth over sport at all competitive levels.

Myth 4: *African American athletes are treated as equals of their white teammates.* In reality, compared with white athletes, African American athletes on average earn lower salaries, receive fewer and smaller endorsement opportunities and less media exposure, and seldom are retained if they are marginal players or substitutes. However, it should be noted that the star African American athletes have reached the pinnacles of their sports. Fame and fortune have certainly come to Michael Jordan, Reggie White, Ken Griffey, Jr., Carl Lewis, and Jackie

Joyner-Kersee. Do white teammates, coaches, sportswriters, announcers, owners, and members of teams' management staffs ever utter racist comments? Are the myths dispelled above perpetuated to stereotype African Americans? Do whites resist consciously or unconsciously any loss of power or dominance over African Americans? Does justice and beneficence require that all athletes receive equitable opportunities and treatment?

Myth 5: *African American athletes have the ability to play only reactive, rather than decision-making or leadership, positions.* In reality, African Americans have historically been restricted to reaction-time positions such as defensive back, outfielder, or power forward. This position shifting by coaches or self-selection by athletes was attributable to role modeling and a perception that African Americans will be allowed to succeed only in certain positions. Such stacking has retarded opportunities to develop the leadership skills needed to play quarterback, catcher, or point guard. Although African Americans have demonstrated the skills required to play every position in football, baseball, and basketball, their percentages in the so-called "thinking" positions consistently remain less than their overall participation numbers.

Racist behavior, founded on myths and prejudices, can be traced to a lack of moral valuing and reasoning and an insufficient determination to change. Most people in sport simply have not been educated for social responsibility. Values do not come to sport managers and athletes—or to anyone—through osmosis; values must be taught and learned. Moral valuing and reasoning and appreciation and understanding of social responsibility evolve only through concerted efforts to instill these values in participants.

RECOMMENDATIONS

As discussed in the first three chapters, the moral values of justice, honesty, responsibility, and beneficence should guide the attitudes and behaviors of individuals involved with sport. Racial discrimination and inequity are antithetical to each of these. Does justice demand that African Americans: (1) receive equal opportunities to play every team position; (2) be hired for coaching and management positions on the basis of their qualifications; (3) receive salaries, endorsements, and media exposure on the basis of merit; and (4) earn degrees even when this necessitates remedial academic support?

Should whites honestly admit to past and present discriminatory treatment of African Americans while seeking to eliminate such treatment? An honest appraisal of interscholastic, intercollegiate, and professional sport reveals that equal employment opportunities and affirmative action directives have failed to permeate whites' stronghold in athletics. Has this occurred because these directives may not have been valued by those who could make a difference?

Honesty also enters the recruiting picture. Given the past exploitation of African American athletes, should recruiters honestly assess young athletes' potential for professional careers, as well as their ability to successfully earn degrees? False promises lead to broken dreams and continued exploitation of athletes' physical talents. If a recruiter pledges an opportunity for a degree, does the institution have a duty to provide the support services that achieving this level of success requires?

Responsibility encompasses an ethical accountability for the care and welfare of another, thus countervailing discrimination. Responsibility includes providing education, at all levels of sport, directed at understanding and appreciating universal values and principles. Will the responsible sport manager treat every African American athlete in the same way as everyone else? Can those who act irresponsibly by making racial slurs, exploiting the athletic talents of African Americans, or discriminating in sport personnel decisions be re-educated?

Beneficence goes beyond treating others fairly. Beneficence means showing kindness. The belief of treating another as one wishes to be treated knows no color. Will the beneficent person in sport oppose intentional and unintentional words or actions that cause hurt or harm? The beneficent person does no harm, removes harm, prevents harm, and does good because doing good is right.

Racial discrimination and inequities cannot coexist with justice, honesty, responsibility, and beneficence. When those in positions of power understand, appreciate, and act on the basis of these four moral values, sport will harbor no color barriers. Consider the following questions in reflecting on racial equity in sport: (1) What do you believe about equitable treatment of people of color? (2) Could you reverse your response to the first question and be able to live with it if you were a person of color? (3) Could you universalize your beliefs to all people in all cultures? (4) Are there any exceptions to your belief statements? (5) Can or should there be any exceptions to universalizibility?

SUMMARY

This chapter provides an overview of some of the past and present inequities suffered by African Americans in sport. Historically, African Americans have been excluded from competition with white athletes because of the color of their skin . . . because of ignorance on the part of whites concerning fair and just treatment. African Americans' physical abilities often have been discounted as inherited, rather than developed through hard work, and they have been accused of being intellectually inferior without any basis other than racial bias. The media often has ridiculed, stereotyped, omitted, or short-changed the achievements of African American athletes. African Americans have achieved only slight movement into the power positions controlling athletics.

Significant progress has been noted, however, in the many sport achievements of African Americans. No longer must they endure blatant discrimination in and exclusion from sport. Certainly, African American superstars enjoy huge salaries and the adoration of millions of fans. Yet few would agree that African Americans below this top level of professional sport have achieved equity in sport. Success will occur only when hiring decisions, team selection, media coverage, and other benefits associated with sport are equitable for all, regardless of race.

Although this chapter focuses on the discriminatory treatment experienced by African Americans and their progress toward racial equity in sport, it does not address the fact that many other minorities are involved in sport. Historically, ethnic groups including the Irish, Italians, and Jews have used sports such as boxing for upward mobility. Many Latinos have contributed their talents in baseball and other sports. These groups plus Asians, Native Americans, Hispanics, and others have had to combat subtle and overt racism and inequitable treatment. With changing social attitudes and renewed emphasis on moral values, the future could be bright. It is hoped that all ethnic groups will soon compete side by side and against one another, with all individuals having the opportunity to display their athletic prowess while playing the game justly, honestly, responsibly, and beneficently.

ISSUES AND DILEMMAS

CASE 10–1

Myron Atkinson played basketball on the courts a couple of blocks from his tenement apartment in Newark, New Jersey, every chance he got. Everybody chose him as a teammate whenever possible because Myron's shooting, passing, rebounding, and defensive skills were the best in the neighborhood. On the courts, he could forget about the loss of his father in a drug-related shooting and about how tired his mother always was from working two jobs to provide for him and his three sisters.

Besides being the star in pickup games, Myron, who was six-foot-five, dominated play on his West Side High School team. For the second straight year, he was named All-State for his 23.5-point scoring average and 10.7 rebounds per game. As he approached his senior year, he was already being recruited by dozens of colleges, including Duke, Kansas, and Kentucky.

Coach McPherson had always ensured that Myron could focus on basketball by getting the teachers at West Side to give him and many of his teammates passing grades. Because Myron respected his coach so highly, he never questioned how or why his white coach managed to keep the best athletes—most of whom like Myron were African Americans—eligible. Myron did not dislike school and always attended classes; it was just easier and more fun to play basketball than to study. Besides, why study when his grades would be taken care of?

At the start of his senior year, Myron learned about the requirements for eligibility to play on a major college team. Myron's dream of starring in college and later in the NBA suddenly evaporated. His 625 on the SAT the preceding year and his marginal grades in mostly non-college preparatory courses left him woefully short of qualifying. Myron questioned Coach McPherson about why he had never explained these requirements and about what Myron could do. Coach McPherson told Myron that staying eligible for the West Side team, which had a good chance of winning the state championship that season, was more important than academics now or later. Coach McPherson told Myron that he would continue to help him academically as a senior, but only if Myron continued to take technical-type courses in which teachers would take care of athletes.

1. What moral values or principles are in jeopardy in this situation?
2. What are the ethical issues, if any, in Myron's situation?
3. Has Coach McPherson treated Myron unethically? If so, how?
4. Who is culpable in this situation, and why?
5. If you were Myron, what would you do?
6. What are the teachers' roles in this moral dilemma?

7. Is it possible that Coach McPherson had good intentions? How and why?
8. Why do good intentions often fall short?
9. If Coach McPherson was in error, what could be done to change his value system?

◆ ◆ ◆

CASE 10–2

Dr. William Simmons wanted only the best for his son and daughter. He especially encouraged them in tennis, his favorite sport, although basketball had paid his way through college and his premedicine studies. Frequently, the entire Simmons family played mixed doubles, various combinations of singles, or just hit for fun at the Forest Hills Country Club.

As the years passed, young Billy became a repeat age-group winner and then the club champion. Because the Simmonses were the only African American members of the Club, Billy had always competed against whites, where skill, not color, determined the outcome of matches. In United States Tennis Association sanctioned tournaments, however, he learned that some people could be racist and unethical. He heard his first racial slurs, uttered by parents of the boys he played. He also realized at a young age that opponents will cheat on line calls to gain unfair advantages. When he first experienced these incidents, his level of play dropped dramatically. Seemingly, the more these comments and behaviors affected him, the more frequently they occurred.

After a long talk with his father, during which he learned about the many abuses Dr. Simmons had suffered while playing basketball, Billy determined that he would block out others' statements and actions. With a greater focus, Billy's game soared as he led his high school team to two consecutive state titles and achieved a top 10 ranking in the 18-and-under class in Georgia.

On the basis of his record, Billy expected to be recruited by the University of Southern Georgia (USG), which had a top-rated tennis program. Although he received numerous athletic grant-in-aid offers to attend less prestigious institutions, Billy chose to attend USG on an academic scholarship. He was sure he could earn a place on the tennis team.

It did not take Billy long to learn why Coach Vines had not recruited him. He was told that Coach Vines had never had an African American tennis player, and some had heard him make disparaging remarks about African Americans when his team played them. Despite learning all this, Billy really wanted to play tennis for USG.

On the first day of practice, Billy arrived at the courts early. Coach Vines first ignored him and then asked him what he wanted. Billy simply asked for a chance to make the team. On the basis of the week-long tryouts, including the matches played, Billy had clearly earned a spot on the team. But the team roster posted the next day did not include the name Billy Simmons. Upset, Billy called his father to ask for consolation and advice. After assessing the situation from Billy's perspective and talking with Coach Vines, Dr. Simmons scheduled a meeting with USG Athletic Director Bruce Holcombe.

Dr. Simmons stated the facts as he viewed them, indicating that he believed his son had been discriminated against because of his race. He asked Holcombe to investigate the situation immediately and intervene, if appropriate.

1. What principles or moral values are in jeopardy?
2. Is this a moral issue, and why?
3. What questionably moral actions are occurring, and why?
4. How had Billy been treated during his early years of playing tennis? What does this tell you about the values of the individuals he played at his club?
5. What were the conflicts Billy experienced in competitions outside his club?
6. On what values did Coach Vines base his recruiting and team selection decisions?
7. What legal and moral values, if any, were violated by Coach Vines in not selecting Billy for the tennis team?
8. What action should Athletic Director Holcombe take if he finds that Coach Vines has discriminated against Billy?

◆ ◆ ◆

CASE 10–3

The Miller boys and their father loved football. Regardless of the season, as soon as Mr. Miller got home from work, Wayne, Robin, Eric, and Jeremy urged him to play with them. All of the boys enjoyed catching their father's accurate spirals. The Miller boys admired their father for all the trophies he had won in football and especially for his all-star performances at Grambling State University, where he had played quarterback.

When Wayne, Robin, and Eric got old enough to join youth football leagues, first Wayne and then his brothers wanted to play wide receiver. As experienced recipients of their father's passes for years, they earned starting positions and did well each year. Jeremy was different; he wanted to be a quarterback just like his father. Each year he tried out for quarterback, and each time the white coach told him that his skills were more appropriate for a wide receiver or running back. Although Jeremy accepted this decision initially, he began to question it when some of his African American teammates hinted that he would never get to play quarterback as long as a white boy wanted to play that position. Mr. Miller encouraged Jeremy to try his hardest in whatever position he was assigned while coaching him at home on how to play quarterback.

When Jeremy tried out for the junior high team, on which Eric played wide receiver, he was eager to play quarterback. The neighborhood Miller-to-Miller combination was unbeatable because the two boys had played together so much. Jeremy was told by the white coach that he was good enough to earn a spot on the team but that he would not get to play quarterback. Again, it seemed to him that skin color, not skill, was the determining factor in who was selected to play quarterback.

Mrs. Miller, a teacher at the junior high school her sons attended, began to inquire about why Jeremy was not allowed to play quarterback, especially because the three white boys who attempted to lead the team had been doing poorly. When Coach Dobbins heard about Mrs. Miller's questions, he informed her that African Americans possessed physical traits such as the ability to run faster and jump higher that enabled them to be superior wide receivers and defensive backs. African Americans, he added, were better at these reactive positions but less adept at thinking positions such as quarterback and linebacker. Everyone who knew football, he assured her, understood that this was a fact based on racial genetics.

1. What, if any, moral values or principles are involved in this case?
2. Is this a moral issue and, if so, why?
3. What morally questionable actions are occurring, and why?
4. What effect, if any, did role modeling have on the football positions that the Miller boys chose to play?
5. Did the Miller boys experience any discriminatory treatment while playing in youth football leagues? If so, what was it?
6. Were the beliefs expressed by Coach Dobbins based on fact or myth, and why did he espouse them so sincerely?
7. Did the position shifting of Jeremy by his white coaches violate the three facets of moral development (that is, moral knowing, moral valuing, and moral acting)?
8. What action if any, should Mr. and Mrs. Miller take if they believe that Jeremy has been discriminated against because of his race?

◆ ◆ ◆

CASE 10–4

Marilyn Scott fell in love with ice skating when she was seven years old. Although she was the only African American child skating at the rink, she was used to this since she attended a mostly white private school in Boston. Every afternoon, Marilyn joined a small group of aspiring figure skaters for the three hours of practice. Marilyn's talent surfaced quickly so that by age eleven she competed for the junior national title. For the next three years, Marilyn continued to improve dramatically, but each time she fell short of winning the championship. By that time, her mother was convinced that Marilyn was the victim of racial discrimination. Several people and even one judge had hinted that if Marilyn had been a blue-eyed blonde she would have won the past two years.

1. Historically, why have some sports been categorized as "white sports" while others have been associated more with African American athletes? Are there any ethical issues involved in this?
2. How are championships selected in figure skating and how could this process have been impacted by discrimination?
3. What recourse, if any, do Marilyn and her mother have?

◆ ◆ ◆

CASE 10-5

Historically, most public schools have offered football, basketball, and baseball for boys and basketball, if anything, for girls. Only in recent decades have opportunities expanded to include sports such as tennis, track and field, swimming, wrestling (for boys), and volleyball and softball (for girls).

An interesting phenomenon in sport participation appears to have occurred concurrently. Many African Americans, prior to and following public school integration, choose football, basketball, and track. Simultaneously, more and more whites have opted out of sport or chosen tennis, swimming, golf, and soccer as their sports. As a result, many high school sports are nearly segregated by race.

1. What have been the contributing factors to this near separation of the races by sport?
2. What role have non-school sport opportunities played in this phenomenon?
3. What role has economics played in the selection of sport by race?
4. Are there any ethical issues involved in this near separation of the races by sport?

REFERENCES

Center for the Study of Sport in Society. 1996, 1997. *Racial Report Card*. Compiled by Richard E. Lapchick. Boston: Northeastern University.

ADDITIONAL READINGS

Aaseng, Nathan. 1993. *The locker room mirror: How sports reflect society*. New York: Walker and Company.

Coakley, Jay J. 1998. *Sport in society: Issues and controversies*. 6th ed. Dubuque, IA: McGraw-Hill.

Hoose, Phillip M. 1989. *Necessities: Racial barriers in American sports*. New York: Random House, Inc.

Lapchick, Richard E. 1991. *Five minutes to midnight: Race and sport in the 1990s*. Lanham: Madison Books.

Lapchick, Richard E., and Jeffrey R. Benedict, eds. 1995. *Sport in society: Equal opportunity or business as usual?* Thousand Oaks, CA: Sage Publications, Inc.

Minority hiring not making the grade in collegiate sports. 1998. *Black Issues in Higher Education* 15(2) (March 19): 6.

Shropshire, Kenneth L. 1998. *In black and white: Race and sports in America*. New York: New York University Press.

CHAPTER **11**

Gender Equity in Sport

◆ How have societal attitudes influenced females' participation in athletics, and have these attitudes related to any ethical issues?

◆ What has been the impact of Title IX on the sport opportunities of female athletes, coaches, and administrators?

◆ What was the educational model of the Association for Intercollegiate Athletics for Women, and why did it cease to exist?

◆ What did the NCAA do to change the governance of women's intercollegiate athletics, and why?

◆ Why are females largely excluded from power positions in athletics?

◆ What are the ethical and moral issues associated with gender equity in sport?

◆ In what ways can greater gender equity in sport be achieved through the resolution of ethical dilemmas?

Societal expectations about appropriate feminine behavior and gender-bound roles curtailed women's active participation in sport until relatively recent times. This country's early laws, such as those prohibiting women from owning property or operating businesses, verified the dominant position of males, leaving females with few rights. Not until 1920 did all women receive, by constitutional amendment, the right to vote. Most females were illiterate until a few in the upper class began to attend private women's colleges in the 1800s. Although only a few pursued careers outside the home, these women threatened the status quo of a woman's "true calling" as wife and mother.

Historically, men have been able to engage in sporting activities but women have been excluded. In some cases, females were permitted and occasionally encouraged to watch, while in other instances they were explicitly banned from involvement in sports. During the past century, a few women disregarded disparaging comments and competed in various sports. Notable among these have been Eleonora Sears (tennis, walking, polo), Babe Didrikson (track and field, basketball, baseball, golf), Billie Jean King (baseball, tennis), and Joan Joyce (softball, golf).

HISTORICAL PERSPECTIVES

Acceptance by men was grudging when women, dressed in restrictive feminine attire, engaged in sports such as golf, tennis, and figure skating that emphasized gracefulness rather than assertiveness.

However, when female participation in sport increased, especially by the upper class, these women were heavily influenced by a staunchly held belief in Victorianism. This dominant societal perspective dictated the boundaries of propriety in a woman's dress and behavior. She was never to be seen sweating (women at the time were supposed only to "glow"), her interest in sport remained frivolous, and social encounters in sporting events always surpassed victories in importance.

During the latter years of the twentieth century and well into the twenty-first century, women in golf, tennis, archery, and equestrian events invariably stayed within societal norms. Helen Wills, Glenda Collett Vare, and Gertrude Ederle, although a part of the 1920s Golden Age of Sport, were probably more accepted for their participation in the traditional women's sports of tennis, golf, and swimming, respectively, than for their outstanding sport achievements. The All-American Girls Baseball League (1943 to 1954) and Hazel Walker's Arkansas Travelers professional basketball team (1949 to 1966) were always concerned about the feminine dress and behavior of their athletes, especially in these traditionally male sports.

The clothing worn by female athletes has constantly been a concern because of the fear that these garments would reveal too much flesh. Athletic attire has been transformed, albeit gradually, from long dresses including yards of petticoats and corsets to tennis dresses. Yet even the latter outfit is believed to render the wearer more feminine than she would be in shorts and a T-shirt. Bloomers for basketball gave way to the "scandalous" shiny, short uniforms of the Golden Cyclones (Amateur Athletic Union basketball champions led by Babe Didrikson).

Even with the dramatic growth in sport opportunities for females in the past two decades, many males still devalue females' athletic prowess, and the media largely ignores their accomplishments. Until 1996 (American Basketball League) and 1997 (Women's National Basketball Association), repeated attempts to start women's professional basketball leagues had failed because of lack of fan support. Radio and television mention girls' and women's game scores infrequently, with the exception of premier golf and tennis events, a few glamorous Olympic sports like figure skating and gymnastics, in 1996 women's sports of softball and soccer, and in 1998 ice hockey.

In retrospect, though, it seems important that males (with some females concurring) have truly believed their attitudes and actions to be proper and appropriate. As protectors of their wives and daughters, men accepted their responsibility to shield girls and women from physical harm, including that in sport. At the time, no moral dissonance even hinted at the issue of gender equality. Quite the contrary, moral education based on unenlightened religious beliefs or an ignorant cultural heritage yielded a sexist social system and structure that largely went unquestioned.

Given the legal, educational, and social model that restricted women's potential involvement in many facets of life, as well as sport, how and why moral change has occurred is the focus of this chapter. This examination includes how and why discriminatory treatment historically, organizationally, and societally has violated ethical standards. Although greater gender equity has been achieved, full acceptance of sportswomen has yet to be achieved.

GENDER INEQUITY IN SPORT

Sport has traditionally been a man's world. Males competed, coached, organized, publicized, owned, announced, wagered on, and watched sport in virtual exclusion from females. Religious, medical, and societal beliefs relegated women to their homes as wives and mothers, or possibly allowed them to watch or lead cheers while men competed. Assertiveness, dominance, toughness, tenacity, and leadership were viewed as masculine traits, inappropriate for women. Many characterized females as too frail, slow, short, or weak to become anything more than recreational players in any sport.

History reveals, though, that these attitudes about excluding women from sport grew out of ignorance or preconceived ideas and medical myths of the time. For example, physicians claimed that "Women's insides will fall out through excessive jumping and running," "Women will become sterile if they participate in vigorous sport," and "Women have limited energy resources that if used up in sport will leave them helpless when they must endure the demands of childbearing." People may have suffered from a lack of reasoned thinking if they believed these myths.

Sometimes by fiat, but mostly by societal constraints, girls learned early in lives that their brothers and male classmates were encouraged, while they were discouraged, to play sports. Toys directed boys into assertive, vigorous, and competitive activities; girls' toys reinforced passive, cooperative, and domestic play. Sometimes girls, disenchanted with inactivity, joined the boys in their games and occasionally surpassed them in skills. Yet, around puberty, most girls faced self-imposed, parentally imposed, or societally imposed choices. Many dropped out of competitive sport, perhaps continuing as fans or cheerleaders. Others continued participation in a more acceptable sport for females, such as tennis or golf, even though they might have preferred baseball. The choice of actively participating in one's favorite sport carried the risk of being labeled a tomboy or having one's femininity questioned.

What seems remarkable in retrospect is that few people questioned this status quo. It seemed as if males possessed some genetic or physiological right to sport that females lacked. Given the valued outcomes thought to be associated with competitive sport, such as teamwork, fair play, cooperation, discipline, and self-control, how could society advocate their development for only males? Considering the ideas of the times, did this societal exclusion of most girls from sport violate the moral principles of justice, honesty, responsibility, and beneficence?

Limited Opportunities

Medical opinion contributed to the perception that females were incapable of taxing their bodies as males did. Many women physical educators in the early decades of the 1900s reinforced the notion that females should be encouraged to play, not compete, because play was healthy. Competition was considered unbecoming to a lady and potentially dangerous.

Before the 1970s, few youth sport programs offered the same competitive opportunities to girls that they did to boys because parents, peers, and societal attitudes failed to encourage most girls to develop their sport skills. Maybe these girls lacked interest, were disadvantaged physiologically compared with the boys, or realized that competitions did not exist at higher levels and became discouraged about developing skills that they would have limited opportunities to use. The few girls who successfully became youth sport athletes, usually in sports deemed appropriate for them, demonstrated self-confidence and determination in surmounting others' discouraging statements and actions.

A lack of opportunities for girls certainly characterized interscholastic sport until the 1970s. Before this time, other than a small percentage of girls who played basketball, usually in rural settings, most girls were considered not to be interested in or skilled enough to become serious athletes.

Similarly, few competitive sport opportunities existed for college women. Most female physical educators staunchly opposed the male model of highly competitive, commercialized intercollegiate athletics. Instead, they claimed that women's activity needs were best met through instructional physical education programs, intramurals, and occasional play days or sports days (where social interaction surpassed even friendly competition in importance). Gradually, however, in the 1960s, it became clear that women with athletic skills wanted to compete. Within a decade, a new model for intercollegiate athletics for women, different from the men's, would begin to challenge the exclusiveness of sport as society questioned the moral basis for excluding females from sport competitions.

Governing Organizations and Policies for Women's Intercollegiate Athletics

Building on evolutionary structures that preceded it, by 1971 the Association for Intercollegiate Athletics for Women (AIAW) emerged as the governing organization over women's sport competition in college. Founded on the principle of an educational model that served women athletes, the

AIAW grew to offer 41 national championships in 19 sports for its nearly 1000 member institutions. Competitive opportunities for women at the state and regional qualifying levels skyrocketed, too.

Most collegiate sport programs for women, however, operated on shoestring budgets. Coaches initially volunteered their services, and players bought their own uniforms and equipment. Teams traveled in undersized vehicles, ate at fast-food restaurants, and stayed four to a room just so they could compete. Because they loved competitive sport, they endured difficulties in scheduling facilities; blocked access to athletic trainers, sports information personnel, and weight training equipment; and few opportunities to receive grants-in-aid.

Title IX

The landmark event in equal opportunity for girls and women in sport occurred in 1972 when Congress passed the Education Amendments Act. Title IX of this legislation stipulated that schools and colleges could not discriminate in their educational programs, including athletics.

The NCAA opposed Title IX vigorously from the outset, lobbying against the initial passage of the legislation and repeatedly attempting to limit the scope of Title IX's application. Nonetheless, through the issuance of "Title IX of the Education Amendments of 1972; a Policy Interpretation; Title IX and Intercollegiate Athletics" in December 1979, the Department of Health, Education, and Welfare (HEW) explained the scope and application of this legislation. In clarifying the meaning of "equal opportunity," HEW specified that compliance must occur in (1) financial assistance (grants-in-aid) based on athletic ability; (2) other program areas such as equipment, travel and *per diem* (daily expenses), practice and competitive facilities and times, recruitment, and coaching, and (3) meeting the interests and abilities of female and male students in intercollegiate sport. Possibly because of the money involved or the extent of male dominance, many colleges and universities resisted complying with Title IX.

On behalf of its member institutions, the NCAA claimed that equal sharing of athletic monies, facil-

ities, and services would threaten the viability of the revenue-producing sports. That is, only an unequal distribution of goods would enable men's revenue-producing sports to earn the capital to support both men's and women's sports. This argument seems flawed because the strength of the economy can never justify a moral injustice. Although no one knows what would happen with complete equity because in the over quarter of a century since Title IX was passed, it has not been achieved. Distributive justice dictates that inequality can never be legitimately defended or justified on the basis of scarcity of goods or an entitlement for those who earn more revenues. The question becomes one of whether monies, facilities, and services are more important than people and how they treat each other.

After the NCAA failed to get athletics exempted from the requirements of Title IX, most colleges and universities began to provide more money for women's athletics. Administrators in institutions that expanded their women's athletic programs stated that their actions were based more on a moral obligation than fear of losing federal funding for noncompliance. Many of the larger universities excluded football from their gender comparisons when reporting on progress in complying with Title IX, even though this violated the law. Others slowly and grudgingly provided more equitable support for women's teams to avoid costly legal battles or negative publicity. Some complied only under the threat of lawsuits alleging discrimination. Interestingly, these same responses continue to characterize strategies for partial compliance with Title IX today. Some women resorted to legal recourse whenever they believed that decision makers in athletics violated moral principles.

A few institutions refused to change. One college claimed that Title IX did not apply to athletics because this program received no direct federal funding. The Supreme Court in 1984 agreed in the *Grove City College v Bell* case. In effect, this ruling eliminated the application of Title IX to athletics, resulting in the withdrawal of, or the Office of Civil Right's suspension of, dozens of cases involving college athletics. Discrimination against women in intercollegiate athletics continued to exist, and in certain instances increased until 1988 when the Civil Rights Restoration Act re-empowered Title IX.

In 1992, the Supreme Court in *Franklin v Gwinnett County Public Schools* strengthened the importance of Title IX by ruling that individuals discriminated against could receive punitive damages. The moral issue, though, is why are congressional action, judicial rulings, and the threat of financial losses required before athletic administrators will treat female athletes equitably?

Some advocate that the NCAA's decision to compete directly with AIAW championships in 1981–1982 was a power move. Given the AIAW's weak financial status and the NCAA's offer to provide more than $3 million in expense reimbursements to competing institutions, the struggle was short-lived. After the defection of 20 percent of its members during the 1981–1982 season, in 1982 the AIAW ceased to exist.

Conversely the NCAA claimed to offer women's athletes greater opportunity through expanded programs, more financial support, and television coverage. Rather than seeing the end of the AIAW as an aggressive takeover, the NCAA viewed its actions positively and in the best interests of women's sports in its member institutions. The NCAA added that Title IX required it to sponsor women's championships.

According to legal cases, most notably the 1996 Supreme Court decision not to hear *Cohen v. Brown University*, an institution must meet at least one of the criteria of the three-part test: (1) participation opportunities are substantially proportionate to the undergraduate enrollment of females and males; (2) if members of one gender have historically been under-represented among intercollegiate athletes, then there must have been a continuing practice of program expansion to meet the interests and abilities of this group; and (3) in the absence of number 2, an institution must demonstrate that the interests and abilities of this gender must have been fully and effectively accommodated. The first of these, called the proportionality test, has three possible issues associated with it. First, gender discrimination could persist if an institution cuts men's teams because no additional opportunities for females have been added (greater proportionally may have been achieved, but such action is judged insufficient to meet Title IX requirements). Second, colleges have been expected to achieve proportional progress even though the schools may not be providing equal opportunities for younger females. Third, just achieving proportionality does not exempt colleges from the moral obligation to eliminate gender discrimination.

Outcomes of Change

With the NCAA in control of women's and men's athletics, males today are primarily the coaches and administrators for women's programs partially due to an increase in the number of teams and partially because of males hiring males to coach. Since 1972, there has been a drop from more than 90 percent to less than 50 percent in the number of women's teams coached by women (see Table 11-1). Similar findings are reported for

TABLE 11-1

Trends in the Gender of Coaches of Women's Teams

National Collegiate Athletic Association Member Institutions*

Year	Female Head Coaches (%)	Division I	Division II	Division III
1998	47.4	46.2	41.7	50.7
1997	47.4	46.7	42.3	50.8
1996	47.7	47.5	41.9	51.3
1995	48.3	47.7	43.2	51.3
1994	49.4	46.9	45.4	53.6
1993	48.1	45.5	44.1	52.3
1992	48.3	46.6	42.3	52.6
1991	47.7	45.9	42.1	51.7
1990	47.3	44.2	44.0	51.8
1989	47.7	—	—	—
1988	48.3	43.8	45.7	53.3
1987	48.8	—	—	—
1986	50.6	45.5	46.8	57.2
1985	50.7	—	—	—
1984	53.8	49.9	52.2	58.8
1983	56.2	—	—	—
1982	52.4	—	—	—
1981	54.6	—	—	—
1980	54.2	—	—	—
1979	56.1	—	—	—
1978	58.2	—	—	—
—	—	—	—	—
1972	90+	—	—	—

National Association for Intercollegiate Athletics Member Institutions[†]

During the 1990–1991 season, 39.5% of the head coaches of women's teams were women.

*From Acosta V, Carpenter L: *Women in intercollegiate sport: a longitudinal study: Twenty-one year update 1977–1998*, Brooklyn, N.Y., Brooklyn College.
[†]From Neal V, Anderson P, Jones S: *1992 NAIA sports program survey: administrators and coaches of varsity teams.*

NAIA institutions and in high schools. The number of females involved in intercollegiate athletic administration has dropped dramatically, too (see Table 11-2).

Women athletes today specialize in one sport, train year-round, and sometimes prioritize athletics over academics, as do their male peers. Sport has been found to negatively influence females' moral reasoning levels in comparison with those of nonathletes. Although female athletes' moral reasoning and development is significantly higher than

that of male athletes, females' scores in these areas decrease the longer they participate in sport.

Recent incidents of the elimination of women's sport teams at many institutions countervail the requirements of Title IX. Sometimes, cuts that are made to save money include a similar number of men's teams slated for elimination. In most cases, the institutions have reinstated the women's teams because of public outcry or legal mandates.

Of significant note, however, has been the argument that the only way women's teams can be

TABLE 11-2

Trends in Females in Athletic Administration.

National Collegiate Athletic Association Member Institutions*

Year	% †	Division I	Division II	Division III
1998	19.4	9.9	18.6	29.4
1996	18.5	8.8	16.7	27.9
1994	21.0	—	—	—
1992	16.8	8.6	15.0	24.8
1990	15.9	7.0	15.2	24.8
1988	16.1	8.4	14.6	23.0
1986	15.2	9.4	15.2	20.4
1984	17.0	10.0	15.9	21.2
1980	20.0	—	—	—
1972	90.0+	—	—	—

*Source: Acosta, R. V., and L. J. Carpenter. *Women in intercollegiate sport: a longitudinal study: Twenty-one year update 1977–1998*, Brooklyn, N.Y.: Brooklyn College.
†Percentage of female head athletic directors of women's programs.

added or increased support provided is to eliminate men's teams. This pitting of the men against the women leads to the question, what is the ethical basis for simultaneously doing good and doing harm?

Interscholastic Sport Changes for Girls

The National Federation of State High School Associations (NFSHSA) and its member organizations traditionally ignored girls' sport. By assuming a lack of interest or skill in females, administrators in most high schools disregarded the activity and competitive needs of half of their students. The 1970s ushered in a new era in the treatment of aspiring girl athletes in the schools.

The impact of Title IX, although gradual, was dramatic in most schools. Girls and boys in the 1980s began to share more equitably the use of practice and competitive facilities, athletic trainers, and weight rooms. Some school administrators, however, have resisted treating all athletes fairly and justly. Credentials and experiences usually govern coaches' stipends in the schools, rather than gender of the coach of the team. However, some schools pay higher salaries to coaches for boys' football, basketball, and other sports.

Teams for girls have proliferated; the number of girls competing increased by hundreds of thousands. Because of a lack of enough females prepared or interested in coaching, the increased number of teams, greater equity in coaching stipends, and male athletic directors hiring men to coach girls' teams, more and more men were hired. Some women eager to coach competitively in the 1970s found that they did not enjoy the pressures of coaching and quit. Others burned out because of multiple team assignments combined with family responsibilities. This trend of men coaching girls' teams has continued to expand to more than 50 percent today. These hiring practices may be attributable in part to the fact that most high school athletic directors have been and continue to be men, who frequently consider men more qualified to coach than women.

The importance of Title IX, along with the Civil Rights Restoration Act, to girls and women is unquestionably critical in the elimination of gender-based discrimination in sport. Would this federal legislation have been unnecessary had people truly valued females' participation in sport? Did decision makers value the educational experiences of sport for males but not for females? Was it fair and just to

refuse to fund competitive opportunities for females? Why did the legal system have to mandate
compliance and threaten with financial losses those
who refused?

Did the possible loss of federal funding and the
negative media attention lead to greater compliance
than did the belief that gender equity in sport is a
moral issue? The establishment and growth of the
AIAW primed the pump, encouraging women to
develop their sports skills. Title IX's mandate for
the elimination of inequities in financial support,
access to facilities, and overall athletic opportunities, has led to significant increases in the quality
and quantity of sport programs for girls and
women.

SOCIETAL ATTITUDES

As discussed in the historical section, societal attitudes have hampered sport opportunities for females. Society teaches girls to not be assertive, independent, or tough, although success in sport
demands each of these traits, as well as other so-
called masculine characteristics. Society heaps praise
and rewards on boys and men who achieve in sport.
To a much lesser extent, girls and women receive
accolades, trophies, and other awards for their sport
achievements. Does the media largely ignore
sportswomen, giving most of its print and broadcast coverage to males? Often when sportswomen's
accomplishments are publicized, the media depicts
them in sexist ways that undermine their seriousness as athletes. Does the media image of female
professional athletes trivialize their accomplishments as athletes? Do male tennis stars receive
praise for their physical prowess and skillful performances, while the coverage of female tennis players
emphasizes clothing, hair styles, and mannerisms?

Although males in general possess physical advantages in sport, whenever females succeed in
competing on equal terms with males—that is, at
similar elite levels or as opponents—often their
femininity is questioned or they are derided as
somewhat less of a woman. Babe Didrikson, the Associated Press' greatest female athlete of the first
half of the twentieth century, had to endure numerous disparaging comments because of her mul-

tisport prowess. Female athletes have been exposed
to stereotypical statements and prejudicial treatments whenever they step outside others' perceived
boundaries of propriety.

These societal attitudes may result from ignorance of physiological facts about women moving
and competing. The discrimination that has occurred will change only if values are challenged
through education, dialogue, and debate. Reasoning must center on challenging those in charge who
hold to unfair practices.

Another illustration of societal or psychological
pressure placed on females is the emphasis on participating in acceptable sports. Supposedly, women
should not play baseball or football, box, race cars
or horses, play rugby, pole vault, or ride rodeo
bulls. It is permissible to play basketball, softball,
volleyball, soccer, or even to run track but with
some risk about how others view these athletes'
femininity. Those who opt for tennis, golf, swimming, figure skating, and gymnastics are more likely
to receive media attention and societal approval.

Homophobia, a fear of those who choose part-
ners of the same sex, has become a major issue in
sport, and especially women's sport. Coaches and
athletic administrators seek to ensure that their
programs are never accused of condoning homosexual behaviors among their athletes. They believe
that such allegations would harm recruiting and
reputations.

Despite Title IX, in many competitive situations
males continue to receive better equipment, facilities, coaching, awards, and other program support
because those in the power positions believe that
male athletes deserve preferential treatment. If people acted justly, would they demand that all athletes
receive equal benefits? In NCAA institutions, male
athletes receive 70 percent of the monies available
for grants-in-aid, an amount disproportionate to
their enrollment numbers and to the number of
athletes by gender. With the usual exception of tennis, there is a disparity between men's and women's
prize winnings. Is this because corporations provide
more sponsorship dollars to men's events or because women's sports do not have a large spectator
following? Can sport managers develop their moral
reasoning leading to gender equity in sport?

RECOMMENDATIONS

Girls and women do not suffer from total exclusion from sport or have to endure many of the discriminatory practices of the past. But, even though over a quarter of a century has passed since Title IX banned gender discrimination in federally funded educational institutions, equity for girls and women in sport remains elusive. Insidious discrimination, threats of lawsuits, and continued under-representation of females in coaching, athletic training, officiating, athletic administration, and sport media persist. Several problem areas are identified below, with possible solutions.

Problem 1: *Should female athletes receive most of their coaching from men or from women at all levels of competition?*

Solution: Many athletes and athletic administrators seem to prefer male coaches over female coaches. Why has the number of women coaching women's NCAA teams dropped (from 90 percent in 1972 to 47.4 percent in 1998)? Does society (specifically, competitive sport) value and appreciate females as coaches and athletic administrators? To facilitate a change in attitudes, women need a mentoring system to provide these individuals opportunities to develop the knowledge and skills for success. Because role modeling helps teach values and develop morality, administrators should hire female coaches to provide their athletes with these same-gender teachers of ethical principles. Perhaps because of the current predominance of males in sport there remains the perception that male coaches are better. The challenge is to encourage women to pursue careers in coaching and to educate young athletes to value women coaches.

Problem 2: *Does financial support for sport programs at all levels of competition inequitably favor males? If so, how can this be changed?*

Solution: Community leaders, school administrators, athletic directors, and others in positions of power over sport should allocate proportionate and equitable funding for males and females on the basis of participation numbers, not on past budgets or the sport. This means valuing women in sport, not to the detriment of men in sport but for the betterment of all. Moral reasoning demands that one examines what is just, honest, responsible, and beneficent when determining the treatment of others. For example, is it honest to claim that men's football finances all other sports and thus that this team deserves a larger budget, when in reality most football teams lose money? Is it just to perpetuate traditional practices of preferentially treating men's programs? Is it responsible to provide men's teams with better facilities, athletic trainers, travel accommodations, and coaches while women's teams experience few of these program support services? Is it beneficent to fail to promote, fund, or expand women's competitive opportunities? Greater opportunities for females demand increased funding. If males should not receive special treatment, as reasoned thinking should lead one to conclude, people should eliminate those benefits that cannot

be justified and redistribute these resources to women's programs. Another alternative obligates administrators to raise more money.

Problem 3: *Should more college grants-in-aid be awarded to male athletes?*

Solution: Grants-in-aid should be awarded proportionately to the interest and participation levels of female and male athletes as required by Title IX.

Problem 4: *Should males have greater numbers of participation opportunities than females at all levels of sport?*

Solution: Sport administrators should increase the number of competitive sport opportunities for females until their interests and needs are met in a fashion equivalent to those for males as required by Title IX.

Problem 5: *Should men control all levels of sport, with only a few women holding administrative positions in sport?*

Solution: Those who hire athletic directors and their assistants, sports information and promotions directors, athletic trainers, and other administrative personnel should seek qualified women for these jobs. They also should actively seek women for internships and assistants' positions to prepare them to become coaches and administrators because of the unique skills, perspectives, and styles these females would contribute to athletics. No longer will only the autocratic, task-oriented, structuring management style of the ex-coach work in athletics. Rather, the building of relationships through encouragement, flexibility, delegation, and nurturing—traits more characteristic of females—will enhance performance in the corporate as well as the sport setting.

MORAL EDUCATION

An overarching solution to each of these problems can be classified as moral education. Athletic leaders need to understand how their personal values and beliefs relate to personal and professional relations. An athletic department's mission statement and purposes, as reflective of its staff's values and beliefs, should match a philosophy that encompasses moral knowing, moral valuing, and moral acting.

The ethical issues pervading gender equity in sport remain, as does the importance of justice, honesty, responsibility, and beneficence. Justice requires that female athletes receive fair treatment. This encompasses all the financially supported services associated with athletics. Is it just to fly the men's basketball team to a competition 250 miles away while expecting the women's basketball team to drive? Would you reverse your response if you were a member of the women's basketball team? Does distributive justice demand equitable treatment regardless of skill level or fan popularity? Are there any exceptions to universalizibility?

Are athletic directors, who are mostly men, honest when they state or demonstrate through their hiring practices that women are not interested in or qualified for coaching or athletic administrator positions? Admitting to past discriminatory hiring practices and aggressively seeking to rectify them verifies that one values and believes in women serving as leaders in sport. Given the discussion about moral reasoning and moral development in the preceding chapters, it appears that one effective strategy could be an educational intervention that helps individuals analyze what they value and why.

Responsibility governs how sport leaders and athletes deal with each other. Both should demonstrate a commitment to making things work for the greater good. If administrators act responsibly on the basis of their beliefs and values, can the existing system enact change and promote gender equity in sport?

Beneficence has the following four qualities: (1) do no harm; (2) remove harm; (3) prevent harm; and (4) do good. On the basis of the preceding historical, organizational, and societal analysis of women in sport, should these characteristics of beneficence be achieved? If people truly believed in beneficence, would they work tirelessly to remove and prevent sexism in sport? Beneficence leads to kind words and deeds. Athletic administrators and media persons should stop demeaning, stereotyping, or ignoring female athletes. Kindness will lead to acceptance of females as equals in the power positions in sport. Beneficent individuals will encourage females to achieve their athletic potentials through increased participation and competitive opportunities in the absence of discriminatory treatment.

SUMMARY

Gender equity in sport has yet to be achieved. Historically, females' opportunities have been limited because of societal perceptions of their lack of interest and ability, physiological myths, and discriminatory exclusion. Many women lack the physiological skills to compete equally with most men. It can be argued, however, that women have sold out to men by not celebrating their biological differences. Instead of playing men's games by men's rules, women should develop their own games that highlight their unique physical talents.

Women's athletic programs remain unequal, even after being combined with existing men's governance structures. Title IX helped females achieve greater equity, but full equality remains elusive because too many people still do not value the right of women to equitable treatment within sport. Females have not achieved significant movement into the power positions controlling sport. However, each new female head coach or athletic director hired signals another victory in the battle for gender equity in sport. Many more are needed, along with equitable treatment, before discrimination is eradicated.

ISSUES AND DILEMMAS

CASE 11-1

Lisa Whitley grew up playing baseball. Despite her mother's attitude that sports were unfeminine and inappropriate for her daughter, Lisa shared her father's love of baseball. He played with her, taught her the skills, and coached her teams. By age twelve, Lisa demonstrated the best baseball skills of any youth sport athlete in Southern California. Although her team lost in the finals of the Little League regional qualifying tournament, Lisa's .725 batting average for the year was the main reason the team advanced so far.

Although she had encountered occasional sexist remarks and disparaging comments about a girl playing with the boys, Lisa disregarded them. She just wanted to play baseball. Unfortunately, the baseball league for boys twelve to fifteen years of age did not want her to play. She and her father were told that only under court order would a girl be allowed to participate in the league.

Because Lisa's family did not have the money to hire a lawyer and file a lawsuit, she was forced to quit organized baseball. Mrs. Whitley was delighted, but her husband had other ideas. Because the local school had just started a softball team for girls, he urged Lisa to redirect her talents into this sport.

At first, Lisa was despondent and unwilling to play what she perceived to be a less challenging sport. Finally, Lisa's competitive spirit prevailed as she enthusiastically embraced softball, especially the opportunity to pitch. Through long hours of practice during her middle school and high school years, Lisa became an outstanding pitcher. She finished with a high school record of 75-2, with an earned run average of 1.31. She led the nation with a .553 batting average.

Lisa chose to attend Southeastern California College (SCC) on a partial softball grant-in-aid because its team had done well in the preceding year's NCAA tournament and her father could attend her games. Once enrolled, Lisa learned that the college only marginally supported softball. The coach was part-time, the budget limited, and the institutional support services for female athletes quite different from those offered for male athletes.

Lisa questioned the situation because, in high school, the girls' softball and boys' baseball teams had been treated equitably. She learned that Mr. Riddick, the athletic director and former baseball coach, had resented the establishment of the softball team three years earlier. He often stated that women had no business playing this sport, especially because money for softball in his opinion could be better spent on baseball. But because Dr. Whitmire, President of SCC, in the face of a threatened Title IX-based lawsuit, mandated having a softball team, one was established. Despite minimal financial support and obvious violations of the requirements of Title IX, Coach Collins had successfully built a competitive team.

Lisa and her teammates resented the preferential treatment given the baseball team and other men's sports. They asked Coach Collins for help, but she said she would lose her job if she complained or requested more financial support. So the players, led by Lisa, asked Athletic Director Riddick for funding for more grants-in-aid, a full-time coach, better facilities, access to athletic trainers and weight training facilities, and an expanded competitive schedule. Mr. Riddick adamantly refused. He then threatened the elimination of the softball team if the issue was brought up again. Undeterred, the team asked President Whitmire to intervene once again. He attempted to placate Lisa and her teammates by citing all the progress made at SCC for women's athletics in recent years. Also, he stated that budgetary constraints precluded providing any additional funding for the softball team.

Dismayed by the unresponsiveness of President Whitmire to their plight, the mother of one of the softball team members filed a discrimination suit based on Title IX against SCC. A furious Mr. Riddick immediately fired Coach Collins and canceled the softball team's schedule, claiming a financial crisis. No other team was eliminated.

1. What are the moral values in this case?
2. What, if any, ethical issues led to Lisa's forced exit from baseball?
3. What are the moral bases for equity in high school sports for both genders?
4. What ethical principles, if any, were violated by SCC's refusal to treat female athletes equitably?
5. What values or principles did Mr. Riddick violate by eliminating the team?
6. Was Lisa correct in what she did? Why?
7. If you were Lisa, how would you feel?
8. What could have been Mr. Riddick's justification for his actions?
9. What would you have done if you had been in each person's position?
10. What underlying values were used by each person in making his or her decisions?

◆ ◆ ◆

CASE 11-2

Sally learned to run by chasing her older brothers. She could never catch them, but it certainly was not for lack of effort. To channel her daughter's high energy and love of running, Mrs. Ramsey arranged for Sally to join the community-based Junior Striders Track Club. She quickly established herself as the fastest twelve-year-old in the club—girl or boy—at short distances. Sally continued to decrease her times as she grew, matured, and trained under the expert coaching of a retired former college coach, Bob Jonas. In age-group competitions locally and throughout the state, she repeatedly won 100-meter, 220-meter, and 440-meter races. Sally was eager to run for Central High School.

Sally's world changed dramatically just before she entered the tenth grade, when her mother's company transferred her. After settling into their new house and enrolling in school, Sally learned that Stegall High School did not have a girls' track team. She was told that girls were not interested in this sport, although there were basketball and softball teams for the few athletic girls in the school. The boys competed in eight sports, including track.

Determined to continue her running, Sally asked Coach Hudson if she could train with the boys' track team. Only after her relentless persistence did he acquiesce, thinking she would quit after a couple of tough practices. Sally handled all of his challenges and endured the snide comments she received from classmates and track team members. Grudgingly, the boys accepted her as a dedicated athlete, but always added that they surely would not want to race against her, lest they be beaten.

After numerous attempts to get the athletic director, principal, and school board to add a girls' track team, Mrs. Ramsey filed a lawsuit against Stegall High School and the Capital Area Conference to permit Sally to compete on the boys' team. She based the complaint on Title IX, stating that females at Stegall and in the conference were denied equal opportunity in sport. Rather than fight this case, the Stegall School Board ruled that Sally must be allowed to compete on the boys' track team. The conference teams threatened to cancel their scheduled track meets with Stegall.

1. What moral principles, if any, are being violated?
2. What moral values, if any, were displayed by Coach Jonas?
3. What were the moral values of the people of Stegall that placed females in support, rather than participant, roles in sport?
4. What were the ethical issues, if any, why Coach Hudson initially resisted and subsequently allowed Sally to train with the boys' track team?
5. Why did Mrs. Ramsey sue Stegall High School, and what was the basis of the lawsuit?
6. Why did the School Board allow Sally to compete? Was this decision a morally reasoned one?
7. What were Sally's moral and legal rights in this situation?

◆ ◆ ◆

CASE 11-3

When Southwestern State University (SSU) merged its men's and women's athletic programs in 1980, Marilyn Graham's title changed from women's athletic director to assistant athletic director for women's athletics. Instead of having administrative authority over the eight women's sport teams, she now reported to Hugh Knowles, the athletic director. Although she was pleased with the increase in program support for the women athletes, she realized that they were not treated equitably.

Budgets for men's basketball and football far exceeded those for any other of the men's sports and all of the women's sports. Throughout the 1980s, she expressed concern that the women's percentage of the athletic budget had reached 25 percent but stayed there despite the fact that females comprised 51 percent of the student body. Whenever she raised questions, the response was always that the two men's revenue sports financed all the other sports. If these were not preferentially treated, then every team would lose support or possibly risk elimination.

Another distressing fact that Marilyn Graham noted was the gradual change in who coached the women's teams. In 1980, all were coached by women because she had hired each one—all talented, committed coaches. In the subsequent decade, six of these coaches had moved to larger universities because of their success at SSU. Although during each search she had recommended qualified women candidates, only twice did Athletic Director Knowles hire a woman. For volleyball, swimming, track, and tennis, he hired men to coach.

After a dozen years of trying to gain greater financial support for the women's teams and to hire women coaches, Marilyn Graham was relieved of her administration responsibilities over women's athletics. Although the only female athletic administrator at Southwestern, she was moved out of day-to-day operations and given the title of assistant director for public relations. Her former duties were reassigned to a newly hired male associate athletic director.

1. What are the moral and ethical issues in this case?
2. What are the legal issues, if any, involved in this situation?
3. Is it ethical to treat female athletes inequitably in program support because they do not play revenue-producing sports?
4. What should the financial support for athletic teams be based on: gender, ability to generate revenue, percentage of athletes involved, percentage of students at the institution, or other criteria?
5. What moral principles, if any, could have been used by Marilyn Graham in her recommendation of women for the vacant coaching positions?
6. What moral principles, if any, could have been used by Hugh Knowles in his decision to hire men to coach the four women's teams?
7. Is it ethical for women's athletic programs to be administered exclusively by men? Why or why not?
8. What recourse does Marilyn Graham have in addressing her change of responsibilities and the treatment of women's athletics at Southwestern?

◆ ◆ ◆

CASE 11-4

Northwest State University (NSU), a NCAA Division II institution, had made some progress in complying with Title IX, but university administrators acknowledged that compliance had not been achieved. There were six teams for women; the college undergraduate population consisted of 60 percent women. Male athletes on six teams received 75 percent of the grants-in-aid.

When the university committed an annual addition of $100,000 from student fees for athletics, the athletic director was asked to submit a proposal to the president for how these monies would be allocated. He proposed the following:

(a) Add a volleyball coach (thus creating two positions
       instead of the former volleyball/softball combination) $40,000
(b) Add partial and full grants-in-aid for women $40,000
(c) Add partial and full grants-in-aid for men $20,000

This proposal would raise the percentage of grants-in-aid for women to 40 percent.

1. What requirements of Title IX were being violated by NSU prior to the new funding? Was this ethical?
2. What requirements, if any, of Title IX would be violated if the proposal of the athletic director were to be implemented? Would this be ethical?
3. What are the relationships, if any, among the number of teams, percentage of students by gender, and percentage of grants-in-aid?
4. If you were the athletic director, what recommendation would you have made?
5. If you were the university president, what would have been your response to the athletic director's proposal?
6. What are the ethical issues associated with this situation?

◆ ◆ ◆

CASE 11-5

When the Rodriquez family moved to Greenville, they were eager to join community activities. Fernando Rodriguez immediately signed his four children up for sports with the city recreation department. He could not understand why the leagues were configured as they were. His six-year old daughter and seven-year old son were placed on T-ball teams comprised of boys and girls. His ten-year old son was assigned to a competitive boys' baseball team, while his eleven-year old daughter's (Maria) only option was a recreational girls' softball team. Since Maria had shown the best athletic abilities of his children, he had always encouraged her to play baseball to challenge herself. Suddenly, she could not play baseball with the boys as she had before.

1. When Fernando Rodriquez questioned the differences in opportunities provided for his children, what rationale do you think he received from recreation department officials?
2. What are the pros and cons of dividing sports opportunities by gender?
3. Is it equitable to force boys into competitive sports leagues and girls into recreational sports leagues? Is it ethical?
4. What recourse, if any, does Mr. Rodriguez have relative to Maria's team placement?

REFERENCE

Acosta, R.V., and L.J. Carpenter. 1998. *Women in intercollegiate sport: a longitudinal study: Twenty-one year update 1977-1998.* (available from the authors, Brooklyn College, Brooklyn, N.Y. 11210).

ADDITIONAL READINGS

Cahn, Susan K. 1995. *Coming on strong: Gender & sexuality in twentieth-century women's sports.* Cambridge: Harvard University Press.

Carpenter, Linda Jean, and R. Vivian Acosta. 1993. Playing by the rules: Equity in sports. *CUPA Journal* 44 (Summer): 55–60.

Greenberg, Judith E. 1997. *Getting into the game: Women and sports.* Danbury: Franklin Watts, Inc.

Powe-Allred, Alexandra, and Michelle Powe. 1998. *The quiet storm: A celebration of women in sports.* Indianapolis: Masters Press.

Priest, Laurie, and Liane M. Summerfield. 1995. Promoting gender equity in middle level and secondary school sports programs. *NASSP Bulletin* 79(575) (December): 52–56.

Tokarz, Karen. 1986. *Women, sports, & the law: A comprehensive research guide to sex discrimination in sports.* Buffalo: William S. Hein and Company, Inc.

White, Kerry A. 1997. 25 years after Title IX, sexual bias in K-12 sports still sidelines girls. *Education Week* 16 (June 18): 1; 20+.

CHAPTER 12

Epilogue: Morality in Sport

This text describes how moral reasoning can address moral issues in sport. Ethical dilemmas surface daily in our personal and sporting lives. Addressing these issues requires good critical examination, which, in turn (1) makes us more tolerant of others' views, (2) gives us intellectual independence, and (3) frees us from dogmatic beliefs. The less reasoned and more dogmatic our thinking, the easier we fall prey to the obstacles and fallacies that impede moral reasoning. The more morally reasoned our view, the more consistent with our beliefs and values are our actions.

Moral reasoning predicated on a system of personal values and beliefs calls for a consistent application of these values, beliefs, and practices within sport. We must take the time to examine our personal values and beliefs, as well as their consistency, and have the courage to take a stand for what we value. Because we do not live, play, and work in isolation, we must have the courage to challenge common beliefs such as, "Who am I to judge someone else's values," "Everyone has the right to their own beliefs," "Everyone else is doing it," and "That's just the way things are." Yet, if we all "did our own thing" without taking into consideration the effects of our views and actions on others, chaos would assuredly result and violations against others would occur.

Challenging others' beliefs may help us (1) better understand our personal values as they relate to our relationships with others, (2) become stronger and more consistent in our beliefs, and (3) better

understand our beliefs relative to the whole. In this sense, the whole relates to sport, school, community, the nation, and in other settings. Consequently, moral reasoning allows us to develop our own value and belief system, while requiring that it be compatible with the whole: the societies in which we live, work, *and* play.

MORAL REASONING: A REVIEW

Moral reasoning, a systematic, logical, and rational process whereby we identify issues, examine opposing views, and attempt solutions, is predicated on our abilities to be impartial, consistent, and reflective. *Impartiality* requires that we consider others' views when making decisions. Although difficult because we see and perceive the world through our own eyes and may hold biases and stereotypes, becoming impartial requires that we deliberately seek to correct our sometimes narrow and distorted perceptions. Inherent within impartiality is the concept of fairness in which we are free from bias, fraud, or injustice and we do not make decisions based on "what's in it for me" or to take advantage of another. *Consistency* requires ensuring that our actions are consistent with what we value and believe relative to the past and present and *universality principles*. *Reflective* thinking, based on a clear understanding of moral and nonmoral values, helps us make careful judgments or observations about an issue. Reflection may also lead to several viable, alternative views. We may not find a correct answer;

however, the reasoning process may free us from our own prejudices, help us discard false beliefs, and enable us to better understand opposing views.

MORAL AND NONMORAL VALUES: A REVIEW

Germane to our discussion of moral reasoning are values, both moral and nonmoral. *Nonmoral values,* things such as money, fame, power, and winning, do not include people, their intentions, motives, deeds, or character traits. In contrast, *moral values,* the relative worth that we place on some virtuous behaviors, are internal, subjective, and immeasurable in an objective sense. Moral values are traits or dispositions that we hope to portray and support. In order, in this text, to address moral issues, we chose as basic moral values justice, honesty, responsibility, and beneficence. We chose these because they are universally understood. The importance lies not in the particular value chosen but in our respective efforts to (1) rank these values by their relative importance and (2) be consistent in using our designated primary value to address our individual moral issues and dilemmas. *Principles,* universal guides or universal rules of conduct that govern our lives, are directly related to the moral values we hold. Examples of universal principles include respect for self and others, respect for others' property, and respect for the truth. Although some issues such as gender and racial equity inherently involve the value of justice and the principle "Do not be unfair," we may choose the value of responsibility with the principle "Do not be irresponsible" and come to a similarly reasoned perspective.

In the process of ranking our moral values and developing principles in which to guide day-to-day action, we also must examine these principles and identify ahead of time any exceptions we may have to the rule. In other words, there may be a very few instances in which we might violate one of our principles in favor of another principle. For example, let's say that you have ranked honesty as your number one value. It is WWII. You are harboring people in your attic, people who are wanted by the Nazis. A Nazi storm trooper comes to your door and says, "Are you harboring any people in your at-

tic?" If you value honesty and hold the principle of "Do not lie, cheat, or steal" you are obligated to say "Yes, I have people in my attic." However, most prudent, morally sensitive individuals would lie and say "no." In this case, you probably made your decision based on another value, such as justice, or beneficence. You have made a decision on another moral value. With exceptions though, we must be careful with how many exceptions we have for any given principle and that the exception is made in relation to another moral value, not a nonmoral value.

The relationship of nonmoral values to moral values is paramount to our moral actions. Essentially, nonmoral values drive our moral actions. What we value nonmorally, such as winning or money, affects our moral actions. If we value winning or money to a greater extent than we value justice, honesty, responsibility, and beneficence, it becomes easier for us to violate others to get what we want.

The approach suggested in this text challenges each of us to examine what we value and believe and then to rationally scrutinize these values and beliefs relative to the issues. Some of you may find the approach of this text uncomfortable; it is a value/principle-based approach. Our purpose is not to moralize, or tell you what to believe, what to value, or how to act; our purpose is to challenge you to discover for yourself values in relation to universal values, principles, and reversibility (the ability to treat others as you want to be treated). Finding the truth and the most reasonable view becomes the goal. Not unlike a physical skill, moral reasoning must be practiced constantly for it to improve.

MORAL REASONING IN RELATION TO SPORT AND SOCIAL ISSUES: A REVIEW

Throughout this text, we have challenged you to develop and practice moral reasoning with common, yet seemingly difficult moral issues in sport, such as gender and racial equity, elimination from sport, gamesmanship and intimidation, ergogenic aids, eligibility, violence, and commercialization. These issues are but a few of those that we encounter daily in sport. Whereas many of the issues have existed throughout the history of sport, others have surfaced and become more prevalent only recently. Essentially, because sport involves participation among and between people, moral issues continually surface and persist. The issues come and go and may change with the seasons, but the reasoning process remains the same. Moral reasoning, the constant in the moral equation, challenges us to examine what is of relative importance to us before an issue or dilemma occurs. Once the dilemma surfaces, it becomes more difficult to sift through the issues as we face emotionalism, controversy, and our personal biases. Thus, we must constantly challenge ourselves through the reasoning process.

Moral issues surface in our personal lives and may or may not involve the same potential conflicts as those in sport. Of importance, then, is that we examine and debate each dilemma; ensure consistency in our beliefs and actions whether they involve social, personal, or sport settings; and find solutions workable for each of us. Solutions to moral issues are not easy to come by because of the involvement of emotions, opinions, circumstances, and personal histories. Each multifaceted issue involves a multitude of questions. Violence in sport, for example, raises several moral questions, such as how important is winning relative to our moral values and principles and how do we view the concept of gamesmanship relative to sportsmanship. If we value the nonmoral value of winning more than our moral values and principles, it becomes easier to harm an opponent, bend the rules, and take advantage of another person.

Moral reasoning opens the door and helps us identify issues, see opposing points of view, take a stand, and attempt solutions. We may not always agree and our beliefs may not withstand rational scrutiny; another position may be more defensible. To withstand rational scrutiny, our values and beliefs must be universal and hold true for all people at all times. They must also be reversible in that we treat others as we would hope to be treated. Relative to issues of gender or racial equality, if our beliefs and actions were equitable, universal, and reversible, we would feel comfortable and satisfied taking the other person's position. For example, this position would hold that coaches or athletes in a men's program would be happy and satisfied taking the budgets, facilities, practice times, or other support services of the women's program (and vice-versa).

Adopting a moral reasoning approach is not easy, though, because we must examine what we value and what we believe. Through this process, we learn to listen and examine carefully all views, and all inaccuracies and half-truths, and take a stand based on our beliefs no matter how popular or unpopular. We may find that what we believe and value is not shared by the entire group. It takes courage to take a stand, because we may be challenging the status quo, with others in strong opposition, or we may be the only one holding this belief. Moreover, through debate and dialogue, we may come to the realization that our beliefs are based on false or inaccurate information. Thus, we must have humility. We must realize we may be wrong and we must reevaluate our beliefs and our position.

Having reviewed how to reason morally, let us examine a real situation with issues and dilemmas and use moral reasoning to see how far we have come. As with most moral dilemmas, we are given little warning and little time to prepare our response. However, we have learned that if we understand our values and beliefs and have examined these beliefs relative to universal principles (such as respect for the self and others, honesty, reversibility, and universality), making a reasoned decision, taking a stand, and acting on that stand becomes easier—and our actions are more consistent.

 ## ISSUES AND DILEMMAS

Keith has just completed his junior year as a grant-in-aid student-athlete. He has been successful this year, not only on the golf team as the number-two man on a 10-member roster, but also in the classroom, where last semester he earned a 4.0 grade-point average, leading to a cumulative grade-point average of 3.87. He believes in justice, honesty, and responsibility and attempts to guide his life by the concomitant principles. He qualified for and played in all but one tournament during the season; he chose to not qualify for the one tournament, giving priority to two academic projects due during the tournament dates. Keith, respected by all team members for his dedication, loyalty, and integrity, was voted team co-captain.

Despite Keith's success in the classroom and on the golf course, he has experienced a difficult year working with his coach. As Keith talks with his team members, he finds that they all share similar concerns such as: (1) The coach calls practices but tells only a select few about the time and place (despite Keith's position as co-captain, he is not told); (2) the coach works with only a select few and is belligerent toward the others; (3) he finds the negative in everything, yelling, screaming, and swearing at players; (4) he seldom coaches, encourages,

or works with players on the course, either during practice or matches; and (5) a written qualification process does not exist for selection to the tournament-travel team. Essentially, the coach changes the process on a whim. He has regularly stated, "I do not care what anyone else says, I can chose any five players I want."

Keith and his teammates decide to talk with the coach about their concerns. Keith, with the support of his teammates, shares their concerns, but these are met with hostile responses from the coach. Unfortunately, practices and coaching do not improve. Rather, quite the opposite occurs. The coach's verbal assaults and negativity increase, with Keith becoming the focus of the coach's wrath. Things become so bad that the team talks in confidence with the assistant athletic director, explains the problems, gives a list of possible solutions, and asks for help and advice. The assistant athletic director assures the team that the discussion will be held in confidence, the problems will be examined, and the team will be notified of results. However, within a half hour of the team's leaving the assistant athletic director's office, the coach knows about the discussion and Keith again receives verbal abuse. In desperation, Keith and his team talk to the athletic director and are again assured that the complaints will be examined.

Two months pass with no change and no response from the athletic director or athletic department personnel. Keith and his teammates leave for summer break, believing they still have their grants-in-aid for the following year. However, on June 30, Keith receives a letter stating that his athletic grant-in-aid has not been renewed. The letter states, "After review, the university athletic department has decided to not renew your academic year athletic grant-in-aid. If you have any questions, you may request a hearing. If you wish to transfer universities, we will assist in any way we can." The letter was signed by the athletic director, the coach, and the director of financial aid.

The letter gives no reason for not renewing Keith's grant-in-aid. At the end of the academic year, the coach gave no indication to Keith that he was considering not renewing his grant-in-aid. Now, in the middle of his summer vacation, Keith has limited opportunities to earn sufficient funds to finance his senior year. He understands that his grant-in-aid can be rescinded at any time without a particular reason. He also believes that there are usually three general reasons why athletes do not have their grants-in-aid renewed: academic, athletic, and attitudinal. Keith knows that his loss of a grant-in-aid cannot be because of grades—he is an exemplary student. He knows that it cannot be because of performance—he is second on the 10-roster, plus he qualified for all but one tournament and has the second lowest scoring average for the team. Only one plausible reason exists; he is a trouble-maker in the eyes of the athletic department and coach. Keith is mad, upset, and frustrated and does not know what to do. He comes to you and says, "I took a stand on what I thought was right and look what happened. I thought that the purpose of higher education was to support critical thinking. It doesn't pay to take a stand when no one else believes in treating someone fairly!"

The following questions, which are guidelines to help you begin reasoning, are not exhaustive, nor do they give a complete picture of the issues and dilemmas. As you examine these issues and look for alternatives and reasoned perspectives, be sure to use systematic and logical approaches.

1. What issues are involved in this scenario?
2. What moral questions are raised?
3. What moral values are involved?
4. What principles may have been violated?
5. What nonmoral values may have been involved in the decision to ignore the athletes' concerns?
6. In the coach's decision to not renew Keith's grant-in-aid, what rights, if any, have been violated?
7. If athletes sign grant-in-aid contracts renewable on a year-by-year basis, what rights, if any, do they have regarding due process?
8. Knowing that those who ask questions are often thought of as troublemakers and that whistle-blowers are usually expunged from the system, what would you do if you felt the treatment of Keith was morally unacceptable?

9. Suppose that you are a young administrator with some training and a desire to approach issues through moral reasoning. What would be your recommendations to Keith? To the coach? To the athletic director? To the assistant athletic director?
10. If you were in Keith's position, what would you do?

From this scenario, several issues and moral questions arise—some obvious, others hidden. These questions listed above challenge you to examine the issues and your nonmoral and moral values and their concomitant principles, as well as your consistency and impartiality.

Keith chose a certain path to address his concerns; the coach and athletic department took another. As you examine the issues, think about what you value. We know that a morally reasoned approach may result in several equally viable alternatives. What possible alternatives exist for Keith, the coach, and the athletic director? It may be easy to identify the principles violated, but do your views or solutions change depending on whether you have job security? Do you change your position if your colleague or best friend is the administrator in charge?

A LOOK TO THE FUTURE

Today, we in sport face questions concerning gender and racial equity, commercialization, gamesmanship, athlete and coach rights, drug use and abuse, and other issues. The questions may be of a moral nature, but more often than not people do not intentionally violate others. Rather, actions may occur as a result of the desire to do what one *feels* is right, rather than what may be *truly* right. Oftentimes, though, actions and responses are based on faulty or dogmatic thinking, generally as a result of poor or nonexistent moral reasoning skills.

We also know that our value systems and the foundations of moral character develop at a very young age and are shaped by diverse factors, most involving environment, modeling, and education. Generally, those environments in which we spend the greatest time have the most impact on our values and beliefs. Because athletes spend much time immersed in the culture of sport and many hours practicing and developing their sport skills, the values and beliefs they hold are often shaped by those with whom they work and the environment in which they play and train. Similarly, modeling, either positively or negatively, powerfully impacts our actions and what we may hold as true and right. Nowhere is this more apparent than in the sport milieu. One need only to watch the corner playground to find children mimicking their favorite sport stars' moves or wearing their favorite teams' jackets, shirts, and hats. For the past forty years, a comprehensive, concentrated moral education curriculum, though, has been practically nonexistent in most schools, colleges, and universities. Although many coaches and administrators state that they stress ethical play, research finds that little or no concentrated moral education exists in sport.

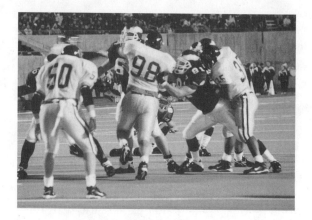

Nor has research been favorable concerning the development of moral character through sport, even though this is universally expressed as a primary purpose of sport. For many years, the belief has existed that sport builds character and promotes moral growth. This belief stems from the nineteenth-century English public school system justification for the development of sport programs based on sport's supposedly inherent ethical values. Most sport and physical education texts, teachings, and programs for the past 150 years have supported this belief. A strong body of qualitative and quantitative research exists, however, supporting that the longer athletes participate in sport, the more their moral reasoning is adversely affected by the competitive experience. Moreover, athletes' reasoning skills are significantly lower than those of their nonathletic peers. It would appear from the research that sport does not model, challenge, support, or teach the critical reasoning skills paramount to making good moral decisions.

Yet, all is not lost for sport. Research has found that a very specific teaching methodology, based on a morally reasoned approach, can significantly affect moral reasoning and moral development. As advocated in this text, participants must be challenged to examine their beliefs and actions, consider others' views, and take a stand relative to universality and reversibility concepts. They are challenged by peers

and others to defend their points of view. The process results in what Kohlberg (1981) called *cognitive dissonance,* a state where we begin to question whether our beliefs and views are the most reasoned for us. Kohlberg and other cognitive development theorists believe that cognitive dissonance is essential to the reasoning process and improvement of moral development.

Currently, few sport organizations, teams, or programs teach athletes sport ethics or moral reasoning. Although athletes may be taught about the dangers of alcohol and drug use and racism, seldom do we challenge them to examine themselves, their beliefs, and their actions. With these issues, rarely do they experience cognitive dissonance. As with athletic programs, few coaching certification programs teach sport ethics or moral reasoning, with the National Youth Sport Coaches Association possibly being the only organization to date with specific sport ethics competency requirements in its coaching certification program. Although some see little reason for such programs, some interesting questions arise. Because of the importance of the situation or setting, what happens to an athlete who reasons from a more developed perspective but must participate in an environment that does not support moral reasoning? If the longer people participate in sport the lower their moral reasoning, and if coaches have been involved in sport for many years, what perspectives do they hold? How do their perspectives affect their athletes' moral reasoning? What role do coaches have in moral education? Finally, can moral reasoning exist in sport if the environment does not value the basic premises of a reasoned perspective? Most research shows that we will have limited success in matching what we know and value to prosocial actions if the environment does not embrace and value the moral reasoning process.

Consequently, if we value the institution of sport and are concerned about the development of honor and integrity through sport, we should use moral reasoning to debate, discuss, and encourage critical inquiry. Moral reasoning must be taught from the moment children enter sport throughout their competitive experiences. We should make a concerted effort to develop moral reasoning skills to the same extent and effort as we do motor skills, strategy, and tactics. The society of sport should value and support ethics, integrity, and honor as the foundation from which all aspects of sport emerge.

Moreover, those of us involved in sport should support an open and honest environment that encourages (1) individuality, (2) the worth of individuals as they participate in sport, and (3) the use of critical inquiry to examine and address the many moral issues that surface daily through sport participation. Finally, would it not be wonderful if we valued and developed moral reasoning and critical thinking skills in our athletic populations to the same magnitude and extent as we do motor skills, strategy, and tactics? A start in this direction would involve nothing more than treating others with dignity, respect, and common decency. If we use common decency as a beginning, the future of sport as a vehicle to support and foster ethical and moral practices becomes brighter.

REFERENCE

Kohlberg, Lawrence. 1981. *The philosophy of moral development: Moral stages and the idea of justice.* New York: Harper and Row.

ADDITIONAL READINGS

Beller, J.M., and S.K. Stoll. 1992. A moral reasoning intervention program for Division I athletes. *Academic Athletic Journal* (Spring). 43–57.

Berkowitz, L. Sport competition and aggression. 1972. In *Fourth Canadian Symposium on Psychology of Motor Learning and Sport,* edited by I. Williams and L. Wankel. Ottawa: University of Ottawa Press.

Bredemeier, B.J. n.d. Sport, gender, and moral growth. In *Psychological foundations of sport,* edited by John M. Silva and R.S. Weinberg. Champaign, IL: Human Kinetics Press.

Bredemeier, B.J., and David Shields. 1986. Moral growth among athletes and nonathletes: A comparative analysis. *J Genet Psychol* 147(1):718.

Bredemeier, B.J., Maureen Weiss, and David Shields, B. Cooper, n.d. Young sport involvement and children's moral growth and aggression tendencies. Unpublished manuscript. Minneapolis: University of Minnesota.

Fraleigh, Warren P. 1982. Why the good foul is not good. *JOPERD* 51(1): (January):41–42.

Hahm, C.H. 1989. Moral reasoning and development among general students, physical education majors, and student athletes. Ph.D. diss., University of Idaho.

Hall, E. 1981. Moral development levels of athletes in sport specific and general social situations. Ph.D. diss., Texas Women's University.

Kretchmar, R. Scott. 1993. Fairplay: who committed the robbery? *Strategies* (May):23–24.

Martens, Rainer. 1978. Kids sports: den of iniquity or land of promise. In *Children in sport: A contemporary anthology,* edited by R.A. Magill, M.J. Ash, and F.L. Smoll. Champaign, IL: Human Kinetics.

Simon, Robert L. 1991. *Fair play: Sports, values, and society.* Boulder, CO: Westview Press.

Stoll, S,K., Jennifer M. Beller, and Sue M. Durrant. 1993. A bill of right for athletes: A novel idea or blasphemy? *For the Record* (July).

Stoll, Sharon K. 1993. *Who says this is cheating? Anybody's sport ethics.* Dubuque, IA: Kendall/Hunt.

Glossary

A

Aesthetic A philosophic term applied when something is "pleasing to the senses," whatever the sense might be—sight, sound, touch, feel, movement, taste, or smell.

Amoral An ethical position meaning one is not able to make a judgment. Such actions are outside the realm of morality.

Anabolic steroid A drug that resembles male testosterone; a controlled substance used for body building or increasing strength.

Applied ethics The practical application of ethical theory directed toward issues in life and certain professions, such as, medical ethics, sport ethics, business ethics, and law ethics.

Athletics The competitive experience of sport, whereby coaching is essential, spectators are present, and specific constitutive, proscriptive, and sportsmanship rules are highly developed within an organized structure. The experience is often likened to that of work with decided aspects of dedication, intensity, and sacrifice.

Autonomy A philosophic term meaning self-governance, whereby one has the right, power, or condition of self-governance. The individual has self-determinism and freedom from external control or coercion.

Axiology The branch of philosophy dedicated to the study of values.

B

Beneficence The ethical position whereby one attempts and is actually obligated to do no harm, but rather to remove harm, prevent harm, and actually do good.

Bias The position whereby an individual shows partiality and prejudice, slanting an opinion in one direction only.

C

Character A moral demeanor that refers to one's outward demeanor as judged by society. Positive moral character refers to one's ability to know the right and to have the courage to follow the right. Character refers to one's virtue or how one lives by a set of moral values. A person of character is known to be just, honest, fair, and decent to others, as well as being a person of honor and integrity.

Choice One of the necessary stipulations (Value, Principle, Obligation, and Choice) to determine whether a moral issue is being presented. A moral dilemma does not exist if one does not have a choice. Coercion, manipulation, or other excusing conditions usually abrogate moral responsibility.

Code of ethics Moral guidelines written for a professional body to follow. These guidelines are always developed by the professional body, monitored by that body, and enforced by that body.

Cognitive dissonance The cognitive process whereby an individual's values and beliefs are challenged. The challenging process is necessary in moral reasoning to wrestle with moral dilemmas.

Consistency Requires ensuring that our actions are consistent with what we value and believe relative to the past and present and universality principles.

Consequential ethics   A theory based on utilitarian philosophy; right and wrong are based on the greater amount of good resulting. The consequences of action play a major role in deciding the greater amount of good. Major philosophers include John Stuart Mill and Jeremy Bentham, both of whom espoused utilitarian ethics.

Constitutive rules   The specific game rules that guide play in a sport. Constitutive rules may have unsportsmanlike conduct explicitly described and violations specifically written to punish such behavior.

Corticosteroids   Steroids developed particularly to reduce inflammation, especially that brought on by overuse syndrome. Corticosteroids do not cause anabolic effects, and they are the only legal form of steroid ingestion or injection presently acceptable.

D

Deductive reasoning   Philosophic reasoning in which the argument moves from the general perspective to the specific.

Deontic ethics (non-consequential)   Ethical theory based on the ideal that we can perceive rightness apart from any consequences. This perspective believes that there is an inherent right that must be followed, regardless of any extraneous factors. Right and wrong are based on the ideal of what should be. Major philosophies include Kantian ethics, the ethical theory of Immanuel Kant.

Determinism   Every event, including human choice and volition, is caused by other events and is an effect or result of these other events.

Discriminatory practices   Prejudical actions that result in inequitable treatment of others.

Dogmatism   The argumentative position based on opinion that is not supported by fact.

Due process   The act of the right to refute accusations or actions and give individuals a just accounting.

E

Epistemology   One of the philosophic branches of philosophy. The epistemologist studies knowledge, particularly addressing such questions as, "Can we know?" "What do we know?" "How do we come to know?"

Ergogenic aids   Any aid, supplement, or ingested material that is prohibited by the letter or the spirit of the rules; used to garner an advantage in the sport experience.

Ethics   The theoretical study of morality. Ethics is also the standard of morality that a profession should follow.

Excusing conditions   An ethical position in which outside factors beyond an individual's control excuse the individual from moral action. That is, if the moral action places one in undue jeopardy, if one cannot readily affect the outcome, or if one is ignorant of the conditions, one is excused from acting.

Extrinsic value   The relative worth that an individual places on objects, things, or actions that have an objective worth. For example, an athlete or others in the athletic community might place much value on an article like a letter jacket, which is a symbol awarded for work done.

F

False obstruction   A reasoning obstacle that does not permit an individual to morally reason through a dilemma. Usually this obstacle is permitting a bias or perception to cloud one's thinking.

Free choice   The philosophic position that individuals have the freedom to choose their moral actions without intimidation, coercion, or manipulation being a factor. Free choice in contrast to determinism supports the concept of autonomy. One can make choices based on values, outside of determinism.

G

Gamesmanship   The perspective of pushing the rules to the limit without getting caught, using whatever dubious methods necessary to achieve an end.

H

Honesty   The quality of trustworthiness in which an individual can be depended on to "not lie, cheat, or steal."

Honor   A virtue or distinguishable characteristic of an individual that implies the individual is obligated to follow a specific set of written or unwritten moral guidelines. Honor implies that individuals have given their word as a guarantee of future moral performance.

I

Immoral   A moral perspective in which the individual knows the good, right, and proper course of action but instead chooses to do wrong.

Impartiality   Requires that we consider others' views when making decisions.

Inductive reasoning   Reasoning from particular facts to a general conclusion.

Integrity   A moral virtue or distinguishable character trait in which an individual is free from corruption. That is, the individual has been shown to have certain positive moral character traits and, even when challenged and tempted to do wrong, will choose the good, right, and proper.

Intimidation   An intentional act done to frighten or inhibit others or render them unable to do certain behaviors.

Intrinsic value   A nonmoral value in which relative worth of an event, object, or experience is placed on some internal, personal satisfaction. An intrinsic nonmoral value in sport might be the internal, personal joy of playing, the joy of success, the joy of experience, and so forth.

J

Justice   A universal moral value in which the essential nature of fairness and equity should be applied to all people. Justice in sport refers to "making a level playing field" either in constitutive rules or for past inadequacies, social injustices, or physical or mental handicaps.

L

Logic   The philosophic branch of philosophy that focuses on the study of language.

M

Materialism   The doctrine that everything in the world, including thought, can be explained only in terms of matter; the individual tendency to be more concerned with material objects than with spiritual or intellectual values.

Meta-ethics   The specific philosophic study of ethics in which the formal academic inquiry is toward the analytical.

Metaphysics   The philosophic branch of philosophy in which study is directed toward questioning the nature of reality; divided into several different directions such as cosmology (what is the nature of the universe?) or ontology (what is the nature of man?). In sport a metaphysician might ask the question, "why do we play"?

Moral   The moral perspective in which one knows the good, proper, and right. The moral perspective is played out through one's motives, intentions, and actions as they impinge on or affect other human beings.

Morality   The motives, intentions, and actions of an individual as they are directed toward others and how these are judged by the greater society.

Moral development   The evolving growth process by which one learns to take others into consideration when making moral decisions. Moral development is usually considered to occur through six different stages in three different levels, from a lower reasoned perspective to a greater reasoned perspective.

Moral judgment   The ability to form an opinion based on moral issues.

Moral reasoning   The ability to systematically think through a moral problem, taking into consideration one's own values and beliefs while weighing them against what others value and believe.

Moral value   The worth each individual places on specific nonmoral values that affect and impinge on others, such as winning. Moral values are usually highly specific—for example, justice, honesty, responsibility, and beneficence.

Motivation   The psychological condition that moves an individual to action.

N

Nonmoral value   The perspective taken toward an issue in which good and bad are determined on the basis of nonmoral issues. The question is based on intrinsic or extrinsic values.

Normative ethics The theoretical study or position of morality in which rightness and wrongness are analyzed and reviewed with a decision specifically stated. For example, that is the wrong thing to do.

O

Objectivity The philosophic position in which one is without bias or prejudice. The position is concerned with reality rather than perceptions or feelings.

Obligation One of the four stipulations that must be met to equate an event to a moral dilemma. Obligation implies that one "should" and even "must" follow one's principles based on one's moral values.

Obstruction Any philosophical condition in which a hinderance is blocking progress or development on a moral issue.

P

Paradox An apparent illogical statement that at first appears to be contradictory but may be true or false.

Paternalism The practice of governing or monitoring adults in a manner that suggests a father-child relationship. The practice ethically violates an adult's status as an autonomous moral agent.

Pedagogy The educational study that is directed toward the art or science of teaching.

Philosophy The deliberate and rational attempt to understand the whole and the sum of one's objective and subjective experiences with a view for effective living.

Pragmatism The practice of testing validity of all concepts by their practical results.

Prejudice A preconceived, usually unfavorable, idea or opinion that is biased and often intolerant.

Principle An affirmation of one's values. Always stated in the negative, a principle says what one will not do based on what one morally values. If one values honesty, the principle becomes, "Do not lie, cheat, or steal." Principles do have exceptions or qualifiers. For example, if a principle violates another principle, qualifiers may exist. "Do not lie, cheat, or steal, unless failing to do so places another human being in personal jeopardy."

Proscriptive rules Game rules that expressly forbid specific actions.

R

Reflective thinking Process of making careful judgments or observations based on a clear understanding of moral and nonmoral values.

Relative worth The individual importance placed on some intrinsic or extrinsic object, experience, or person.

Relativism The popular position that states either that (1) there is no standard of right and wrong, (2) no one has the right to make moral judgments, (3) right and wrong are unknowable because of different societies and cultures, or (4) no one should judge others concerning right and wrong.

Respect The moral value in which one holds someone or something in high regard.

Responsibility The moral value in which one is answerable, accountable, and possibly liable for actions in the past, present, and future; a statement of character that one is trustworthy to carry out deeds.

Reversibility The moral perspective of placing the burden on oneself or the ability to treat others as we would hope to be treated. It is asking the question, "What would it feel like if this were done to me?" Reversibility in common usage is the Golden Rule.

Rules Individual day-to-day moral guidelines, written or unwritten. Rules are usually based on specific First Rules or principles. Rules are divided into three different types—constitutive, proscriptive, and sportsmanship. Constitutive rules guide play within a specific game. Proscriptive rules expressly forbid specific actions. Sportsmanship rules are to be followed while in the game and out of the game.

S

Situational ethics The position that every ethical or moral decision is made on the spot and no consistency is shown between individual decisions.

Skepticism The doctrine that the truth of all knowledge must always be in question or doubt.

Spirit of a rule   Usually refers to the intent of a sportsmanship rule or what was intended by the rule. No rule can take into consideration all possibilities, hence the spirit of a rule is to cover the possibilities.

Sports   Games and activities directed toward the play experience in which organization and rules play a significant role.

Sportsmanship   The quality inherent in playing a game in which one is honor-bound to follow the spirit and letter of the rules. Sportsmanship rules are rules of conduct explicitly written or implicitly believed that adhere to this principle.

Syllogism   Reasoning in which a logical conclusion is drawn from two premises.

T

Teleologic ethics (consequential)   Matters of right and wrong are decided on the issue of the greater amount of good.

Trust   To have confidence or trust in someone or something.

U

Universality   An ethical perspective in which decisions are based on whether the decision can be applied across all societies and cultures in every instance.

Utilitarianism   John Stuart Mill's perspective on teleologic ethics in which ethical questions are decided on the amount of good generated by the decision; usually stated as, "The greatest amount of measurable good for the greatest number of people."

V

Validity   A measurement of sound reasoning whereby consistent, impartial, and reflective logic is the standard.

Value   Individual relative worth placed on some intrinsic or extrinsic object, experience, or persons.

Violence   Physical force exerted to injure another.

Virtue   The quality of living by one's stated moral values. Person have virtue if they are fair, honest, responsible, and beneficent.

Index

Note: Page numbers in *italics* refer to illustrations.